SEVILLE

SEVILLE

Sarah Jane Evans

SINCLAIR-STEVENSON

For Richard, Consola and Seraphina

First published in Great Britain by
Sinclair-Stevenson Limited
7/8 Kendrick Mews
London SW7 3HG England

British Library Cataloguing in Publication Data
A CIP catalogue record for this book is available from the British Library.

ISBN: 1 85619 112 5

Typeset by Rowland Phototypesetting Limited,
Bury St Edmunds, Suffolk
Printed and bound in Great Britain by
Butler and Tanner Limited, Frome and London

Contents

Acknowledgements

This book has been twenty years in the researching, though I did not realise back in 1972 where my affection for Seville would lead me. For their hospitality and friendship over most of those years, my first debt must certainly be to Pepe and Jackie Martin, and their daughters Tanya and Clara. This book is tangible evidence of the fun we have had together.

I am especially grateful to Antonio Lara and his wife María Asunción García, his mother Pura Molina, his sister María Carmen Lara and her family for welcoming me into their homes and for all their kindnesses. Paco Hortal was immensely generous with his time, his contacts and his friendship, while Jesús Casada was an enthusiastic and entertaining interpreter of his city's foibles. They all deepened my understanding of their city, and I had a good deal of fun with them in the process.

Many of those who have helped me appear within the pages of this book, and I am deeply grateful to them for their help. There are others who also deserve a mention: Manolo Marín, the late Luis de Soto, Hawys Pritchard, Joaquín Andrade of Asociafruit, Canon Paul Jobson, Michael Kettle, Lourdes Alemán and Antonio Ponce de León. I am greatly indebted to all of them for the ideas and information they gave me; any errors are entirely mine.

Douglas Matthews and his staff at the London Library have been a great help. The library has a varied collection of books by nineteenth-century travellers to Spain; it's well worth venturing through the basement to find them. I should also like to thank the librarians at Canning House and at the Spanish Institute for their help.

I was particularly fortunate to be assisted in the picture research by Jackie Guy at *History Today*, who was generous with her time, her experience and her collection of photographs. George Anderson at the Mansell Collection also made me welcome and hunted for pictures enthusiastically.

I am very grateful to Graham Hines of the Sherry Institute for all his hospitality, and his help and advice over the years, lubricating the wheels of my research, and to Patrick Gooch and María José Sevilla of Foods from Spain.

I should also like to thank GB Airways who generously assisted me in my research.

At Sinclair-Stevenson my thanks go to Penelope Hoare, Caroline Taggart, Vicki Traino and James Woodall, and I owe especial thanks to my agent, Jennifer Kavanagh.

Finally, my greatest debt is to my husband for his unflagging support and inspiration, and to my daughters, who adopted the Macarena and *tortas de aceite* as their own. I hope that when they are old enough they will use this book to discover the pleasures of Seville for themselves.

Picture credits
Anderson Roma, p. 1; María los Angeles Ruiz and the sisters of the convent of Santa Paula, p. 15; Bodleian Library, p. 6 (shelf mark G. A. Oxon, c.106); Sarah Jane Evans, p. 14; *History Today*, p. 2, p. 3; Mansell Collection, p. 4, p. 5; Patronato Provincial de Turismo de Sevilla, p. 9; Popperfoto, p. 7, p. 8a, p. 8b, p. 10, p. 11, p. 12, p. 13a, p. 13b, p. 16.
Maps drawn by Leslie Robinson.

Illustrations

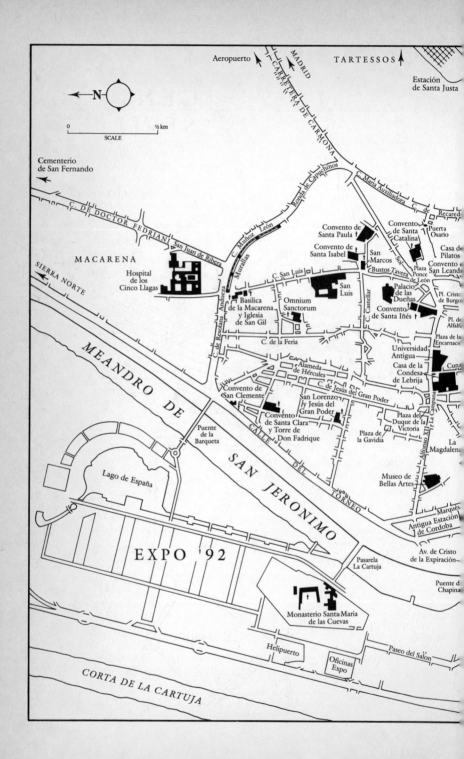

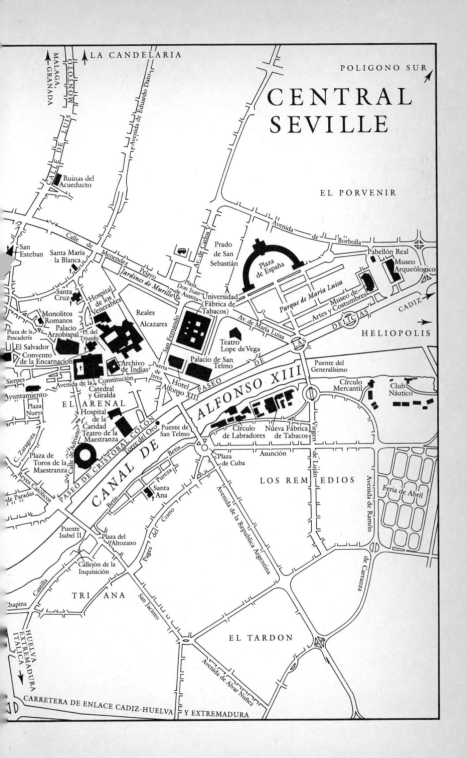

CENTRAL SEVILLE

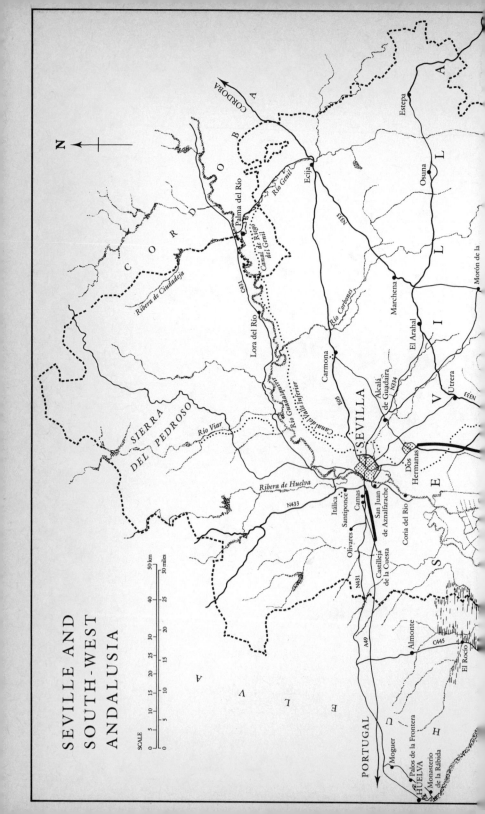

SEVILLE AND SOUTH-WEST ANDALUSIA

SCALE

0 5 10 15 20 25 30 40 50 km
0 5 10 15 20 25 30 miles

N

PORTUGAL

CORDOBA

Palma del Río
Canal de Riego del Genil
Río Genil
Écija
Ribera de Cinúadejn
Lora del Río
Río Viar
SIERRA DEL PEDROSO
Río Guadalquivir
Canal del Valle Inferior
Río Corbones
Carmona
Ribera de Huelva
Itálica
Santiponce
Olivares
Camas
San Juan de Aznalfarache
Castilleja de la Cuesta
Coria del Río
SEVILLA
Alcalá de Guadaira
Dos Hermanas
Marchena
El Arahal
Utrera
Osuna
Estepa
Morón de la
Moguer
HUELVA
Palos de la Frontera
Monasterio de la Rábida
Almonte
El Rocío

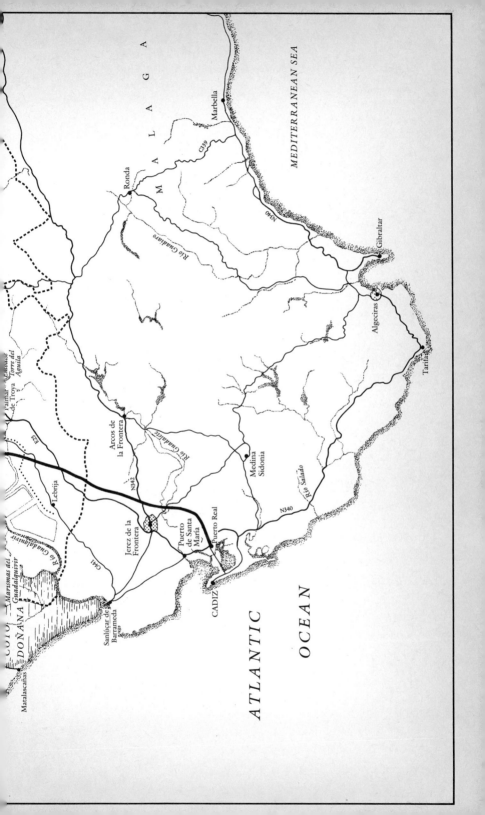

Introduction

Seville – 'the Spanish Athens', the birthplace of Carmen, 'the most beautiful city on which the sun shines in Europe' . . . and 'the cradle of marmalade' – has captivated the imagination for centuries. Even St Teresa admitted one could be forgiven for committing a sin in Seville. In the sixteenth century gold was carried through the streets in ox carts, and so much gold was landed in 1556 that it had to be stored in stables. Seville was the gateway to the New World and as such it flourished, providing a stimulus for some of the greatest art of the period. Seville symbolises the triumphs of Spain, once the greatest nation on earth. Inevitably, it also reflects the fall from that state of grace.

I first saw Seville from a train. It was twenty years ago, in the twilight time of Francisco Franco Bahamonde. His shadow had fallen deep over Seville, but I noticed only the heat, the scorched plains and the palm trees. I was enchanted. The city, I was aware, was not entirely alluring: there were tawdry gift shops, then, as now, selling bedside lamps of the Giralda, and tasteless, overblown imitations of traditional painted ceramics. Poverty and decay were everywhere, and civil war veterans with mutilated limbs begged on the streets. Yet all that I remember – or choose to remember – of that first visit is the architecture, the food, the people and the general excitement of a sparkling city. I adopted Seville then with an affection that has only deepened over the years. To paraphrase what the poet Paul Hyland has said with equal feeling of the Isle of Purbeck: Not one square foot of Seville has ever belonged to me, but I have been happy to own it. The more I have come to know it, the more the enchantment has grown.

On that first trip I had an introduction to the Madres Irlandesas, who ran, as they still do, a very up-market school on the outskirts of Seville at Castilleja de la Cuesta. As I later recognised, my visit symbolised most of the contrasting elements that make the city so attractive and surprising. A beautiful young Irish nun gave me an excellent lunch in the room where Hernán Cortés, the conqueror of Mexico, died (the white-washed convent with its airy patio was once his palace). The nuns were avid readers of the magazine *¡Hola!* (launched in the UK as *Hello!*) and fed me wondrous gossip about the royal families of Europe and the aristocracy of Seville. The village had a dusty, impoverished air, though luscious fruits grew in its orchards. Apart from its convent, Castilleja was renowned for two things: its distinctive sweet biscuits, and for being the birthplace of Rita Hayworth.

That day contained the Catholic Church in general and nuns in particular, beauty, food, hospitality, the explorers of the New World, clues to Seville's sixteenth-century pre-eminence, death, architecture, gossip, the aristocracy, poverty, dust, fertile soil, abundant fruits (and vegetables) and famous daughters (and sons). Over the years the list has changed only slightly. Politics, of course, was missing. Since 1975 Spain has made the transition to democracy, and its prime minister Felipe González, who was first elected in 1982, is a *sevillano*, as is Alfonso Guerra, who was his deputy until he was forced to resign, tainted by a scandal, in 1991. Today, with the massive investment for Expo 92, the fortunes of this formerly provincial city have revived. Seville once more takes centre stage, a model of the economic and political changes that are sweeping through Spain.

In 1972 I came to Seville on an exceptionally slow *rápido*

from Mérida. These days I'm more likely to arrive by air.
Nothing could be worse than the drive into the city from the
airport, which takes you past a jumble of advertising hoard-
ings, ugly flats, waste land, furniture warehouses and car
showrooms. Can this really be the city of gold? Stop in the
centre, drop into the nearest bar, order a beer or a cool glass
of sherry and a *tapa*, such as a little dish of crisply deep-fried
squid rings, or some cured ham, and you can be reassured
that you are back in George Borrow's 'most interesting town
in all Spain' beneath 'the most glorious heaven'.

Seville lies on latitude 37° 22′ N and longitude 6° W, only 7.8
metres above sea level, on the banks of the river Guadalquivir;
it is Spain's only river port. The river runs south-west through
marshes to the sea at Sanlúcar de Barrameda. To the north,
in the distance, lies the Sierra Morena, which separates Andalusia from the rest of Spain, and whence come the fine cured
hams that make such succulent *tapas*. To the east are the hill
towns of Alcor. To the west are the verdant hills of the Aljarafe, farmed by the Muslims, whose villages have become popular suburbs for the *sevillanos*. Beyond, at the coast, lies the
industrial city of Huelva, once enriched by the trade of the
Rio Tinto mines. South lies the port of Cádiz, and beyond it
the straits of Gibraltar. The Guadalquivir valley is Spain's
prime agricultural region, ideal for wheat, cereals, vegetables
and fruit, including olives and bitter oranges. This is good
land for sheep, cattle, pigs and horses. Finally, the region is
important for its wealth of minerals. In the Sierra Morena
mountains and the hills of Rio Tinto, there was iron, copper,
silver and lead to be mined. The Guadalquivir blessed Seville
with good communications and good soils. But it also brought
floods, from which its occupants suffered for centuries, and
disease, from the stagnant water left after the flooding. Only
in relatively recent times have its waters been brought under
control.

Traders and colonisers from earliest times were tempted by

Seville's possibilities: Phoenicians, Greeks, Romans, Visigoths, Muslims, Christians, and last of all Europeans, in the shape of the EC. Under the Visigoths, the Muslims and the Christians, Seville was several times Spain's capital. It may now be 'only' the regional capital, but it has known a more powerful past. The Muslims built on the Romans' achievement, and Muslim Seville became literally and figuratively a glittering city. In the sixteenth century it controlled the trade to the New World, Spain's greatest painters and sculptors of the day worked in the city and it was the cultural as well as the commercial and political capital. However, the Guadalquivir eventually silted up and, as the ships grew larger, Seville lost its monopoly on the New World trade. Felipe II moved the capital to Madrid, and decline set in. The aristocracy clung on to the memory of past successes in the years of empire and the city lay dormant for generations.

Today the city is moving forward once more. Seville is the capital of the autonomous community of Andalusia (created in 1982), the home of the Andalusian Parliament, the base of the Southern Military Region. It is Spain's fourth largest city, with a population of just under 700,000. As host to Expo 92, it has undergone an unparalleled phase of intensive new building: roads, hotels, telecommunications networks, an extended airport, a new railway station, new bridges over the Guadalquivir. The result has been to propel Seville into the twenty-first century with a force which has alarmed many of its citizens.

The *sevillanos* have not been slow to make their feelings known on this, as on anything else. Right or wrong, they have an opinion and defend it against all comers – as they also defend themselves. I am a foreigner, but I speak the language of *sevillanos* and care for their city, and I have been welcomed warmly. In my acknowledgements I have expressed my great indebtedness to all those *sevillanos* who have helped me so generously and been so hospitable. Yet at the same time, as they would be the first to admit, Seville is a closed society. *Sevillanos* have plenty of acquaintances, but few close friends.

One admitted: 'I'd go out and buy an acquaintance any number of drinks, but I'd never have him home.'

A famous *Frost Report* sketch ridiculed the class consciousness of the British – 'He looks down on me and I look down on him' – but they could just as well have been speaking of the *sevillanos*. The philosopher Miguel de Unamuno summed up the *sevillanos* perfectly: *'finos y fríos'* – 'cultured and cold'. They know how to enjoy themselves at a party as well as any, and they have enough fiestas in the year to prove it, but at heart they lack the real openness that characterises, say, their near neighbours, the *gaditanos* from Cádiz.

The *esnobismo* inevitably gets worse the further you climb up the social ladder and reaches its zenith in the year at the *feria*, the spring fair. This is Seville at its party best, laughing and dancing the night through, with the hospitality freely flowing. But the invisible wall is there: you need to be known to join in.

There is one other brake on the gaiety and *alegría*. This is the 'black' side to the Spanish character, which is particularly marked in the *sevillano*. The paintings of Zurbarán typify this for me. They were my first introduction to the ever-present foreboding in culture and society. The red carnation in the gypsy's hair blooms, but then it dies. Christ walks through the streets in Holy Week, while the city commemorates his death – for a whole week. Resurrection Sunday, by contrast, is over in half a morning. The bull runs into the arena, in a conflict that ends in the death of either animal or torero. The flamenco singer laments her lost love or the pain of the Virgin. It is easy to become too sentimental about these things, but there is no ignoring them. While some cultures celebrate the glories of the world to come, Seville seems transfixed with the decay of earthly delights.

Being English, I cannot avoid mentioning the weather, but then, neither can the *sevillanos*. Seville is either very hot or very cold, ranging from $-7°C$ to $45.5°C$. As the writer Antonio

Burgos puts it, 'in Seville you either die of the cold or you die of the heat'. The city streets and its homes are designed for warmth, so when it is cold there is no escaping it. I have gone to bed in the city in March in a nightdress, two pairs of socks and a couple of shirts on top, desperate not to touch the floor in bare feet, because of the cold marble. Yet a few weeks later Seville turns into spring and almost immediately into summer. I have also been silly enough to visit Seville in spring without an umbrella. When it rains, it does so with a monsoon intensity, and it has had an unpleasant habit of doing so in recent years during the *feria*. Spring is, nevertheless, the best time to visit the city, with many flowers in bloom, and the midday temperatures supportable. But summer does not have to be avoided. So long as you have somewhere comfortable to shelter from the frying-pan hours of the afternoon, you will be able to enjoy a city designed with the heat in mind, sharing the way of life of a people who know how to cope with it.

With the heat comes the intense light. Many writers have been enchanted by Seville's luminosity, just as many have been attracted to the Greek Islands for the same reason. In a rational world, one would say that every city across Andalusia and the Mediterranean could rightly lay claim to special qualities of light. What makes Seville different is the play of the light on historic streets and squares in the old city that were perfectly designed for the scorching heat. The Giralda in their midst changes its character throughout the day, from pink to white and grey as the sun passes across the sky.

The heat and the light are a perpetual feature of the city. So once were the scents of the orange blossom and jasmine, extolled by every visitor. Today, those smells can be enjoyed only in the secretive patios of private houses and the rare opulent gardens, such as the Casa de Pilatos and the Alcázar which are untroubled by traffic. Seville has become a city much like any other: full of the fumes of cars, dark tobacco and fried food. Elsewhere, in smaller, quieter Andalusian towns, I have sat out at midnight, intoxicated by the *dama de noche* – the 'lady of the night' – which fills the dark with its heavy scent. No longer is Seville the city filled with the perfumes of one's dreams. In this, at least, it is that lesser thing, the city where one dreams of the perfumes. Alternatively, one can buy the scent in a bottle: 'Agua de Sevilla' is a twentieth-century perfume supposed to reproduce the odour that, when he remembered it, brought tears to the eyes of the exiled poet-king of Seville, Al-Mu'tamid.

Seville contains every cliché of Spain: the geraniums, the white-painted houses, the flamenco-dressed beauties, Don Juan, Carmen, bullfighting, Islamic architecture, bitter oranges, olives, sherry. This book has been written to help you look beyond the cliché and find the city beneath. Part 1 answers the historical questions that always spring to mind in Seville. It also puts Seville's great monuments into their historical context, and introduces its literary and artistic figures.

Part 2 uncovers the living city. It is all too easy to glorify Seville's collection of dead monuments. Franco's policy on historic buildings certainly encouraged that. But the city has a life of its own, if you know how to join it. This book enables you to enjoy life in Seville to the full. It also paints a picture of the city to be enjoyed at leisure. Stretch out with a glass of dry, salty *manzanilla*, the sherry from Sanlúcar de Barrameda, and a dish of olives, and luxuriate in the life of one of the world's great cities. *¡Que aproveche!*

London and Corfe Castle, August 1991

Note on Spellings: Sevilla has been anglicised to Seville and Andalucía to Andalusia, but all other Spanish place names have been left in their original forms. Spanish names have not been anglicised; Fernando does not become Ferdinand, nor Felipe Philip, nor Pedro Peter.

PART 1

1. Hispalis, Isvilia, Sevilla

The history of Seville begins with the great river, the Guadalquivir, on whose banks it stands. Until several thousand years ago, the river ran into the Atlantic at Coria del Río, just below Seville. The site was attractive to the early settlers, being sheltered but close to the sea and lying in the midst of an immensely fertile valley. The region contains some of the most important mineral deposits in Europe and from early times its natural riches lured trader and empire-builder alike. While Spain is a frequently harsh, unforgiving land, the Guadalquivir valley seemed a haven.

There are traces of early settlements scattered across Andalusia. Recent research suggests that predecessors of *Homo sapiens* may have crossed from Africa almost two million years ago, a million years earlier than had been previously estimated. Whatever the exact date, the region has long been a source of romance. The land of Tartessos (the biblical Tarshish, whither Jonah was fleeing from Yahweh when he was intercepted by the whale) with its 'silver mountains' was the stuff of Greek legend. According to Plato, the inhabitants had a taste for bullfighting. Here was the home of the three-headed man-monster Geryon and his herds of cattle whom Heracles killed. In the mountains of Tartessos, Gargoris, King of the

Cunetes, in an unsavoury story typical of the times, repeatedly tried to get rid of Habis, the son/grandson born through his incestuous love for his daughter. He failed, fortunately, for the apparently ill-starred Habis went on to bring law and order to his people and to found the Tartessian monarchy. A good deal of scholarly energy has been spent in locating this fabled land. The essential point for the storytellers was that it was at the far end of the known world, somewhere beyond the straits of Gibraltar. The legends of its mineral wealth would locate it in the region between Seville and Huelva.

In 1958, at El Carambolo, now the Sevillian suburb of Camas, builders discovered an astounding treasure store of golden jewellery, as well as ceramics. Now displayed in the Museo Arqueológico, it gives some substance to the romance. Nevertheless, as late as the eighth century, while this may have been an Eden, it was no promised land. The population was ripe for contact with the first wave of peoples from the East. (This 'orientalising' influence, as it is known, from a Semitic people, was naturally not a popular theory under Fascism. But it has been once more restored to the textbooks.)

The very first traces of settlement found in Seville itself date from the eighth and seventh centuries BC, when the Phoenicians made contact with the indigenous people on the southern shores of Spain and a number of other cities in western Andalusia – Huelva, Córdoba, Carmona – were also founded. The rash of restorations of palaces in the old city in time for Expo 92 uncovered many traces of Seville's early history. Sadly, this could only be rescue archaeology, carried out relatively quickly before the ground was covered over again. The evidence, therefore, is for the textbooks rather than the visitor. For a city with such a historic past, Seville is depressingly bare of remains of its early years. There are tempting clues: for instance, a patch of ground in the Cuesta del Rosario just off the Plaza del Salvador showed that a building had been burnt during the time of the Punic Wars. Was part of the city perhaps destroyed in warfare?

As a settlement, despite its good communications and its fertile land, Seville had – and has – its drawbacks. Most important was the risk of flooding, a constant threat. The early city was bounded to the west by the Guadalquivir, to the south by the Guadaira, and to the east by the tributary, the Tagarete. It was also crossed by a branch of the Guadalquivir which ran along today's Alameda de Hércules, and calles Trajano, Campana, Sierpes and Tetuán, crossing the Plaza Nueva and turning down through El Arenal to the river. At times of flood the island that remained was on a patch of 'high' ground some 17 metres above sea level – the highest point of which is today's calle del Aire. This became the first city and we can walk its boundaries today, beginning in the Plaza del Salvador and following calles Francos, Placentines, Argote de Molina, Segovia, Abades, Angeles, Mateos Gago, Rodrigo Caro, Plaza de Doña Elvira, Gloria, Plaza de los Venerables, Lope de Rueda, Santa Teresa, Ximénez Enciso, Fabiola, Federico Rubio, San Nicolás, Muñoz y Pabón, Plasencia and Cuesta del Rosario. There is one sector of the population which annually gives thanks for the level streets – the *costaleros* who carry the *pasos*, the floats, in Holy Week. The relatively steep climbs in the old city centre cost them much effort.

The next wave of colonisers were the Greeks, who particularly directed their attention to founding settlements on the Mediterranean coast. There are traces of the Greeks until around 550 BC. (Their lasting monuments are the olive and the vine, which they introduced into Spain. As we shall see later, these are just two of a number of what have become 'typical' Seville foods which are not indigenous.) Certainly by the end of the sixth century BC Tartessos' social and economic basis had collapsed. What we find instead is a mass of disparate kingdoms in the Guadalquivir valley, its people known to the Romans as the Turdetani, often at odds with each other though they shared the same antecedents and cultural heritage. The geographer Strabo rated the Turdetani highly. He wrote that they 'rank as the wisest of the Iberians; and they make use of an alphabet and possess records of their ancient history, poems and laws written in verse that are 600 years old'.

The Carthaginians, from just over the Straits of Gibraltar

in Africa, were eager to exploit the territorial advantages of Andalusia, unlike the Phoenicians who had been content to trade. At first, Rome was prepared to overlook Carthage's influence in Spain, but in the third century Rome broke its treaties. Spain was too valuable. The outcome of the first Punic, or Carthaginian, War (264–41 BC), was that the Carthaginians lost Sicily, Sardinia and Corsica. To defend his country's interests the Carthaginian Hamilcar Barca landed in Cádiz in 237 BC and went on to establish a Spanish empire. The Carthaginians built the Via de la Plata, the Silver Road, linking Seville and Mérida with Salamanca, to transport gold and silver, as well as to be a route for the army. It is also said that it is to the Carthaginians that Seville (and the rest of Spain) owes its taste for eating fish with chick peas. Carthaginian influence in Spain spread up the Mediterranean coast, threatening Rome's colonies of Emporion (Ampurias) and Massalia (Marseilles).

Rome could not ignore these invasive upstarts for long. When Hannibal besieged and sacked its ally Saguntum (Sagunto), it was forced to act. With the Second Punic War (218–206 BC), the Carthaginian threat was destroyed. In 218 BC the Roman general Scipio landed at Emporion and worked his way down and across Spain. The people of Spain fought on opposing sides, as they were to do so often in their history. Their methods of fighting across rough terrain gave their name to *guerrilla* warfare. Seville was conquered around 205 BC. Scipio and his brother died in the campaign in Spain, but his son eventually completed the task at Zama, in Africa, in 202 BC, earning the title of Scipio Africanus, and bringing in the *Baja* ('Low') *Epoca*.

This is an emotive phrase, used to describe the period between 200 and 19 BC when Rome first entered Spain, by those who believe Roman 'civilisation' impoverished the indigenous cultures. From their beginnings the peoples of southern Spain had been a great variety of tribes, with different languages, different political cultures and different ways of organising land ownership. Though the Greeks might once have called them collectively Tartessians, and later scholars

Iberians (after the great river Ibero, which is now the smaller Ebro), they did not see themselves as a tidy unity. Then came Mother Rome, who dominated the country for 600 years. It is instructive to contrast the repression of Rome with Islam's more permissive approach seven centuries on, and to contrast it again with Spain's own attempt at colonising the New World seven centuries after that. The Spaniards might have suffered under the Romans, but in the name of God they applied many of the same impoverishing techniques to the alien peoples of the New World.

The conquest of Spain took the Romans 200 years of bitter campaigning. But it was never complete and was followed by endless skirmishing. The peoples of the peninsula would rise up in fairly regular rebellion against greedy provincial governors or enforced enrolment in the army. However, Spain, with its natural resources, was a prize worth the fight. The province of Baetica alone (from Betis, the Roman name of the Guadalquivir), roughly the same size as present-day Andalusia, was a veritable treasure house for the empire, providing wheat, wine, olives and olive oil, as well as silver, copper – and gold. Imperial Rome took more gold from Spain than imperial Spain took from America. Olive oil was an important export for an empire that relied on oil for light, as well as for cooking and medical purposes. Oil production, especially in the region between Seville and Córdoba, began in the first century AD. Another export was garum, made from the abundant local fish. The viscera and blood of the tuna, or whole mackerel, were pounded to a black sauce to spice up food. It was thought to be nutritious and to have curative properties. Tuna, *atún*, is still fished along the coast – the historic industry is recorded in the name of the coastal town of Zahara de los Atunes – and is just as popular, but it is more likely nowadays to be served in steaks, *a la plancha*, or served dried as *mojama*, or in a wine and onion sauce as *atún encebollado*.

The practice of the Romans was to take land from conquered towns to settle demobbed soldiers, enabling Rome to keep an eye on the vanquished. Seville was one such which had land appropriated. This system introduced a structure

7

of landowning which has persisted in Andalusia to this day, forming a static aristocracy of landowners and freezing progress in agriculture. Yet for the first, and – as historian Henry Kamen put it – arguably the last, time some sort of political and moral unity was imposed on Hispania, Roman Spain. Roman rule brought with it a common coinage, a common tongue (the basis of Spain's three officially recognised modern languages: Castilian, Galician and Catalán), improved communications and the establishment of Spain's role as a trading nation. Christianity also filtered in.

Julius Caesar raised Seville to the status of a colony in 45 BC. Yet at the outset it was overshadowed by Itálica, to the west, Spain's first Roman colony. Scipio Africanus had founded it in 206 BC as a home for his veterans, and its role as the subsequent birthplace of two Roman emperors, Trajan and Hadrian, won it great fame. However, Seville ultimately became the dominant city and Itálica is today renowned as Seville's prime Roman archaeological site. As a (reasonably) enthusiastic classicist I found it a dreary, dismal place on my first visit as a student, and one to be avoided at all costs in the heat of summer, given the lack of shade. It was the kind of place that gives ancient monuments a bad name. Given that it is probably the most extensive Roman site in Baetica, it was remarkably uninteresting. This seemed a pity, for the great value of Itálica is that, unlike so many of Spain's great Roman cities, it was never built over by later generations. Today, Itálica is under new management and the research being carried out under its energetic new director, José Manuel Rodríguez, is changing my negative view of the place, even if he cannot change the weather.

The puzzle is why Itálica was so important in Roman times, and why two such apparently important towns as Itálica and Seville should have been founded as colonies so close, apparently in competition. Seville may always have suffered from the risk of flooding, but the Guadalquivir gave it vastly superior communications. Itálica, on its hill, was safe from floods, but a good journey from the bountiful river. Simon Keay, from Southampton University, who has been working on the multinational research project at the site, explains that Itálica owed its fame to two factors. First, two emperors came from there, and Hadrian in particular was keen to aggrandise his home town as part of his personal PR. The expansion Itálica underwent under Hadrian was entirely political. Thanks to him it abounds in public buildings, including the largest amphitheatre in Spain, and the fourth largest in the Roman world; a theatre; a temple; baths – and there are traces of many private houses, of the mosaics that decorated them and of the streets and drains that connected them.

But Itálica was a typical example of Roman dominance over the 'barbarians' of Spain. It was a Roman city, not obviously Spanish, and it was abandoned when the Romans left, and used as a quarry. Eighteenth-century travellers found wheat being grown in the amphitheatre. José Manuel Rodríguez is nevertheless keen to emphasise that Itálica is no Marie Celeste. It lives on still in Santiponce, the neighbouring town. He may be investigating the homes of the long dead, but their descendants are all around him.

Itálica was an imperial project. It acquired its prestige from the state funds that Hadrian poured into it. In that sense it has some similarity with the Expos and the effects they have had on Seville. It is these which have given the second major boost to Itálica's fame. The Ibero-American Expo of 1929 gave Itálica, by its proximity to Seville, a PR push which promoted it above some of Roman Spain's other outstanding cities. Similarly, the preparations for Expo 92 gave the impetus for change in the management of the site. By the end of the 1990s, our understanding of Itálica will have been transformed. As it is, from its very earliest years Itálica has been the pawn of public relations. Even now, says José Manuel Rodríguez, 'the guides who bring parties in will tell you something about Trajan to get a clap and 1,000 *pesetas*'.

For an idea of the grandeur – albeit shortlived – that was Itálica, it is necessary to visit the Museo Arqueológico, housed in what was the Renaissance Pavilion for Expo 29. The building is noteworthy for being one of the few public buildings in Seville that is falling apart. It is all the more noteworthy amid the frenzy of renovation, restoration and building for Expo 92. The roof is leaking, and the elegant doves that perch in the eaves have whitewashed the facade in droppings. There are imposing sculptures of Trajan, the city's imperial son, and of Mercury, Diana and Alexander the Great. The large mosaic on display is equally grand. By contrast, there are relatively few domestic items on show. Nevertheless, standing by the jewellery case, it is easy to make romantic connections between the women who wore the beaded necklaces and earrings all those years ago, and the *sevillanas* today in the streets outside with their colourful jewellery. History lives when modern versions of the red ceramic ware they used are sold in every street market throughout Spain, and used in every bar and kitchen. The ironwork, too, shows clear links with the grilles that decorate the windows and patios of the picture-postcard Seville of today.

The hardest part for any museum is breathing life into dusty remains. But there is one item from Itálica in the Archaeological Museum which calls out from down the centuries. Centuries before the Hollywood stars starting immortalising their fame with their feet, casting their prints in pavement cement, they were doing it at Itálica to propitiate the gods. The priests who organised the games in the amphitheatre had their footprints carved in stone, an offering to Nemesis to ensure that they were successful in their task. They needed the support. Today there are shows at the amphitheatre once more, but of a more restrained variety. The international dance festival in the summer has replaced the wild beasts.

Hispalis was the Roman name for Seville. The name may come from 'Spal', which is probably Phoenician. Some say that Hispalis is Carthaginian for 'flat land'. San Isidoro, the great *sevillano* bishop, later canonised, had it that Caesar called the city Julia Romula (after himself and the founder of Rome). The name Hispalis, he says, comes from the fact that the city was built on 'these piles' (*his palis*), to protect its buildings from the risk of flood. However this is straining the Latin just too far. Another myth holds that Hercules erected six great stone pillars in Seville and Caesar subsequently founded Hispalis. Thus Caesar and Hercules were the joint founders of the city and statues of them top the two columns that adorn the Alameda de Hércules, the promenade that was created in the sixteenth century. These columns are thought to have come, not from Hercules, but from the portico of a temple built in the time of Hadrian or his successor. One column was broken being transported to the Alcázar, and three remain in calle Mármoles on the edge of the Barrio de Santa Cruz. These must be the most depressing of the meagre remains of imperial Rome in the city. As you walk down the narrow street, there's no sign of them. A newly refurbished apartment block has a small half-column of grey marble in its patio. For a desperate, irrational moment you panic that they have been removed and that this has been left as a cynical souvenir by the architect. And then, right at the end of the street, hemmed in by buildings, stand the granite monoliths. Their feet are paddling in a stinking, stagnant pond. A couple of urchins are throwing rubble from the inevitable skip of builders' detritus into the greenish water.

More impressive are the 500 metres of Roman wall which run between the Puerta de la Macarena and the Puerta de Córdoba, with six rectangular towers, and a vaulted gallery inside. The walls were subsequently restored by Moors and Christians alike. The problem now is that they look too well restored. It is hard to believe that they might really have belonged to a Roman city, and that Seville might once have been walled as Avila still is.

The layout of the Roman city continues to be debated, though it is known to have been on the same higher, drier ground of the Phoenician settlement. There is general agreement that the commercial forum would have been near the present cathedral, with another forum nearby, possibly in the Plaza de la Alfalfa. Of the theatre, the amphitheatre, the circus, the appurtenances of civic life, there are no traces, though a number of hypotheses have been made.

There are some remembrances of life in Roman Seville – for instance, of the guilds. The emperors, like many managers, were not keen on workers combining for mutual benefit. They could be a source of political instability. However, there are records of the guild of Sevillian copper refiners, as well as the local firemen, who were essential for protecting the warehouses of the port. There are records, too, of an early youth club. One Fabia Hadrianilla left a bequest of 50,000 sesterces in her will, giving an annual income at five or six per cent interest, to buy food for twenty-one free-born girls (at forty sesterces each) and twenty-two free-born boys (at thirty sesterces each) who belonged to a *collegium iuvenum* in the city. In a bid for posterity, she specified that the money was to be distributed twice a year on her birthday and that of her husband.

Once Julius Caesar died, Spain never regained its importance for the power brokers of the Roman Empire, though it produced four emperors and remained an important source of food. The ordinary people were regarded as close to being barbarians by the Romans, who created an élite of their own people and certain favoured Iberians who had full citizenship. It was not until the emperor Caracalla was strapped for cash that an emperor could bring himself to grant the Spaniards full citizenship. But the eventual outcome of this magnanimous gesture was to alienate the people from involvement in political life. Rather than live in the cities, they preferred to withdraw to large country estates or *latifundia* which exist to this day: isolated farmhouses with their own flour mills, olive presses, bodegas and livestock.

Seville was the foremost port on the Guadalquivir, with its direct access to the sea, and was also noted for its shipbuilding. As well as traces of the shipyards, the remains of many potteries have been found along the banks of the Guadalquivir. The potters made the jars for exporting olive oil and other produce. (At Rome's port of Ostia, the journey's end, a corresponding hillock of broken Andalusian pottery has been found.) Olive oil is no longer transported in jars, but the potters' descendants keep up their trade. Today, though, their customers are more likely to be tourists than businessmen.

Baetica had been at peace for 200 years, but in 171–3, the Mauri (from Mauretania in North Africa) invaded. In 177–219 they invaded again. The empire's economy teetered as the emperor Septimus Severus debased the silver coinage. In 262 Frankish tribesmen crossed into Spain. The emperors were incompetent. The Roman Empire was not invincible.

Around this time Seville acquired its first Christian martyrs. Justa and Rufina, the story has it, were potters from the Triana district. The Christian sisters rejected a pagan god, or possibly the ceremonies in worship of Adonis provoked them. Whatever it was, Rufina was burned to death and Justa probably died a prisoner. Seville gained its martyrs, and the potters their patron saints. Murillo has enshrined them for all time in a famous painting which now hangs in the Museo de Bellas Artes (*see Plate 1*). Justa and Rufina gaze soulfully from the frame, holding the martyrs' palms; around their feet are the products of their trade. In the thirteenth century when the city was taken from the Muslims, it was claimed that the sisters' grave had been found.

In the fourth century Constantine restored a grip on the empire, and Christianity flourished. The Holy Hispalensian Church of Jerusalem was built in Seville, but it – like so much of the city's history – lies buried, in this case under the cathedral.

In 409 Germanic invaders – Vandals, Alans, Suevi – poured over the Pyrenees. The Vandals moved down into Baetica, and plundered a number of cities, including Seville. Seville was again sacked and pillaged in 428. The Vandals' leader Gunderic died after desecrating the church; clearly, San Isidoro noted in his history, this was an Act of God. From Seville the Vandals moved on to Africa. It is from this period that the name Andalusia dates. The Arabs thus called Spain, the country from which the Vandals came, 'al-Andalus', 'belonging to the Vandals'. Not long after, in 443, Seville was attacked by a plague, the first of a number which were to devastate the city over many centuries.

The Visigoths followed on from the Vandals and set up their court in Seville in the middle of the sixth century, attracted, as the Romans had been, by the city's natural resources and its pretty face. The first Visigothic king of Seville was soon murdered; his successor died the same way, at a banquet, just eighteen months later. Subsequently, under Athanagild, the court was moved to Toledo, and Seville, as was to happen repeatedly, lost its primacy.

With the Visigoths, the stratified, urban-dwelling, land-owning, Catholic, Roman patricians were confronted by an individualistic, tribal, warlike, nomadic people who followed the Arian heresy. The religious split between the two was never entirely resolved, and this and the accompanying political disputes finally weakened Visigothic rule and allowed the Muslims into Spain.

The Visigoths were unable to impose anything like the same unity on Spain that the Romans had. They did, however, contribute several saints to the calendar. The first was Hermenegildo, who was appointed to rule Seville by his father Leovigildo. Leovigildo followed the Arian heresy and it was his son's adoption of Catholicism that led to civil war. Hermenegildo finally refused to co-operate with his father, minted coinage proclaiming his Catholic kingship and called in help from the enemy Byzantines. Leovigildo set up camp in Itálica and besieged Seville for nearly a year. Hermenegildo was eventually captured and taken prisoner, having ruled for just two years. Not long before Leovigildo's own death, Hermenegildo was murdered to ensure that he was not alive to jeopardise the succession of his brother Reccared. A millennium later, in 1585, the martyr Hermenegildo was canonised.

The greatest figure in Seville of this period was undoubtedly the bishop San Isidoro (560–636). (His was an influential family, for his brother San Leandro was Bishop of Seville immediately before him. San Leandro gained immortality in the *yemas de San Leandro*, the sweets based on egg yolks that the nuns make in the eponymous convent.) In this period it was the Catholic church and the indigenous élite who provided the intellectual leadership. Amongst their achievements was the publication of the *Fuero Juzgo*, a code based on Roman law. Isidoro's learning turned Seville into one of the great centres of Visigothic life. He founded a universal library and an ecclesiastical school, and his *Etymologies* catalogued all that was known at the time, in a scholarly enterprise reflecting the last gasp of the ancient world. As the friend and adviser of King Sisebut he also became politically powerful. Sisebut is sometimes rated as the most literate and liberal king in the history of Visigothic Spain. He shared with Isidoro a zeal to reconstruct the secular and spiritual life of the country. But this also meant bringing heavy pressure to bear on the Jews.

There had been Jews in Spain from early times, following in the footsteps of the Phoenicians. Over the centuries they had been allowed varying degrees of freedom to practise their faith, but in general they had been excluded from public office unless they recanted. In the later part of the fifth and for most of the sixth century they were treated with reasonable tolerance. But Isidoro stressed the need to forbid Jews to marry Christian women, or to hold authority over Christians, or to have Christian slaves. Sisebut passed a law confiscating the goods of any Jew who converted a Christian, and of any Christian converted by a Jew. When the differences between the Visigoths led to one side inviting in the Arab-Berbers from North Africa in 711, the oppressed minority of Jews greeted the invaders gladly. This action was inevitably used against the Jews in later centuries: in times of crisis the Jews always got the blame. The last years of Visigothic rule crumbled in enmity and disagreement; not just the Jews, but the slaves and many of the rest of the population suffered. The religious dissent that had given rise to civil war rumbled on. For many, indeed, the empire-building Muslims were welcome.

The Visigoths ruled Spain for three centuries. In Seville practically nothing remains of their passing, whether works of art or buildings. There are some Visigothic pillars to be found in the old city, for instance in calle Corral del Rey, and in the patio of the church of San Salvador. The Alcázar contains some stones of the period. In the Casa de Pilatos, the little statue of the Good Shepherd on the altar in the chapel is also Visigothic. Most notable of all, perhaps, is the fountain in the centre of the Patio de los Naranjos at the foot of the Giralda, striking for its size, if not the quality of its ornament.

Depending on your point of view, the arrival of the 'Moors' (taken from Mauretania, in North Africa, and always used in Spain with a derogatory meaning) could be either a Good Thing (bringing Art, Culture, Science), or a Bad One (bringing Homosexuality, Book-burning, Bloodshed). The latter view was urged upon me by a former stalwart of the Franco years who lent me the work of the Spanish historian Claudio Sánchez Albornoz, who has argued this case eloquently. The former view has been espoused more recently, typically by the small town of Puerto Real, near Cádiz, which commissioned the Ecuadorean artist Osualdo Guayasamín to create a monument 'in homage to the victims of the European invasion in 1492'.

The 'Moors' were in fact a mixture of Berbers (hence 'barbarians') and Arabs (their colonisers), as well as Syrians and Egyptians. The Berbers were described in one Muslim history as a great people, on a par with the Arabs, the Persians, the Greeks and the Romans. A confederation of tribes, they had acquired no empire of their own but had been taken over successively by the empires of Carthage, Rome, Byzantium and Islam. Among their number were the emperor Septimus Severus and the church fathers Tertullian, Cyprian and Augustine. Once under the influence of Islam, they remained divided and continued to create their own schisms: successively Fatimids, Almoravids and Almohads.

Spain was the obvious next step for the Arab empire spreading its new faith. Once a Visigothic faction had asked the Berbers for support, a party crossed the straits to Spain and occupied its southern tip in 710. The party's leader was Tarif; his memory is preserved in the name of the town there: Tarifa.

The following year Tariq ibn Ziryab led a full expeditionary force. Their disembarking point came to be known as Jabal Tariq, the rock of Tariq, or Gibraltar. The conquest of Spain took the Romans 200 years, and the Christians 400 years. But in just seven years the Arabs took control of most of the country, though they never managed to conquer northern Spain, from La Coruña to Barcelona. This failure left a pocket of Christian opposition which was ultimately to be their downfall.

Seville was a prize for the invading army: 'The best and most important of cities in Spain' as the Muslim history *Akhbar Majmu'a* described it. The historian of Seville, Santiago Monoto, put it more floridly, illustrating the romantic passion Seville arouses in so many of its natives. Noting that under the Arabs, Hispalis was called 'Isvilia', which is the source of the modern-day 'Sevilla', he declared:

> The city had been transformed into a seductive beauty, with a gorgeous body and a refined mind. It was no longer a girl, it had become a woman . . . As it abandoned the clothes of childhood, so it gave up the name with which it had been brought into the world . . .
>
> The city liked its new name, and made it its own. Wearing it like a diadem, it called at the gates of History with so lustrous a title, that it was that name which had to be engraved on the pages of gold in the great book in which only the chosen may appear. And History, seduced by the enchanting city which wore its river like a necklace, wrote in letters of light, Isvilia: Sevilla.

Seville fell to the general Musa Ibn Nusayr, who entrusted the keys of the city to the Jews. Soon after Musa left, eighty Arabs were killed in an uprising. The rebellion was rapidly quashed by Musa's son Abd al-Azis, who governed Muslim Spain from the city as emir. He, however, only lasted a couple of years before being decapitated, on the grounds, so it is said, that he had converted to Christianity. In the early years of Muslim Spain, the Arabs and Berbers were in constant conflict, and the Arabs only defeated the Berbers by drafting in a force of <u>Yemenis</u>. Under Muslim rule Seville's importance as a trading centre continued to grow. Its harbour was crucial not just for trade, but for importing quantities of soldiers to feed the endless battles and skirmishes.

Al-Andalus was the name given to the whole of Muslim Spain. Its centre of administration was restored to the south from the Visigothic capital of Toledo, which was on the 'frontier'. The capital was briefly in Seville, and then moved upriver to Córdoba. Within half a century of the arrival of the Muslim invaders, al-Andalus had become a province of the Umayyad caliphs of Damascus, who ruled until 1031. In 929 Abd al-Rahman III proclaimed Córdoba the capital of the western caliphate. Córdoba became the most important city in Western Europe, with a population of half a million. The *mezquita*, or mosque, in Córdoba is a triumphant symbol of that great city.

During this period Seville flourished and was particularly famous for the manufacture of musical instruments. The Umayyads laid the foundations for what is remembered as best in Muslim Spain. The arts, science and medicine blossomed, and trade and commerce increased alongside. The Umayyads brought stability – though there was never peace between so many conflicting peoples and interests – and religious tolerance, enabling the Jews to become influential in society once more. Not all was entirely calm; in 844, the Normans came upriver and plundered Seville.

Umayyad rule finally collapsed in 1031, and al-Andalus was split into twelve kingdoms or *taifas*, of which Seville was one. The poetry of this period is as sensuous as its more famous architecture and art. Under its poet-king al-Mu'tamid (1069–95), Seville once more became pre-eminent. In 1078 tragedy struck when the Guadalquivir once more burst its banks; as a result, more than 6,000 homes were flooded and several hundred people died. Hardly had Seville recovered from this than the city was shaken by an earthquake, which brought down a number of buildings. Al-Mu'tamid paid out handsomely for the repairs, but when it came to paying the customary tribute to Alfonso VI, King of Castilla, and his daughter's husband, the coffers were almost empty. The grandeur of Seville had been bought at great cost. The only solution was to send debased coinage. The trick did not work. Alfonso initiated a campaign against the Muslim possessions, culminating in taking Toledo in 1085. This was the beginning of the end for Muslim Spain. The *Reconquista*, or 'Reconquest', had begun, though it should more appropriately be called a Conquest, since the Christians were campaigning against a people who had been under Muslim rule for almost four centuries. Arabic was the official language, the majority had converted to Islam; al-Andalus was a province of the Arab empire.

Al-Mu'tamid's only solution was to call for help from North Africa, from the Almoravids. The story has it that his son begged him not to, knowing the fanaticism of the Almoravids, but al-Mu'tamid replied, 'I'd rather be a shepherd looking after the camels of the emir of Morocco, than run a pigsty in Castille.' The Almoravids rapidly defeated Alfonso's army near Badajoz, and then returned to Africa. But two years later, they were called in again and they arrived this time not as allies but as conquerors. Al-Mu'tamid was taken prisoner and sent to Africa, where he died.

Santiago Montoto notes that Seville must have been an appealing prospect to the Almoravids. He paints a colourful portrait:

> The spectacle of the city, so striking with its fertile fields populated with farms, with its market gardens irrigated by the great river, surrounded by its strong walls, with its white houses, amidst which sprang up hundreds of mosques, as well as minarets, domes of the great houses and towers of the royal palaces, made a vivid impression on the Moroccans, who were used to the crudities of a civilisation which looked very backward in comparison with this brilliant kingdom.

Under the Almoravids religious repression returned for the Jews and for the Christian minority, who were known as Mozarabs. The Almoravids lasted a century and were succeeded by another fanatical tribe of Berbers, the Almohads. They lasted no longer than the Almoravids and were finally resoundingly defeated by Alfonso VII at Las Navas de Tolosa in 1212. Thereafter the 'Reconquest' was assured. Seville returned to Christian control in 1248 and by the middle of the thirteenth century Granada was the sole – though enduring – outpost of Muslim Spain. It was not until 1492 that the Nasrid dynasty in Granada fell. The forces of Aragón, Castilla and Portugal were too preoccupied with internal dissension and overseas expansion to complete the conquest of Spain.

One must not underrate the achievements of Muslim Spain. In the Generalife, the gardens of the Alhambra in Granada, the Arabs are sentimentalised as great gardeners and fountain-makers. Indeed they were, but this had its practical side. To feed the gardens and the fountains of Seville, they had to continue the work of the Romans, restoring the aqueduct and introducing new technology to increase and improve the supply of water into the city and its farms. In the Aljarafe they planted figs and olives; they also introduced oranges, rice, sugar-cane and cotton, all products which are grown to this day. They continued the mineral trade, and across al-Andalus built up industries, including wool, silk, glass, paper, weapons and leather. They enhanced the vocabulary, introducing words into Castilian (such as *alcázar*, royal palace; *alcalde*, mayor; *arroz*, rice; *sandía*, water melon) and into English (such as almond, orange, sugar, algebra and alcohol). They introduced the technique of making *azulejos*, the polychrome glazed tiles which became and remain such a distinctive feature of Andalusia.

What remains in Seville of its Muslim past? It is hard to say, for there has been little research, says Reyes Ojeda, a young archaeologist working for the Junta de Andalucía, the Andalusian government. She grabbed my arm, eagerly pointing out one trace of the past, a part of the ninth-century wall of the *mezquita* in calle Alcaicería, round the corner from the Plaza del Salvador. As we stood there shoppers hurried past, heedless of their ancient city around and beneath them. 'There are no civil buildings from Islamic Seville at all,' Reyes told me. 'Until very recently everybody in this region was interested in either the Roman and prehistoric city, or in Seville after the Reconquista. Much more work has been done on the Islamic period in Granada, Jaén and Almería, in eastern Andalusia. There was a problem, too, that nobody took archaeology very seriously. They were interested in the restoration of later buildings rather than in excavation. Consequently much more work has been done on Islamic ceramics.'

What does remain is the irregular layout of the old city. Its narrow streets keep out the sun, but they also defy the map-reader. It is to Seville's Arab rulers that we also owe the city's prominent landmark, an orientation point for the confused traveller. This is the Giralda, a structure particularly remarkable for its state of preservation, given the grubbiness of the cathedral and the decay of those palaces which have not yet been restored.

The Giralda was built, not in the golden years of the Umayyads, but under the harsher Almohads, between 1172 and 1195. It was originally, of course, the minaret to the *mezquita*, or mosque, but became in due course the cathedral's bell tower. Souvenir manufacturers have done much to debase their city's prime marketing tool. Seeing it for sale as a table lamp in 'ivory' or 'gold' from fifteen to ninety centimetres high, or as the pattern on a set of three stacking mugs, does not endear me to it. Equally, the hordes of tourists milling round its feet are an irritant. But the Giralda rises above everything that subsequent generations have done to it. Thanks to sensible town planning, there are no buildings near it which come to more than two-thirds of its height (just over a hundred metres). This is the building to watch to appreciate the much-hymned luminosity of the city.

The Giralda has withstood successive earthquakes, where its neighbour, the cathedral, has suffered damage. One of the reasons for this may be its design. The façade is perpendicular, but the inner walls get thicker – and thus heavier – as the

21

building rises. This counteracts the natural tendency of walls to separate the higher a tower rises. The charming feature of the Giralda for the visitor is that inside there is a ramp, rather than steps, making the climb a good deal easier, especially since the incline gets less steep as one wearies at the top of the building. So easy is it, in fact, that Fernando I is said to have ridden his horse to the top, as did elderly *muezzins*. The Giralda was originally finished off with four bronze spheres, one at each corner. They were the only casualties of earthquakes, when they fell off in the middle of the fourteenth century. In 1395 they were replaced by a small tower. The present belfry with twenty-four bells was added by Hernán Ruiz in 1568, and topped by the 'Giraldillo' or weather vane, which gives the tower its name. There is some debate about what it represents, whether fortitude, victory or faith. The actual weather vane is inside the cathedral; the statue on the Giralda is a copy.

At the foot of the Giralda is the Patio de los Naranjos, with its Visigothic fountain basin. A romantic site shaded by orange trees, it was once a popular spot for the merchants of the city – and for pickpockets. The merchants have gone, but the pickpockets are still on the look-out for an incautious tourist.

The Torre del Oro, built a little later, in 1220, seems vastly overrated by contrast to the Giralda, though in any other city it would be worthy of attention. The novelist Camilo José Cela had it exactly right when he declared that the Torre del Oro was permanently humiliated by the Giralda. The tower was built at the end of an Almohad wall that ran down to the Guadalquivir from the Alcázar. It is in three tiers, the top tier having been added in 1760. Perhaps it is the epithet 'del Oro' that misleads. The tower may have been 'golden' because it housed the gold from the ships that came back from the Americas, or more likely because it was covered with golden tiles. Either way, there is no sign of that splendour now. It houses instead a small nautical museum and is the embarkation point for uninspiring boat trips up the Guadalquivir. Further up the river there used to be an accompanying Tower of Silver. The Torre del Oro is best enjoyed as the sun is setting, across the river over a *tapa* at the Río Grande or the Kiosco de las Flores.

The Alcázar is more of a jewel. The first building on this site was an Arab fortress begun in 712. In the ninth century Abd al-Rahman II had a palace built here, and the surrounding walls, which run from the Barrio de Santa Cruz to the Plaza del Triunfo, are eleventh century. The Almohads extended the buildings in the twelfth century, and after the Christian conquest the kings set up a court here and used it as a basis for campaigning against Muslim Granada. Ironically, it was Pedro el Cruel who created the palace that is so admired today, building over the ruins of one destroyed in the earthquakes of 1356. He used *mudéjar* craftsmen. The term refers to Muslims who continued to live under Christian rule without converting, but it became extended to the architecture of the period, to describe the work of the Muslim craftsmen in Christian Spain. They made this palace, for it was never a fortress, into the outstanding example of its kind in Spain. Practically every century since then the kings of Spain have added to it and adjusted it, not always for the better. Despite the tourists and the tamperings, it is a complex building of enormous beauty, with alluring, scented gardens.

Backing on to the silent walls of the Alcázar is the Barrio de Santa Cruz. We owe its present condition to the Marquis of Vega-Inclán, who in the interests of tourism had the *barrio* restored in the 1920s. It has a certain stage-set quality, enhanced by the brilliance of the light. So manicured is its beauty that I expect to find a theatrical performance round every corner or the eponymous Barber bursting into song. Nor am I always mistaken. More often than not there are some youths dressed as troubadours to entertain the public, or some giggling girls in flamenco outfits. To be sure, many of the houses are still lived in, but for every home there is a touristic bar, a shop of bijou artefacts and a couple of hotels.

Each street in the *barrio* has its own anecdote, its own famous resident. In calle Pimienta the Jews fixed the exchange rates; in calle Susona lived the Jewess Susona who loved a Christian. When she learned that her father and his friends intended to kill several inquisitors, her beloved included, Susona told her lover. There were fierce reprisals against the Jews, and Susona's family were killed. Susona ordered her skull to be placed over her door upon her death as a punishment and an example to others. The story has it that the skull was still there in the eighteenth century. In this sanitised heritage centre where the bougainvillea blossoms, it is easy to forget that this was once the home of a sector of the population who suffered bitter persecution.

Claudio Sánchez Albornoz has asked us to consider what might have happened if the Arabs had stayed. He points out that without the 'Reconquest' we would not have had the *conversos*, the Muslims who converted to Christianity, whose grandchildren include Fray Luis de León, St John of the Cross and St Teresa of Avila. Furthermore, he argues, the experience of the 'Reconquest' gave Spain the power to conquer America, which once more refreshed the culture of the country. There would have been no pilgrimage to Santiago de Compostela, for St James, after all, was the *matamoros*, the slayer of the Moors, who was said to have appeared miraculously to lead the Christians to victory against the Arabs. There would have been no cathedrals, no *Cantar del mío Cid*, no *Don Quixote* nor *Celestina*, no El Greco, no Velázquez, no Goya. This is a wonderful game to play, on a par with naming famous Belgians, but gets us nowhere. The achievements of Muslim Spain are with us still and the influences of so many years of civilisation are profound.

It was Fernando III who took Seville for the Christians and he was later canonised for his pains. It was a difficult siege, finally broken by destroying the bridge of boats, the city's last supply line. The king made his triumphant entry on 2 December 1248. He gave the Muslims a month to leave the city, providing them with ships to sail to Africa, though many preferred to flee to the remaining parts of Muslim Spain. Fernando's short reign was characterised for its religious tolerance. Typically, therefore, his epitaph is written in four languages, Spanish, Hebrew, Latin and Arabic, and he called himself 'King of the Three Religions'. His embalmed body is displayed in the cathedral three times a year, on 14 and 30 May and 23 November, and his statue is paraded in the Corpus Christi procession.

The city the Christians took over was seriously underpopulated. Some 100,000 Arabs had been expelled and the population numbered no more than 14,000. Fernando *el Santo's* son, Alfonso X, *el Sabio*, 'the Wise', moved quickly to counter this with a resettlement policy of veterans, echoing the Romans before him. He settled 200 knights from his father's campaigns in large houses in the city, which became some of the seigneurial palaces of Seville. The city was repopulated with Cataláns and Castilians – it was Alfonso *el Sabio* who established Castilian as the national language. As trade picked up after the war, foreign merchants moved in, as the city's street names still reveal: Francos, Placentines, Génova – the French, the Plasencians and the Genoese all settled here. The Genoese bankers and merchants were given a mosque in the plaza de San Francisco to carry out their business.

The port made Triana and El Arenal on both sides of the river very cosmopolitan, with sailors and traders arriving from all over the world. Alfonso X himself recorded the ships that came: from Tangiers, Ceúta, Alexandria, Genoa, Portugal, England, Pisa, Lombardy, Bordeaux, Bayonne, Sicily, Gascony, Catalonia, Aragón, and 'from Christian and Moorish lands'. The Jewish quarter was given three mosques to use as synagogues, and a farm in the Aljarafe. The remaining Arabs also had their own mosques and baths in a district known as the Morería. The city was reorganised into 24 parishes which remain today. Seville may have grown, but its old centre stays much the same. Over the next centuries the *mudéjar* craftsmen combined the prevalent Gothic style with their own Muslim traditions to build a panoply of churches, outstanding in their quantity and quality, among them Santa Ana (the historic church of the Triana district) and San Gil in the thirteenth century; Santa Marina, San Vicente, San Isidoro, San

Lorenzo, Omnium Sanctorum, San Andrés, San Esteban, San Marcos, Santa Catalina and San Pedro in the fourteenth century; and San Martín, San Juan de la Palma and San Isidoro el Campo, in the fifteenth century.

Over the coming years, Seville as capital of Castilla became embroiled in bitter disputes between contending branches of the royal family. These came to a head with the illegitimate twin sons of Alfonso XI by the aristocrat Leonor de Guzmán. Henrique and Fadrique (he of the Torre, or tower, of that name, which is the only Gothic civil monument standing in the city) of Trastámara campaigned against their legitimate half-brother Pedro, born to María of Portugal, whose family went to war in protest at the way her husband Alfonso was treating her. (María is buried in the convent of San Clemente, close to the Barqueta Bridge, a former Moorish palace which is being excavated and restored.)

Pedro went down in history as 'the Cruel' and had, unfairly, as bad a press as Richard III. The stories about him which terrify little children are legion, and are most vivid in the history of calle Cabeza del Rey Don Pedro ('Head of King Peter Street'). The legend goes that the king murdered an enemy. He promised to kill the man who did it, not knowing that his deed had been witnessed. He had the 'head' displayed in a box. Only after his death was it discovered that the box contained a bust of the murderer, Don Pedro himself.

Then there is the legend of doña María Coronel, the foundress of the convent of Santa Inés in the street that bears her name. Running away from the lustful King Pedro she buried herself alive in calle Hombre de Piedra (Man of Stone Street) in the garden of the Convent of Santa Clara, today confectioners and bakers like the nuns of Santa Inés. God made the grass grow over her to confound the king, and she made her escape when he had gone. The alternative version has her disfiguring herself with boiling oil in desperation. Either way, a person who creates such beauty as the Alcázar surely can't be all bad.

The history of the time also records the dynastic feud between the Guzmáns and the Ponce de Leóns, the families of Arcos and Medina Sidonia, two ruling families of Seville. Their descendants live in the city still. There's a charming Ponce de León who practises in Seville as a neurologist. He dresses as an English gentleman, as the upper classes are wont to do, but cares nothing for this aristocratic legend.

The Jews meanwhile suffered vicious attacks throughout Spain. The Judería, in the Barrio de Santa Cruz, though charmingly picturesque today, was not so pleasant in the fourteenth century. The palaces we can see were not built until the fifteenth and sixteenth centuries. The previous houses were cramped and poorly ventilated. In 1391 the rabble were roused and 4,000 Jews were killed. Much of the Judería was destroyed and two of the three synagogues were taken back by the church authorities.

In these years the generally insanitary conditions all over the city led to a number of epidemics. Whenever the Guadalquivir overflowed, rising on occasions almost as high as the land round the cathedral, it left stagnant lakes of water which did not drain away. There were at least fifteen epidemics between 1350 and 1488, and a similar number of famines. The city reeled under the repeated blows. These calamities, together with the occasional earthquake, most notably that of 1356, led the moralising to believe they were justified punishment from God for popular excess. According to one document of the time:

[in the streets there were] monasteries of bad women who misused their bodies in the sin of luxury or who ran the brothels like abbesses and they would fraudulently or to order hire out these bad women who were there to perform this wrongdoing, and sometimes it happened that these women who were together in a sort of school did their sins and wrongdoings more fraudulently than those who did it in public, and that some were wives and widows and virgins who entered these houses and they would perform these horrors, which is a great affront to God and gives a very bad example.

The clergy themselves committed the sin of pride, deciding, on 8 July 1401, to build 'a church so large that those who see it shall think that we are mad'. Seville Cathedral became the world's largest Gothic church and the third largest Christian cathedral (beaten only by St Peter's in Rome and St Paul's in London). It was, not surprisingly, more than a century in the building, and is the incarnation of the words 'In my father's house there are many mansions'. The cathedral has a multiplicity of nooks and crannies, containing amongst other things the largest reredos in Christendom; the body of San Fernando; the original of the Giraldillo; the wooden copy of the crocodile, popularly known as *el lagarto*, 'the lizard', which the Sultan of Egypt sent Alfonso the Wise in exchange for his daughter's hand in marriage (he was unsuccessful); two of the largest organs in the world; and the cathedral's certificate of its unique dimensions from the Guinness Book of Records. It is a building that dwarfs all who enter, and it contains one monument that shrinks the visitor to the size of Alice in Wonderland and the scuttling clerics to mice. This is the remarkable monument – though not the tomb; the body is in Santo Domingo – to Cristóbal Colón, Christopher Columbus, who takes his place in Chapter 2.

2. The New Babylon

In Franco's time the Reyes Católicos, the Catholic Monarchs, were a popular propaganda tool. The endless plaudits for a pair of Catholic Monarchs were mystifying to visitors. Why should these two have been singled out when a good few monarchs before and every monarch after had been Catholic? The point, of course, was that Fernando and Isabella threw out the Arabs and the Jews, and laid the heavy hand of Christianity over all. From an initially reasonably open-handed stance they rapidly became more repressive, and were followed in this by their successors. The Inquisition, which began as an instrument for uncovering Jews, ended up as a tool of state terror. The Catholic Monarchs were creating the kind of holy Roman society that appealed, something over four centuries later, to a fascist dictator, who adopted their yoke and arrows for his own symbolism.

Twenty years on from my first visit to Spain, the changed status of the Catholic Monarchs is a sign of the times. Even the Pope has finally refused to canonise Isabella, though it was a Pope who had originally granted the pair the title of Reyes Católicos. The Catholic lobby might have been strong, but there are enough Jews and Arabs in the world who take an opposite view to give even the Holy See pause. Fernando and

Isabella can now take their place as a remarkable couple who by their marriage united Spain, and by a mixture of luck and design oversaw the arrival of a Golden Age in Spain, the last time that Spain was truly great. But there are few who would return them to the pedestal on which Franco placed them.

The marriage of Fernando II of Aragón and Isabella I of Castilla in 1469 ensured that the militarist ethos of Castilla, the spirt of the Conquest of the Arabs, triumphed over the more outward-looking, commercially minded Aragón. In the long term, this was to have a damaging effect on Spain and on the growth of its empire. In the short term, however, Fernando and Isabella took Granada, the last, glorious stronghold of the Arabs, thus finishing off the Reconquista which had begun four centuries earlier. It was 1492, a year of extraordinary importance for Spain, and for the rest of the world. On 3 August Christopher Columbus sailed from Palos de la Frontera at the mouth of the Guadalquivir with the *Niña, Pinta* and *Santa María*, making landfall in the Bahamas on 12 October. (The sailor who caught sight of land was Rodrigo de Triana, named, as was the custom, after his home town. He has his memorial now in the street named after him, which runs by the church of Santa Ana. Other sources suggest that he was actually from Lepe, but the name Triana sticks. Columbus never paid the large reward owing to him as the sailor who first sighted land, and he is said to have left Seville for Morocco and to have disappeared from the history books.)

Columbus did not actually discover the mainland of South America on his first trip, nor on his second, nor did he immediately encounter the riches which he so eagerly sought. That was left for Hernán Cortés and the other explorers who came after. But Columbus opened the door to the enormously profitable trade which ensued, and of which Seville had the important initial century of monopoly, through the Casa de Contratación, the commodity exchange. For the city, the economic and cultural pay-off of Columbus's of discovery was enormous. The inevitable decline that Seville underwent in the late seventeenth and eighteenth centuries seems all the more shocking by contrast with the glory that had gone before it.

The unity that Fernando and Isabella brought to Spain by their marriage was not binding. In her marriage contract Isabella stressed her rights as an equal, and she intended to keep the rewards of Columbus's discovery for Castilla: *'A Castilla y León, nuevo mundo dio Colón'* ('Columbus gave a new world to Castilla and León). When she died in 1504, the nobles of Castilla eased Fernando out and he went back to Aragón. But when their daughter Juana's husband died suddenly he had to be recalled as regent, because she was mentally unfit to rule.

Júana had married into the Habsburg dynasty and her son Carlos was brought up in the Netherlands. By the time he was nineteen, the young Carlos was not only King of Castilla and Aragón and its empire in America, but also Holy Roman Emperor. (Although he was the first King Carlos of Castilla, he was the fifth emperor of that name. Thus he is known as Carlos V.) Carlos was a foreign king, who brought his foreign advisers with him, to the displeasure of the Spanish courtiers. His early years on the throne were marked by popular uprisings, the *comunero* riots, across Spain. During his reign many of the greatest discoveries of the Americas were made. In 1519 Hernán Cortés conquered Mexico, and in the same year the Portuguese Magellan sailed from the Las Mulas wharf opposite the Torre del Oro for the first circumnavigation of the world, completed by Juan Sebastián Elcano. In 1532 Pizarro conquered Peru.

Even before the trade with the Indies began, Seville was a bustling city, the most populous in Castilla. Arenal, running from the cathedral to the river, was the fishermen's and sailors' quarter. Inevitably, therefore, it was also thronged with peddlers, prostitutes and down-and-outs. The shipbuilders on the river banks were furiously busy. By the city walls were the dirtier trades, such as the tanners. And drifting from the east, beyond the Tagarete river, came the stink of the city's rubbish tips and the slaughterhouses. Around the church of San Salvador there was a variety of markets selling foods and domestic items. Records list some ninety categories of artisans in the city at this time, making everything from fans, helmets, cabinets, crossbows, muskets and quilts, to saddles, mirrors and combs. There were 2,000 men in jobs connected with wine alone: working in the vineyards or as hauliers, running taverns or waiting at table. Triana, Seville's principal suburb, was renowned for its manufacture of soap, which had been a royal monopoly until the fifteenth century, and was exported for four centuries under the 'Castilla' brand. The industry exploited two local resources, olive oil and potash. The factory itself was in calle Castilla, close to the Castle of the Inquisition. In 1988, during the demolition of number 24, some of the huge vaulted 'caves' of the royal soap factory were uncovered in the basement. Republican supporters used them as hideouts during the Spanish Civil War.

For those with the money, life was very good. So good that the Crown was obliged on a number of occasions to issue decrees forbidding such excess. Society was headed by royal officials and important families, most of them landowners who preferred to live in the city than on their estates, and a number of whom have descendants in Seville today.

At the end of the fifteenth century the annual income of the Dukes of Medina Sidonia was 10,000 *maravedis*, four times the city's own substantial income. The extensive clergy flourished. (The Church was an extensive landowner and would let property to merchants, who would then sublet, creating a chain. Thus by the end of the sixteenth century even brothels were ultimately owned by the Church.) The merchants were also able to spend lavishly; many were foreigners, and had settled around the cathedral. The Jewish *conversos* were successful entrepreneurs, integrated into the highest levels of Seville life. Toledo was the best example of the flowering of Jewish culture, in the arts and sciences, but Seville came a close second. Gradually, though, the envy of the Jews, and the mistrust of the *conversos*, could not be contained. In their search for unity the Catholic Kings declared *limpieza de sangre*, purity of blood, and unity of faith the cornerstones of their policy.

The first Inquisition in Spain was set up in the Castillo de San Jorge, or Triana Castle, in 1480. The castle was at the

west end of what is now the Isabel II Bridge, between the
bridge and the Plaza Callao, and was excavated in 1989/91.
The peaceful Callejón de la Inquisición beside it, amid the
shoe shops of the calle Castilla, is today an unexpected
reminder of those terrible years. The Inquisition was set up
to root out false *conversos*, who were known as *marranos*
(from the word for 'unclean' food, i.e. pork), and is renowned
for its public burnings of convicts, the *autos-da-fé*. Records
differ over how many suffered at its hands: between 700 and
2,000 *conversos* are said to have been put to death between
1481 and 1490; 5,000 were imprisoned or sentenced to pen-
ances, while so many left the city that the gates had to be
closed. Then in 1492, after defeating the Nasrids in Granada,
Isabella had expelled the remaining Jews. The Genoese
piloted 8,000 Jews from Granada; many thousands of others
went overland to Portugal or Italy and the Ottoman Empire.

Patrician *sevillanos* will talk with sentimental affection of
the *sevillano* Jews scattered across the world: how some still
keep the keys to the homes in Seville that their ancestors left
as hastily as the Jews of the first Passover left theirs; how a
very high percentage of Sephardic Jews are of Andalusian
extraction; how they maintain a romance language. The
language in question is Ladino, a relation of Yiddish. Today
there is a Ladino newspaper in Israel, where there are some
200,000 Ladino speakers, and Ladino speakers keep the
language alive across the world.

The *sevillanos'* enthusiasm for their Jewish compatriots
sounds paternalist to an outsider's ear, as anti-Semitic as ever.
They vehemently deny any racism, and stress their multi-
cultural origins in defence of this. Nicolás Salas, one-time
editor of the centre-right newspaper *ABC* and historian of the
city, assured me that racism is not an issue. Yet in a city where
– as in most of Spain – a black face comes as a shock, and
where the only black people are usually the young Africans
selling African knick-knacks and hippy jewellery on the
streets, I wasn't convinced.

At the beginning of the sixteenth century, the expulsion of
the Jews and the Muslims created a hole in a population

already depleted by plague. That's one view. There's another, says Nicolás Salas, one that can be traced down to the present. Immigrants from other regions, Basque and Catalán, revived the city. Their names can still be traced today, making use of the passion for surnames which absorbs *sevillanos*. *Sevillanos* in the middle and upper classes are great ones for examining each other's names and family trees (much as the British are fond of discovering whether complete strangers share any common bonds of friendship or education with them). Since Spaniards bear two names – the father's father's surname and the mother's father's name, shortened for ease to the father's only, as in Francisco Franco (Bahamonde), or Miguel de Cervantes (Saavedra) – there is room for energetic genealogical investigation on first meeting. So at this period the name Ybarra, now one of the great families of Seville, nationally known for their eponymous olive oil and mayonnaise, begins to appear in Seville records. The Ybarras were Basques: both Basque and Catalán traders moved south to Seville to exploit the new possibilities for trade, and are just one example of the immigrants who filled the gaps. On the other hand, the Jews had been an essential part of the economy, while the Muslims had been artisans, and had also done many of the jobs the *sevillanos* had no ability for or wish to do. It took the city some years to recover its equilibrium in its search for purity.

In the first part of the sixteenth century, the benefits of the New World were yet to be widely enjoyed. Seville still suffered from floods and plagues, and the population was equally depleted by the number of men who died on or never returned from the sailings to the New World. Andrea Navagero, the Venetian ambassador and author of colourful pen-portraits of Seville, wrote in 1526 that so many men had left for the Indies that it was as if the city had been abandoned to the care of women. In addition, the plague of 1507 had decimated the city. More than 1,500 people were buried in the church of La Magdalena in one week in May alone. With such a reduction in population, grass started to grow in the formerly bustling plazas of San Francisco and San Salvador. Plague hit again in 1529. The largest parishes were in the environs of the cathedral (Santa María and San Salvador), and in Triana (Santa Ana) and they accounted for more than a third of the city's households. The population reached its peak in the 1580s, at about 100,000, and began to decrease slowly, as economic decline and a series of plagues took their toll.

It wasn't just sailors who went to the Indies; merchants wanting to exploit the new markets would send deputies, factors or relations. Nevertheless there were still plenty of wealthy traders and rich families left in the city, as well as a substantial sector of less prosperous artisans. Beneath them was a drifting underclass, and many Negro and Berber slaves – Seville was renowned in this period for the size of its slave population. There was also a substantial transient population, speaking many languages, from many lands: sailors, merchants, beggars, travellers. No wonder the playwright Lope de Vega called it the New Babylon. If Seville was, in Cervantes' words, 'an asylum for the poor and the refuge of the outcasts', it was also a magnet for anyone on the make. For one writer of the period, Seville was the city where 'the silver flowed as freely as did the copper in other parts'. Manufactured goods went out from northern Europe and Italy; in return came bullion, gemstones, sugar, drugs, hides and cochineal for distribution in Spain and across the Old World. For those who had access to money, almost anything could be bought. The *hidalgos, hijos-de-algo* or 'sons-of-someone', for instance, were able to buy their way up the social ladder. This practice was pilloried by the writers of the day, but that did not prevent it. Merchants were ennobled, aldermen and councillors bought their posts, all of their payments filling the needy royal coffers.

One of the most famous merchants in early-sixteenth-century Seville was the German printer Jacobo Cromberger, also known as Jácome Alemán ('the German'). He and his family dominated printing in the city for almost half a century. Under him Seville had the most flourishing book trade in Castilla and was the centre for popular printing, until Felipe II moved the capital to Madrid in 1561. Jacobo Cromberger acquired the monopoly on printing liturgical books, which he held until his death, and became immensely prosperous. Clive Griffin's absorbing and detailed study of the family, *The Crombergers of Seville*, gives a clear picture of the life of a successful immigrant merchant. His initial workshop was close to the calle Génova, which was famous for its silversmiths and bookshops. Records show that the street at this time was a closely knit community of artisans, merchants, apothecaries and retailers who were linked to each other by marriage or by common business interests:

> The most suggestive glimpse we are given of the Calle de Génova's residents is in 1520, on the day after the outbreak of the short-lived *comunero* riots in Seville. A large number of them met in the house of a local *converso* silversmith, Juan de Córdoba, and there formed a vigilante group to protect their lives and property from the mob, which they feared would make the street one of their first ports of call. Five of the signatories were booksellers, one a printer, and at least two were silversmiths. Three were immigrants, and the names of most of the others suggest a *converso* origin which in some cases can be proved. All were prosperous and half of them were connected in some way or other with Jacobo Cromberger . . . They were right to suspect that, had the *comunero* movement gathered the momentum in Seville which it had in other Spanish cities, the Calle de Génova, peopled as it was by foreigners and *conversos*, would have been an obvious target for the rebels; pickings for looters would have been rich into the bargain.

Jacobo started the trade with America. His son Juan set up the first printing press in the New World in 1539. However, in the early days, the Crombergers had been obliged to use a third party, since non-Castilians were forbidden to trade with the New World. They were finally granted special dispensations by Carlos V. By the time of his death, aged forty, Juan had acquired investments and interests not only in Spain, but also in northern Europe, Mexico, Peru and elsewhere in South America, as well as the monpoly on books exported to the Indies. He owned a house in calle Marmolejos, four printing presses and the slaves who worked them, stock of unsold material, vineyards in nearby Castilleja de la Cuesta and the Vega de Triana, and several houses and shops in Seville. He had at least ten slaves, some of whom worked in the house rather than the printing office. The inventory, as Clive Griffin shows, illustrates the luxurious lifestyle of a successful merchant of the times:

> The furniture of the house, including the money chests, was mainly imported from Flanders, while the family's extraordinary number of clothes were of velvet, silk or fine cloths from India and were frequently embroidered with gold thread. The latest fashions such as 'pairs of new Valencian chopines' were imported for the womenfolk. Gold jewels set with precious stones, especially pearls, abound . . .; the family dined off silver and gold plate, using silver cutlery and pouring their wine from silver jugs. They possessed religious paintings and icons set in gold and richly decorated with gems, and they even had sacred objects originating from a source as distinguished as 'the reliquary full of most authentic relics which Fray Bernardo [Bernardino] de Laredo took from the Queen of Portugal's reliquary, all worked in gold and enamel and surmounted by a crown'.

For those to whom the entrepreneurial life did not appeal, the Church was a reliable route to social advancement. There was always a chance of a job in a city where there were (in 1579) 176 cathedral chaplaincies and 812 parish posts. An ecclesiastical career was especially popular with the younger sons of noble families. The Church was as corrupt as the legal system, and nepotism was rife. One family of Pichardos controlled an office of prebendary for a total of eighty-three years. A Cardinal Castro in 1590 secured the three highest posts in the cathedral for his nephews. He was, nevertheless, said to be popular, because 'he understood the Sevillians and gave them what they wanted – preference in ecclesiastical appointments'.

Despite the statute requiring *limpieza de sangre*, there were still many *converso* clerics at the beginning of the sixteenth century. The *conversos* were also well known as financiers, but they were typically silversmiths, scribes and doctors. By intermarriage, *converso* families had become part of the intellectual, merchant and governing sectors of the city. The Inquisition's original task was to root out these unbelievers, but it soon moved on to eradicate the Protestant heresy which was sweeping Europe. In these campaigns, some outstanding thinkers were put to death. On 24 September 1559, the Plaza de San Francisco was filled with onlookers for the *auto-da-fé*. The ceremonies were presided over by the bishops of Taragona, Lugo and the Canaries, and by the auxiliary bishop of Seville. Twenty-one people, including one of the Ponce de León family, were burnt, along with the effigy of one man burnt in his absence. There were also eighty penitents, most of them Lutherans.

Booksellers and printers looked on this virulent anti-Protestantism with dismay. In the first half of the century there had been few controls on printing. But in 1551 the first Spanish *Index* of banned books was published in Seville and other cities in Spain. A few years later, in 1557, a man was caught attempting to smuggle Protestant books into Seville, and Protestant cells were soon uncovered throughout Castilla. In 1562, a Seville printer had his effigy burned in an *auto-da-fé* – he had already fled the city. Books joined heretics as candidates for burning. The Inquisition demanded that they inspect all books printed in Spain, and all imports, and declared that it was a capital offence to print books in the vernacular without a licence. Each page of a manuscript had to be inspected by a censor before it could be set up in type. The printers in Seville were particularly affected because they published so many popular works. The Inquisition was beginning the big freeze of intellectual life and inquiry.

The largest sector of the population were the workers, though they are inevitably least well-known. Some of the playwrights of the time came from the working class and cast light on the lives of the ordinary people. There were skilled artisans, as befitted such a rich city: embroiderers (there are still a few embroiderers in Seville today, working in gold threads and precious fabrics, creating the vestments for Christ and the Virgin in Holy Week), engravers, sculptors, painters, silversmiths. Under the Catholic Monarchs, the trades were organised into guilds, though there were already a number of guilds in the city. The reorganisation helped to create a rigid structure, just at a time when Spain would have benefited from greater industrial diversity. This, combined with the distaste of the upper classes for commerce, laid the foundations for Spain's future economic weakness. The guild members also belonged to a *cofradía*, which watched over their spiritual lives, as the guild did their working lives. Many of these brotherhoods ran hospitals for their members; the buildings have long since disappeared.

Beneath this layer, life was as tough as ever: the destitute at the bottom of the pile led hard lives in the insanitary city.

After Felipe II made Madrid his capital, Seville was never the first city again. But initially it retained its pre-eminence. It still had, after all, the monopoly on trade with the New World. This was a time of intense building activity, to cope with the doubling of the population and the enhanced aspirations of its merchants and great families. In subsequent centuries the palaces became derelict, as their owners could not afford to keep them up. It was not until the 1980s, under a socialist government and with Expo 92 round the corner, that a serious programme of renovation and restoration was begun. Today, a number of the departments of the Andalusian government are housed in seigneurial palaces. To the regret of the archaeologists, many of these great houses have been gutted. The typically spacious layout of rooms opening off a patio, reminiscent of the Roman villa, has been lost. The pressure for space in the old city is so great that there is no room for sentiment.

In the sixteenth century Seville had some eighty plazas. A writer of the times remarked that 'There's no *caballero* in Seville who doesn't have a little *placeta* in front of his house.' The Casa de Pilatos, begun in the late fifteenth century, opening on to its own plaza, is a grand example of this and a model for the great houses of Seville. According to tradition it is a copy of Pilate's house in Jerusalem, though it is a curious blend of Renaissance and *mudéjar* styles. It belongs to the Dukes of Medinaceli, one of the great families of Seville, who live there still.

The present dukes have remodelled a seventeenth-century lodge in one of the gardens for their own use, but the work does not blend with its surroundings. Nevertheless the gardens are a peaceful haven from the dusty streets, and worth remembering since they are among the very few private monuments open to the public throughout the day (the house itself follows the usual museum opening hours). The Casa de Pilatos may not be as heartbreakingly lovely as the Alhambra in Granada, but it does have that precious atmosphere that comes from still being a home. In summer the air in the gardens is ripe with the scent of figs. The tissue blooms of the bougainvillea accumulate in forgotten corners, a typically *sevillano* reminder of the transitoriness of wealth and life.

In the boom years of the trade with the Indies the city commissioned a collection of public buildings that still resound with its past glories. The Ayuntamiento or City Hall, on the Plaza de San Francisco, begun in 1527, reflects the grandiose dreams of local government. It was built in the noisily exuberant plateresque style. This technique of adding sculptured detail to Gothic façades took its name from the work of silversmiths, who worked in *plata*, silver.

Further along towards the cathedral, the Biblioteca Colombina occupies the east side of the Patio de los Naranjos. It was founded in 1552 by the bequest of Christopher Columbus's son Fernando, whom the French diplomat Bourgoing noted 'would have been considered a great man had he been the son of a less great father'. It houses the papers of Christopher Columbus, as well as 3,000 books collected by Fernando. In all, it now contains some 60,000 volumes.

La Lonja, or the Exchange, on the other side of the cathedral, was built for the city's merchants in the time of Felipe II, by one of the architects of El Escorial, Juan de Herrera. Up until then merchants had traded outside the cathedral, on the steps, known as *Las Gradas*, which surround it – and occasionally inside it. Genoese bankers had their stalls, slaves were sold, several notaries had thriving businesses drawing up contracts between bankers and merchants. This unholy union of God and Mammon, with its biblical antecedent, clearly could not be allowed to continue. *La Lonja* was the solution. The merchants were moved to this outwardly severe building, with its impressive staircase and elegant long rooms with vaulted ceilings. When the Guadalquivir silted up and the newer ships became too big to sail up the river, the exchange was moved to Cádiz on the sea coast, which became the new port for the Indies. Thus in 1758, the building was instead used as the Records Office, or Archive, of the Indies. It is an extraordinary resource of maps, documents and drawings; the Spaniards hoarded *everything*. The building today is a gold mine for scholars of the city that was *puerto* and *puerta* to the New World. Here can be found the papers of Magellan, Cortés, Vespucci and Columbus, as well as Cervantes' (failed) application to Felipe II for a job in America, and the original treaty in which the Falkland Islands were sold by Spain. For the scholarly bounty hunter it is invaluable. Eugene Lyon, for instance, a Florida historian, researched the records to locate the ship *Nuestra Sra de Atocha*, which sank in 1622, sixty-five kilometres off Key West. His first searches yielded $400,000-worth of silver.

At the entrance there is a plaque, erected by the Council

Seville

for Missionaries in 1952, which resounds still with the spiritual confidence of the Franco dictatorship:

> To the missionary queen, Isabel the Catholic, who opened the way and gave direction to the apostolic impulse of a people.

> To the Spanish missionaries who, in the service of a universal destiny of salvation, were servants of Christ and extended the territory of the world to east and west under the sign of the cross.

> In this Archive of the Indies, documentary treasure-house of our missionary epic, Spain records the distinguished names of the propagators of the faith.

Not all missionaries felt the same, of course. Most famous is the sailor's son Fray Bartolomé de las Casas, who subsequently became a bishop. His father sailed with Columbus, and Bartolomé caught the Indies 'bug'. But where his father saw the people of the New World as slaves, the young missionary disagreed and he fought for years on their behalf. His book denouncing the behaviour of the Spanish colonisers created the undying 'black legend' of Spain's cruelty in the New World.

The historian Henry Kamen takes an even-handed approach to an event that many prefer to call genocide:

> Almost unintentionally, Spain achieved the destruction of America's finest civilisations, annihilated the greater part of the native population and implanted a new culture, one in many ways more savage than those it replaced.

But, he concludes:

42

When surveying the tragic consequences for America of the Spanish invasion, it is worth bearing in mind that this was Europe's first great adventure overseas, and that the errors, like the achievements, were inevitably on an heroic scale.

Also at this time, the Alameda de Hércules, always known as 'the Alameda', was created out of a lagoon, nicknamed the 'duck pond', which had to be crossed by boat in winter. Many *sevillanos*, and a number of guidebooks, are inclined to talk of the Alameda as a kind of Sevillian Hyde Park or Central Park. At the time it must have been a marvel. Today, it is a snare and a delusion. Seville has its Hyde Park in the gracious Parque María Luisa, though that was not created until the late nineteenth/early twentieth century. While it is indeed green, the city does not lack for trees, even if there are few domestic gardens. The Alameda is nothing now but a scruffy, dusty, open space, with a useful taxi rank, which houses a Sunday flea market (see Chapter 6). The surrounding district down to the river is the run-down historic haunt of the city's prostitutes. What gives it a touch of class are the two Roman columns taken from the temple on calle Mármoles, topped by statues of Hércules and Julius Caesar.

The lasting monument to Seville's greatness is its art. The mercantile boom did not crush the creative instinct; quite the reverse. This was the Golden Age, in all the arts from painting and sculpture to literature and architecture. The outstanding painter of the period, one of Spain's greatest ever, was Diego de Velázquez, although he spent most of his working life away from Seville, in the court at Madrid. Velázquez foreshadows the coming corruption of Spain, in the decadence of his court paintings and the degeneration of his portraits of the down-and-out.

Velázquez's father-in-law, Francisco Pacheco from Sanlúcar de Barrameda downriver, was the founder of the 'Sevillian School'. An important painter in the city, he also ran one of the artistic and literary societies popular at the time, whose members included Lope de Vega, one of the world's most prolific playwrights. Among the painters who came to practise in Seville at the beginning of the seventeenth century was Francisco Zurbarán, whose paintings on religious themes were enormously popular with the ecclesiastical authorities and who therefore overshadowed the local artist Francisco de Herrera. The guild of local painters, led by Alonso Cano, irritated by this newcomer's success, demanded that Zurbarán pass the examination necessary for all painters to work in Seville. Zurbarán refused, but his reputation continued to grow despite his colleagues' jealousy. (Alonso Cano himself had come to Seville from Granada to study under Pacheco and was a good friend of Velázquez, but in such an exceptional school of painting he could never match Zurbarán's reputation.) Francisco Zurbarán is perhaps the greatest of Spain's religious painters, portraying the saints with a darkness that has come to symbolise the torments of the Spanish soul.

In the mid-seventeenth century Bartolomé Esteban Murillo rose to fame in Seville. He ran an art school in *La Lonja*. His religious painting seems to take a backward step from the greater realism of Zurbarán. Adept at devotional painting, he produced a chocolate-box spirituality that appealed to the public and his patrons. It is a style that palls if you consume too much of it at one sitting. Far more interesting are his paintings of real people, Sevillian street urchins and beggars, which speak through the centuries. They are also full of detail about contemporary items of the day such as pots and bowls. In nineteenth-century England, Hazlitt approved the naturalism of Murillo's children, and their expressive faces and realistic attitudes. Ruskin disagreed – violently, saying they were 'repulsive and wicked'.

Juan de Valdés Leal was Murillo's contemporary. Like Murillo, he worked under his mother's name and followed many of Murillo's themes. But in Valdés Leal the chocolate box gives way to the toasting fork: his saints are altogether more anguished. Inevitably he is contrasted with Murillo, and he comes off worse. His work seems uneven, melodramatic, overloaded with people. The church of the Hospital de la Caridad near the new Maestranza opera house is the place to go to compare their work. Its collection includes the two of Valdés Leal's most famous paintings, *Finis gloriae mundi*, of which Murillo is famously reported to have said that it made one hold one's nose to look at it, and *In ictu oculi*.

The hospital was founded by the aristocrat Miguel de Mañara, who has been popularly identified as the model for Don Juan/Don Giovanni. Unfortunately for the legend, Miguel de Mañara was still a boy when Tirso de Molina wrote *Condenado por Desconfiado*, in which the character of Don Juan Tenorio first appears. Legend has it that one night Miguel de Mañara witnessed his own funeral procession, and this shock turned him to God and away from his former licentious ways. Certainly he joined the society of La Caridad (Charity), which cared for the down-and-out and buried executed criminals. He ended his life a peaceful, God-fearing man. Yet his tomb in the crypt is still visited by those who want to believe the legend of the reformed lover.

The real Don Juan is much more likely to have been the son of the Marqués de Tarifa, who abducted a woman from a convent. The chapel of Nuestra Sra del Carmen off the Alameda is said to stand on the spot where he was killed by the woman's family in a sword fight. The character of Don Juan, if not the actual person, is commemorated in a statue which was erected in the Plaza de los Refinadores in the Barrio de Santa Cruz in 1974, in acknowledgement of the fact that Don Juan gave Seville a notoriety which that other theatrical and operatic favourite, Figaro, the Barber of Seville, never achieved.

In sculpture, Seville was also going through a Golden Age. The work of Seville's sculptors is still fresh in the public mind today, for some of their finest work is taken out on the streets each year for the Holy Week processions. Foremost are Juan Martínez Montañés, his student Juan de Mesa, Pedro Roldán, and his daughter Luisa, *la Roldana*, who endowed the city with masterpieces of devotional sculpture. The ceramicist Niculoso Pisano, though no *sevillano* but an Italian, was an important influence, for he introduced Italian techniques to Seville's ceramic artists.

Miguel de Cervantes towers above the writers of his day. Yet there were others: Mateo Alemán was an exponent of the picaresque novel, in which satire and social realism were combined, as in his *Guzmán de Alfarache*. The theatre was growing; Seville's leading playwright was Fernando de Herrera. The early theatres were known as *corrales*, and were much like the London inns, where the actors performed in a patio in the open air, working without scenery on Sundays and holidays. Cervantes himself was not born in Seville, nor did he spend many years there. He was imprisoned in the city, though, for non-payment of an incorrectly calculated tax debt. It is thought that he dreamed up his masterpiece *Don Quixote* while in prison and for this good fortune, and for having set some of his other works in the city, most notably *Rinconete and Cortadillo*, he has been adopted as a favoured son. The plaque on the Banco Hispano-Americano in calle Sierpes marks the site of the jail where he was incarcerated. Cervantes' biographer Richard Predmore writes of it:

> Built in 1569, the royal prison of Seville was one of the newest, largest and most populous of all Spain. Contemporary documents describe it as a living hell of noise, confusion, violence and stench. The whole range of criminality was represented there, and it was widely believed that the warden and his staff were as corrupt as any of the involuntary inmates. Food, drink and special privileges were for sale and living was tough for any of those unable to buy.

Cervantes published *Don Quixote* as the Golden Age was in its dying years, and it reflects something of the corruption and decay of that regime. With the seventeenth century the economic crisis had begun. The costs of sustaining such a vast empire could not forever be paid out of American riches, and Spain underwent a period of steep inflation. In 1609, the *moriscos*, the Arab converts to Christianity, were expelled from Spain. This was something of an own goal for the Spanish authorities, since the *moriscos* had supported important parts of the economy. Andalusia was hit particularly hard. Spain signed a peace treaty with England and made a truce with the Netherlands, but the peace was short-lived. Some twenty years later, under Felipe IV, Spain plunged into what was to become the Thirty Years War. The king's adviser at the time was the *sevillano* Conde-Duque de Olivares. Olivares, perhaps the most famous of all Spanish royal advisers, was an influential figure who attempted to introduce some centralisation into Spain. But by 1640, Spain had lost Portugal, and Catalonia was in revolt. The attempted union had crumbled again. A series of uprisings and defeats lost Olivares his job, and cost Spain her pre-eminence in Europe.

The economic slide in Seville was worsened by natural causes. In 1649, the city was attacked by a plague which had swept Andalusia and which killed almost half the population of Seville. People prayed in desperation to the Cristo del Buen Fin (literally 'good end'), now in the church of San Antonio de Padua in calle San Vicente, and the Cristo de la Buena Muerte ('good death'), the work of Juan de Mesa, now in the chapel of the university.

Spain's decline was accelerated by its increasingly feeble kings. There was now no masking the effects of inbreeding in the royal family. The degeneracy of the Habsburgs achieved greater and longer-lasting fame than was perhaps its due by reason of its having been portrayed by such masters as Velázquez and Claudio Coello. This, combined with an inability to rule, eventually led Spain on the eve of the eighteenth century to the brink of war as faction fought faction over the head of the sovereign.

In the course of the War of Succession, which ensued as a result of the death of the childless Carlos II, Spain lost Italy and the Netherlands and surrendered Gibraltar and Menorca to England. Felipe V, the first of the Bourbons, the present-day royal house of Spain, became king in 1707. Ten years later, Seville lost the Casa de Contratación, the monopoly of trade with the Americas, to Cádiz. The ships had got larger, and the Guadalquivir had begun to silt up. These two factors combined to speed Seville's decline. Spain's only inland port discovered there were disadvantages in its site, which for two millennia had seemed ideal.

In 1759, Carlos III, already King of Naples for nearly a quarter of a century, came to the throne of Spain. His reign has been called a time of enlightened despotism. The Inquisition was still in existence, but its influence was greatly reduced amid the influx of foreign thinkers and their philosophies. When asked why he retained the Inquisition, the king replied, 'The Spaniards want it, and it does not bother me.'

Under Carlos III, Spain's largest civic building, the Real Fábrica de Tabacos, or Royal Tobacco Factory, begun fifty years earlier, was finally completed, to process the plant that thrives in the climate of Seville province. The principal façade is adorned with busts of Columbus, who discovered the lands from which tobacco originally came, and Hernán Cortes, who enjoys the uncertain fame of having been Europe's first smoker. (He may, however, have been beaten to it by Rodrigo de Triana, the sailor who first caught sight of dry land.) The factory was a lure for foreign travellers, tempted by the stories of the luscious *cigarreras* who worked there. In the early years of the twentieth century, the excitable Pierre Loüys wrote:

The women showed no reserve in taking advantage of the permission to undress as they wished in the unbearable atmosphere where they lived from June to September . . . Those with most clothes on had only their shirts on (these were the simple prudes); almost all worked with a naked torso, and a simple cloth underskirt pulled down from the belt and sometimes pushed back from the upper thighs . . .

I beg you to believe that they did not mince their words when they had pulled down their blouses, and they added to their words certain gestures with a shamelessness or rather a simplicity which was a little disconcerting . . . Because their nakedness consorted badly with the idea of their wretched work, I had the idea that I was seeing all these active hands rapidly manufacturing innumerable little lovers out of tobacco leaves. What is more, they did everything they could to suggest this.

There were some observers who were repelled by the insanitary conditions and the nicotine-laden atmosphere, and they found little allure in the women. Willis Baxley remarked in 1875 that the *cigarreras* looked 'as if they had breathed the deadly malaria of the Pontine marshes and were becoming prematurely mummified. Sallow, shrunken, shrivelled specimens of humanity, life seems to have but little hold upon the older of the operatives.'

On the west side of the Tobacco Factory is the Palacio de San Telmo, another grand edifice of the period which was begun in 1682. It was intended as a school for navigators, of whom San Telmo was patron. Its porch, an apparent confection of icing sugar and high hopes, is a fine example of churrigueresque, an ornate decorative style named after the Churriguera brothers.

Over beside the cathedral, the *sevillanos* erected a monument to commemorate the earthquake of 1 November 1755. This *triunfo* gave its name to the plaza in which it stands. It is Seville's oldest monument, for the *sevillanos* were never great ones for commemorative statues. It was not until the nineteenth century that they finally caught the civic disease.

* * *

In 1778 the trade with the Americas was liberalised, and all of Spain's major ports became free to trade, with consequent benefits to industry and commerce in those ports. But this only accelerated Seville's economic decline. Agricultural Andalusia meanwhile was in difficulties. With no restructuring of the landowning system, the landless rural workers suffered great privations. Fortunately for the aristocracy, the French Revolution directed minds elsewhere. When the republicans in Paris declared war on Spain, it was said to be one of the most popular wars in Spanish history. The nation united against the republicans. The king at this time was Carlos IV, whose chief minister was Manuel Godoy. Like Felipe IV and his court before them, they were both immortalised by a great painter, in this case Goya, the witness to the sufferings of the poor and the degeneracy of the aristocracy. The French crossed into Spain, but were stopped by a treaty in which Spain gave up Santo Domingo to France. Godoy was obliged to sign an alliance with France against England. This only served to intensify British aggression against Spain's American territories. By the end of the eighteenth century Spain's colonies in the New World were effectively lost. The final blow came in 1805 when Spain's maritime power was defeated by Admiral Nelson. Though such a profound moment in British history, there is nothing at Cabo (Cape) Trafalgar, near the town of Barbate beyond Cádiz, to betray the famous sea battle that was once fought off its shores.

3. Constitutions, *pronunciamientos*, abdications

With the advent of the nineteenth century Spain embarked on almost 150 years of upheaval, culminating in the civil war of 1936. Throughout most of this time, Seville was in decline, at least in contrast with its former glory. The spotlight shifted to the industrialising cities of Catalonia, especially Barcelona. Writing in 1973, the historian Henry Kamen remarked, 'Spain was thrust into the nineteenth century and has never quite emerged from it.' Some twenty years on it is at last possible to disagree.

Back in 1808, the court of Carlos IV was disintegrating. His adviser Manuel Godoy was deposed. On hearing the news, a band of *sevillanos*, stirred up by some of Godoy's many enemies, marched down calle Sierpes to the church of San Juan de Dios, a religious order which Godoy sponsored, broke in and defaced a painting. Carlos' abdication in favour of his son Fernando VII, which followed hard on this event, was greeted in Seville with joy and bell-ringing, but the delight was short-lived. Fernando and Carlos were forced to go into exile in

France and to hand over the throne to Napoleon, who gave Spain to his brother Joseph. On 2 May 1808, the people of Madrid rose up in anger against the French in the uprising whose brutal suppression was immortalised by Goya as the *Dos de Mayo*.

One of the heroes of the day was the *sevillano* Luis Daoiz, an artillery man who died in the French attack on Montelón Park in Madrid. A statue by Antonio Susillo depicting him at the moment when he called on his men to charge the French was erected in the Plaza de Gavidia in 1889. (Susillo sculpted a number of famous statues in Seville, among them a crucified Christ for the San Fernando cemetery. He committed suicide while still young. Legend has it that soon after he killed himself, honey was found to be oozing from the mouth and down the chest of his Christ. It seemed more than coincidental that of all the places and all the times that the bees could have chosen to make a hive in the cemetery they had settled on the Christ then. As a result of this the Christ became popularly known as the Honeyed, or Sweet, Christ.)

The bloody revolt of the Dos de Mayo triggered off the War of Independence (from France), which the British call the Peninsular War, and established the role of the common people in fighting for their rights. The people rose up quickly against the new king. Joseph told his brother, 'My position is unique in history. I have not a single supporter here.' In fact he had more supporters than he knew, for there were radicals who looked to Joseph as the only means of breaking with the decaying traditionalism of the country.

A stranger appeared in the city at this time, 'a mysterious person', as the *sevillano* historian José María de Mena puts it, who was therefore known as *El Incognito*, 'the unknown man'. He was financed, it seems, by the English, who wanted to encourage opposition to the new regime. With the help of the Seville garrison, he set up a 'Supreme Council of the National Government' in the Alcázar. The 'True Government of the Spanish Nation' then declared war under the slogan, 'Religion and patriotism will triumph over the French', and set up an alliance with the English. The new government established itself in Madrid, but was forced back to Seville when Napoleon took the capital. The French forces came south, and the government finally had to flee from Seville to Cádiz. Marshal Soult entered Seville on 1 February 1810.

In the summer of 1812 there was a terrible famine in Andalusia, but on 27 August the sufferings were tempered by the good news that the French had been driven out of Seville, after a battle on the ground between Triana and La Cartuja (the fifteenth-century charterhouse which is now part of the Expo 92 site). In three years a number of old buildings were demolished, which served to create more open spaces in the city. The city was also denuded of some fine works of art by its French occupiers and its English liberators. These included works by Zurbarán from the Cartuja, and by Murillo from the Hospital de la Caridad. The Hospital de la Caridad today displays a prominent notice at the entrance to the church, illustrating the missing pictures and citing their current homes in foreign art galleries. This is another case of the Elgin marbles and almost as hotly felt.

In 1810 Cádiz had set up a *cortes* or parliament, representing all the parts of Spain not occupied by the French, as well as the American states. The word 'liberal', says Raymond Carr, was first used to describe these radical patriots in Cádiz. In 1812 it declared a historic constitution, which the new authorities in Seville were quick to adopt. Its features included the establishment of a constitutional monarchy. The constitution was a rallying point for Spain's liberals, and remained so in the confusion of the century that followed. Constitutions were declared again in 1834, 1837, 1845, 1852, 1855 and 1876, each one a mere shadow of the achievement of 1812. The Cádiz *cortes* abolished the Inquisition, which had been reduced to censoring literature and issuing regulations prohibiting locks on the insides of bedroom doors in the country's inns. The abolition was not achieved without argument: the Inquisition was later reinstated and finally abolished in 1834. The constitution was not so long-lasting. When Fernando VII, *el deseado*, 'the longed-for one', returned to Spain in 1814, he did not delay in repealing it. His return may have been long-awaited, but this rejection of the work of those who had run Spain in his absence was seen as a sign of the 'blackest ingratitude'.

Fernando returned to a changed country. Try as he might to impose a conservative order, the people had experienced the freedom of exercising their own power and the liberals had had a taste of how different Spain could be. Seville only echoed the popular discontent felt across the land. In the heat of the times, the body of King Joseph's finance minister, who had been buried in the cathedral, was taken out and thrown into the public pit.

Seville's greatest literary figure of the early nineteenth century was, without doubt, José María Blanco Crespo (1775–1841), said to be the only Spaniard to have an entry in the *Dictionary of National Biography*. He was of Irish stock, from among those who had emigrated to Spain after the Battle of the Boyne and become *hidalgos*. (Their names remain today: O'Neill, O'Donnell, Donoghue. Cardinal Wiseman, Archbishop of Westminster in the 1850s, was among their number, born in the calle Fabiola in the Barrio de Santa Cruz in 1802, though he left Seville in his infancy.)

On the urging of his parents Blanco went into the Church, but early acquired a distaste for its practices. He disliked the 'cloying and mawkish devotion' expressed, and, says the *DNB*, the material imagery which it used to stimulate the emotions. Despite his misgivings, he was ordained a priest and was soon appointed to the post of Royal Chaplain to the Royal Chapel of San Fernando in the cathedral. At the same time he began to build a reputation for himself as a writer and thinker. As his liberal ideals came into conflict with the decay and absolutism of the Spanish court, he found his faith more difficult to sustain. His sister's death as a result of the 'unwholesome life of the convent' in which she was a nun further set him against the Catholic Church. When the government was set up in Seville during the War of Independence, Blanco wrote a poem in praise of it. He won great acclaim for this and was nominated chaplain to the government. To his dismay, he then discovered that the real radicals and liberals were on the French side, while the government that he had hymned represented everything he so disliked. In despair, he abandoned both Church and country in the middle of the war for England, where, because of his ancestry, he could claim citizenship. There he became a priest in the Church of England, for which he was long derided by the Catholic Church as an apostate. He also added the English translation of Blanco to his name, thus becoming Joseph Blanco White, the name by which he is remembered.

Blanco White was bilingual, able to wrote poetry and prose with equal skill and elegance in both English and Spanish. He joined the English literary establishment and became a good friend of Robert Southey, particularly because of their shared views on Anglicanism. In England he published a newspaper, *El Español*, attacking the Spanish government and subsequently Fernando VII, and supporting independence for Spain's American colonies. In 1822 he published his most famous work, *Letters from Spain*. He wrote the entry on Spain for the *Encyclopaedia Britannica* and was befriended at Oxford by the people who were subsequently to found the Oxford Movement. Coleridge called his sonnet 'Night and Day', written in English, 'the finest and most grandly conceived sonnet in our language'. For all that, Blanco White found life in England difficult and contemplated suicide. In the end he died alone, an outcast from both the Church of England and the Church of Rome, who had turned to Unitarianism. After his death the Catholic Church ignored him and critics in Spain attempted to build up a 'black legend' against him. This has taken years to dissipate. The Church in Spain is only now taking an interest in him, and his status has been restored by some major biographies, transforming him from heretic to heritage.

Writing just before the exaggerations of the romantic era, Blanco White is a useful guide to eighteenth- and nineteenth-century Seville. He may have rejected his native city, but he did not forget it. The leading authority on Blanco White, Antonio Garnica, stresses his skills as an observer, saying he is 'like a Goya with the details he gives'. He finds that Blanco White is nearly always reliable on his facts. For instance, the *paso* or float for Corpus Christi runs on wheels; it is not carried by *costaleros* as the *pasos* of Holy Week are. It was assumed that this had always been the case. Blanco White makes it clear that the *pasos* were carried. As subsequent research has discovered, the wheels are a twentieth-century innovation. But there are times, says Antonio Garnica, when Blanco White lapses into the romantic. Give him a few trees, for instance, and he will turn them into woodland. 'The one thing that stops Blanco White being really popular in Spain today', he adds, 'is the language barrier. Because so much of his best work was in English, it's not immediately accessible over here.'

In 1820, in Las Cabezas de San Juan to the south of Seville, the army officer Rafael del Riego staged a *pronunciamiento*, an insurrection, the first of many which were to become typical of Spain in the nineteenth and twentieth centuries. These insurrections always come from the army, the one body that is sufficiently well-organised to carry out its intentions. Riego's was an – unsuccessful – liberal uprising in defence of the constitution. During these events, a mass of people stormed the prison of the Inquisition in the Alameda de Hércules, destroyed the instruments of torture and set fire to the building. Fernando quashed these uprisings with excessive repression. As a result, on his first visit to Seville, the people received him in complete silence. Many liberals went into exile, creating a pattern typical of Spanish politics for years to come.

In 1823 the *Cortes*, meeting in Seville, declared Fernando unfit to rule, but Fernando overruled them and they were persecuted for their insubordination. Despite his absolutism, there were still those who thought that Fernando was too moderate. They chose to support Fernando's younger brother

Carlos, thus causing a split which continues to this day. The claims of the Carlists today are muted by the obvious achievements of the present king, Juan Carlos, but they still maintain the legitimacy of their cause.

Fernando's daughter Isabella II succeeded in 1833, but she was too young to rule. The Carlists took immediate advantage of the regency to rise up against it. Broadly, the Carlists were strongest in the north and west, but there were Carlists throughout the country and they represented a demand for traditional, Catholic values. The civil war between the two factions was a bitter struggle which lasted until 1839. In 1836, in a 4,000-kilometre march, which Spanish historians compare to that recorded in Xenophon's *Anabasis*, the Carlist general Miguel Sancho Gómez de Damas led his soldiers across Spain. But though he took many towns and cities in Andalusia, he could not defeat Seville. The Carlists were renowned for their barbarities. They revived a sinister secret society, 'The Exterminating Angel', which had been started under Fernando VII and was used by the Church. The Church would go to any lengths in its fights against liberalism. This conflict between liberalism and Catholic traditionalism, with religion as the intermediary, preoccupied Spain's politics to the extent of severely delaying the nation's entry into the industrial era.

The Church was certainly not above reproach. A Scottish tourist in 1830, Henry Inglis, found that morals in Seville were 'at the lowest possible ebb', 'the worst example being set by the churchmen. It is a common saying in Seville that the reason why one sees so few pretty women in the street is that they are all in the houses of the clergy.' He also suggested there were close links between the church and the *contrabandistas*, who, with the bandits, so scandalised the romantic tourists of the eighteenth century. Inglis noted that there were 'several convents on the outskirts of the city, and in particular a nunnery, active as depots for smuggled goods and of course keeping a liberal share of the profits'.

In 1836–7 the Church suffered a severe blow, when the government nationalised all monastic property, and started to sell off Church land, and it also abolished the system of *mayorazgo*, or entail, by which property was handed on within families. These were radical reforms, and nowhere more so than in Andalusia. Seville had and still has the largest number of convents and monasteries in Spain. Before these *desamortización* reforms, there were some thirty-three convents and twenty-nine monasteries in Seville alone, as well as a number of seminaries and training colleges. Sadly, the outcome of the redistribution of Church lands was to make the poor even worse off than before. Church property simply passed into the hands of the rich, and the agricultural workers were left with less than ever. In Seville, 6,000 families had farmed the Church land before the reforms; after the sales the number fell to 400.

The distinction between *latifundia* and *minifundia* became even more vivid. On one side were the wealthy landowners, with estates even greater than those of the Middle Ages; on the other were agricultural workers, individuals doing subsistence farming of the most primitive kind. In addition, there were many who had no land at all. Survival in Andalusia for the poor was precarious. Many left for the Spanish territories in America; others migrated to the cities. The desperate landless were left with their demands for *reparto*, the fair distribution of the *latifundia* lands to those who had no land of their own. The British traveller Richard Ford, writing in the early nineteenth century, recalled that he 'once beheld a cloaked Spaniard pacing mournfully in the burial ground in Seville. When the public trench was opened he drew from beneath the folds the dead body of his child, cast it in and disappeared. Thus half the world lives without knowing how the other half dies.'

Isabella's new regent after the Carlist War was General Espartero who was to be Spain's first military dictator. The moderates, led by Generals Narváez and Prim, soon rebelled against him, Seville included. The city was besieged and grenades fell on the Convent of Santa Inés and the Casa de Pilatos, among others. Espartero's attack on the city was stopped by the news that the moderates had taken power in Madrid. The army dispersed in disorder and Espartero fled to London. The thirteen-year-old Isabella II came to the throne and Spain embarked on a period of fundamental economic change, though it also endured a second, shorter Carlist War. Industry, formerly powered by firewood, was transformed by coal from Asturias. Andalusia provided a number of Spain's great industrialists, but ultimately it was Catalonia which benefited most from the Industrial Revolution. One *sevillano* told me, with a strength of feeling expressive of historic *sevillano* disdain for the northerners: 'They needed it. In Catalonia, they were still up in the trees.'

Seville's principal industries were soap, steel and cork, but it remained hobbled by its primitive agriculturalism, and beset by droughts, famines and floods. Without the finance it could not transform its primary goods; instead it was obliged to send them away and buy them back, processed, at higher prices. By the end of the century the divide between the rich north and the impoverished south seemed ineradicable.

Seville's profile was changed little by new building in the nineteenth century. During Isabella's reign the Plaza Nueva, now a dusty central bus station belying its important title, was constructed. More significantly, an iron bridge, the Isabel II or Triana Bridge, was built over the Guadalquivir to replace the old one made of boats, first created by the Almohads in 1170. Now that the Guadalquivir is crossed by so many bridges, it comes as a surprise to note that until 130 years ago there was only one bridge linking Seville and Triana. It was not for want of trying. Back in 1631 the *sevillanos* had (unsuccessfully) lobbied the Conde-Duque de Olivares, the powerful adviser of Felipe IV and himself a *sevillano*, for a stone bridge.

In 1868, the year of the revolution and Isabella's abdication, the city council demolished extensive sections of the remaining walls and a number of the fourteen gates to the city. Some of them are still remembered on the maps – Osario, Carmona, Jerez. Others had vivid names – Oil, Coal, Meat. The enthusiasm of the council did not extend to demolishing the old city. Much of the working population lived in *corrales de vecinos*, rooming houses around a central courtyard, sharing water, cooking facilities and lavatories. Many of these lingered on into the twentieth century, and there were a few still remaining in the 1970s. The growing city extended into new suburbs. The water supply was also renovated. The new supply of drinking water was contracted to an English company for ninety-nine years, until 1965, when it returned to the City Council. But as a result the water was often known as 'Englishmen's water'. This is somewhat ironic, given the fact that English travellers have always been so cautious of the water in Seville – as elsewhere in Spain.

Miles of railway lines were laid, often on the advice of British engineers, opening Spain up to a new wave of tourists. Most of them came to wallow in the antiquated romance of 'backward' Spain, a relief from the galloping industrialisation of northern Europe. The most famous of these were Théophile Gautier, Alexandre Dumas, Prosper Mérimée, George Borrow and Richard Ford, whose learned and opinionated *Handbook for Travellers in Spain* (1845) and *Gatherings from Spain* (1846) set new standards for guidebooks and travel writing.

In the mid-nineteenth century, Gustavo Adolfo Bécquer came to prominence as a romantic poet. His father, José Domínguez, was the head of the *costumbrista* school of painters, whose work exploited all the clichés of Seville: dark-eyed, dark-haired girls, gypsies, and the *feria*, which had been set up in 1847. The younger Bécquer exploited this in his verse and was echoed in this fashion by his brother Valeriano, who was a painter. The monument to Bécquer in the Parque María Luisa typifies the romantic sentimentality of the era. The poet stands on a pedestal, while at his feet sit three women intent on love. The whole marble conceit is constructed round a water cypress planted in 1870, the year Bécquer died.

The unrest and *pronunciamientos* escalated, forcing Isabella to leave Spain. She was replaced by Amadeo of Savoy, the King of Italy's son. But his was an uneasy monarchy, with disruption from the Carlists, rivalry between his ministers and popular disturbances. In just three years Amadeo too abdicated, and a republic was proclaimed in 1873.

Sixteen years earlier a group of a hundred young *sevillanos*, fired, it is said, by the romantic ideals of the day, had already proclaimed a republic. Lightly armed, they had marched round Andalusia from town to town. The army eventually caught up with them at Benaoján near Ronda, where twenty-five of them were shot dead. The rest were returned to Seville, where all except one, who was fourteen and therefore under age, were executed. Seville had its own wailing wall in calle San Laureano that day, where the mayor wept for the city and its sons.

The First Republic did not last. It had three presidents between April and September 1873. In June of that year, however, a group of left-wing *sevillanos* declared the city independent, calling it a federal social republic. This was quashed by the Madrid government, but Seville replaced it with a Council of the Andalusian Canton. The government was finally forced to suppress the separatists by bringing in the army. Six months later the republic itself fell and Isabella's son Alfonso XII was brought back from London to be king. His adviser, Cánovas del Castillo, attempted to establish a constitutional monarchy, making the king read the political essayist Walter Bagehot to assist the process. But the Spanish–American War in 1898 interrupted the new stability. Spain lost her last great colonies: Cuba, Puerto Rico and the Philippines. This was the end of the Spanish Enterprise, and the humiliation was resounding.

A group of radical intellectuals came together in reaction to this reversal in Spain's fortunes. The 'Generation of '98' sought a solution in the regeneration of the individual. The Basque philosopher Miguel de Unamuno was the most famous of the group. Two other eminent members were *sevillano* poets, the brothers Antonio and Manuel Machado. They were born in the Palacio de las Dueñas, the home of the Dukes of

Alba, for whom their father was working. Antonio is particularly linked with northern Castilla, for his wife, who died young, came from Soria. To the poets of the 1920s, Antonio Machado was immensely influential. Manuel felt the ties of his Andalusian roots more strongly. His inspiration may seem to be the clichés of Seville – bullfighting, flamenco, gypsies – but in work such as the *Poemas del cante jondo* he treats them with a depth and originality that foreshadows the work of the Granadan poet Federico García Lorca.

An idea of the ideological ferment of the times is given by the sheer number of papers published in Seville – and their titles. In 1900 there were twenty-five: *El Liberal, El Posibilista, La Región, La Monarquía, El Crisol* (Crucible), *La Andalucía Moderna, La Iberia*. . . . For the impoverished Andalusians one of the few ways out of the crisis seemed to be anarchism, which had spread rapidly in the later part of the nineteenth century. Anarchism was in tune with the Andalusian personality, in the way it favoured the individual over the collective. Yet after violent demonstrations Andalusian anarchism was crushed, though it went on to flourish in Catalonia, where the powerful Confederación Nacional de Trabajo (CNT), the anarchist trade union, was created. Also founded in the late nineteenth century were the Unión General de Trabadores (UGT), the socialist trade union, and the Partido Socialista Obrero Español (PSOE), the socialist party. Conditions for the Andalusians remained harsh. In 1905 there was a severe drought; many only survived by eating the bread that was handed out in the villages. Even the great cardinal archbishop Spínola went out begging in the streets on behalf of the starving.

At the beginning of the twentieth century, one per cent of the landowners held forty-two per cent of the capital value of the land. Most agricultural workers, then as now, were employed seasonally. Productive land was left fallow, or used for hunting, rearing bulls, growing cork oaks and olive trees, or the dry farming of wheat. The Medinacelis had been using 15,000 out of 16,000 hectares of good land for hunting. Between 1900 and 1930 the average daily earnings of the *bra-*

cero, the day labourer, were three *pesetas* (by 1913, a family with two children needed 5.75 *pesetas* to survive), and workers were employed for no more than 100 to 150 days a year. The problems of agricultural unemployment persist to this day, with the government of the 1990s embroiled in accusations and condemnations of its programme of subsidies to agricultural workers.

In the city itself life was hardly more advanced. As evidence of this Raymond Carr notes that, by contrast with the industrialised cities of the north, there was no typewriter to be found in Seville in 1906. No wonder Lenin saw Spain as the next country for a revolution. It had the textbook features: an agricultural economy, with an outdated aristocracy and a weak middle class. It was ripe for proletarian takeover.

Alfonso XIII came of age in 1902 and took the throne as Spain was subsiding under the pressure of uprisings and political dissent. He seemed doomed to fail. The portraits and photographs reveal a weedy, dapper self-important man, with a moustache of which he was obviously proud. Who would not prefer a republic when presented with such a monarch? Alfonso decided to ignore the practices of constitutional monarchy and kept his own counsel. Political unrest in Catalonia culminated in a general strike in Barcelona, which ended in a nightmare of bloodshed and violence.

Spain had stayed neutral during the First World War and had therefore prospered, though it lost its important foreign markets. But in 1923, the very last of Spain's imperial hopes in North Africa was almost lost. In the uproar at the military and political incompetence of it all, General Miguel Primo de Rivera, Captain-General of Barcelona, made a *pronunciamiento* against the government and became dictator. He lasted for seven years and instituted a number of reforms. But eventually not even the army would support him. He resigned and died two months later.

* * *

The year before Primo de Rivera resigned, Seville hosted the great Ibero-American Exhibition of 1929, which Primo de Rivera himself had so enthusiastically sponsored. The exhibition was long overdue, but by the time it arrived the world was in the middle of a financial crisis and the host country's politics were unstable. Expo 29 left Seville bankrupt. The city only finished paying off the debt in the early 1980s. Some of the empty pavilions of Expo 29 lurk today on the edge of the Parque María Luisa, a warning to the financiers of Expo 92 of the risks they were taking.

Yet for all its financial catastrophe, Expo 29 had its advantages, most notably enhancing the face of Seville. The Lope de Vega Theatre was built, and close by, the Plaza de España, a haunt of speed cyclists and roller skaters. Pedestrians escaping from the sun can shelter in the shade provided within the semi-circle it describes. And visitors from other parts of Spain can play 'spot the province' with their children, looking for their home province in the charming tiled alcoves that skirt the building – if, that is, they can see beneath the layers of muck and grime. Nor is the Plaza de España just a jolly boating lake-cum-playground; there are a number of government and military offices here, which accounts for the fully armed soldier on the central steps.

Expo 29 encouraged hotel building for the anticipated visitors. The most notable of these was the Alfonso XIII, a mixture of Moorish and Andalusian styles, which comes close to rivalling its neighbour, the Tobacco Factory. It was designed to be the grandest hotel in Europe and remains the grand hotel of the old quarter of Seville.

Over the same period, Seville's *barrios* were extended. Heliópolis appeared to the south, at the other end of the Avenida de la Palmera. To the east, the district of Nervión was begun in 1910 by the Marqués de Nervión. It remains a distinctly up-market development today. Within it lies the 'golden mile' of the most expensive housing in Seville.

The delightful former railway station at the Plaza de Armas had already been opened in 1901, a mad Moorish confection of brick, worthy of the architects of London's most grandiose railway termini. Seville used to have trams and converted them from mules to electricity in the early twentieth century. At the start the electricity ran through the track on the road, but this soon had to be stopped because of the risks to pedestrians. It is hard to imagine trams in Seville's streets today. But the one track remaining in the city, by the pavement in calle Hernando Colón opposite the cathedral, is solid proof. In 1910, the telephone, or rather 200 of them, came to Seville. Soon after came the radio, which was to be used extensively in the Civil War, the first war in which radio was important. Finally, one must not ignore the founding at this time of the two rival football teams, Sevilla and Betis (or, rather, Real Betis Balompié, 'Royal Betis Football'), the Arsenal and Spurs of Seville.

Alfonso Zbikowsky was one of the city's more memorable mayors of the period. His innovations included requiring the sellers of seafood and fried fish to wear white coats for reasons of public health. He also abolished the wearing of the sabre by the municipal guard, replacing it with a truncheon. This gave rise to a humorous rhyming *copla*, typical of those sung at *carnaval*, the fair held around Shrove Tuesday:

> *Tres cosas tiene Sevilla*
> *que no las tiene London*
> *el Alcázar, la Giralda*
> *y los guardias con bastón*

('There are three things Seville has which London doesn't: the Alcázar, the Giralda, and police with truncheons.')

Another eminent figure of the time was Blas Infante, who established the idea of Andalusian nationalism. The arguments were spelled out in his book *El Ideal Andaluz*.

To the Seville of the late 1920s, with its enthusiasm for the Exhibition and its rash of new building, came a group of poets and writers, 'the Generation of '27'. Their name, clearly, came from the Generation of '98 from whom they also took much of their inspiration. The Generation of '27 came to Seville to celebrate the tercentenary of the poet Luis de Góngora. Seville was, in the words of one of their number, Juan Ramón Jímenez, the 'ideal capital of poetry', because of the special qualities of the place and its people. The group included Rafael Alberti, García Lorca, and the *sevillanos* Vicente Aleixandre and Luis Cernuda. Many of them were published in the magazine *Mediodía*. Aleixandre in fact left Seville aged two for Madrid, but is claimed as a favoured son on account of his having won the Nobel Prize for Literature. Luis Cernuda was a homosexual poet from a middle-class family, whose sexuality was deplored by the establishment. His friendship with the other writers of the Generation of '27 introduced him to a freer world, but after the Civil War he left Spain for permanent exile in Mexico, where he died in 1957. His works, most especially 'Ocnos', reveal a longing for his homeland of Andalusia, and for his lost youth. Some of them have recently been adapted into a powerful play by a group of young gay writers and actors in Seville, several of whom were drawn to Seville in the late 1980s just as the Generation of '27 had been. With the investment in the infrastructure, as well as in the arts and architecture, the city is jumping.

By 1930, the king's position was weak. He was too closely identified with the failure of Primo de Rivera. An attempted *pronunciamiento* against him was discovered, and the ringleaders were executed. This served only to harden public opinion against him. In the municipal elections (held on the grounds that they would be easier to control than general elections) the socialists and republicans were overwhelmingly successful. General Sanjurjo, commander of the Civil Guard, in what Raymond Carr calls a negative *pronunciamiento*, made it clear that the army would no longer defend the monarchy. The army had no wish to be the whipping boy of the republic.

Two days later the king slipped out of Spain and sailed to Marseilles. The Second Republic was declared.

Seville had already declared for the republic before Alfonso abdicated. Surely this time the republic would hold? The elections certainly showed that the people wished it to. But the democracy was unwieldy, with twenty-six parties in the Cortes of 1931. Coalition governments were inevitable when no party had more than 115 out of 470 seats. The divisions within and between the parties and particularly within the left did for any hopes the left had of survival.

There are four distinct phases to the Second Republic. The constituent period ran from April to December 1931 and ended with the promulgation of the republican constitution and the collapse of the provisional government. The second phase was the republican-socialist coalition under Manuel Azaña which ran until November 1933, when it was defeated in the elections. Then came the *bienio negro*, the two black years, when the republic moved to the right. This ended in defeat for the government in February 1936 by the left-wing coalition, the popular front. This phase culminated five months later in civil war.

The difficulty the republic faced was resolving the inevitable demands for quick action to remedy centuries of deprivation and maladministration. The far left, for instance, demanded the expropriation or nationalisation of land for redistribution. But the Institute of Agrarian Reform only had enough money to be able to hand over to peasant settlers the equivalent of one huge estate. By the end of 1933, fewer than 10,000 landless families had been resettled. The Church paid for its centuries of supremacy in the violence of the popular reaction to it. Raymond Carr comments:

With the benefits of hindsight we can see (especially since the Vatican would have gone a long way to come to terms with the new government) that the attack on the Church was a mistaken priority. Article 26 of the new constitution and the subsequent legislation separated Church and State, expelled the Jesuits, and clipped the Regular

Orders' control over education. It must be admitted that, however conciliatory the Vatican may have been, Catholic influence over education was one thing it would not surrender and this was, at the same time, the one thing that the left republicans were determined to destroy.

At the time the Church was teaching some 600,000 pupils. The arguments between Church and State over education continue to this day. To receive a valuable state subsidy, the church schools have to conform to government standards, and the regulations arouse frequent debate at Church conferences.

The pressure to act against the Church was intense. Hardly had the republic begun than left-wing extremists set fire to convents and churches in Madrid, and their actions were soon copied in Seville and throughout Andalusia. Seville was a centre of communist activity, and Francoist survivors remember those days vividly. 'Remember, the reds set fire to our churches,' they remind me, as if it was yesterday, from the peace of their *casinos* or clubs.

In 1932 General Sanjuro had risked his hand with a *pronunciamiento* in Seville against the faltering government. He was four years too early. He was sentenced to death, but reprieved and soon after escaped from prison. (Sanjurjo would probably have been the monarchists' choice as leader after the Civil War in place of Franco, had he not been killed, just three days after war broke out, in a plane crash.) The republic became still weaker and the authorities frequently lost control as faction fought faction in the streets. The Church was naturally not immune. In 1934, only one float, the Virgen de la Estrella, from Triana, dared to go out on the streets in Holy Week, and was a target for the disaffected bystanders. Yet again Spain was preparing for bitter war, a war that would capture the romantic imagination of foreigners, as so often it had before.

4. From Franco to Felipe

Seville's part in the Civil War was over almost before the war began. The country had been uneasy, expecting action. In Seville the tension was heightened by the weather, which was unnaturally hot and humid. The city was ready to boil over.

Franco's coup began on 17 July 1936, a day earlier than planned, in the Spanish North African territory of Melilla. The conspirators ran the risk of being discovered and had to jump the gun. By the night of the next day Ceuta, Tetuán and Larache in Morocco had declared for the nationalists – for Franco – and so had Seville and a number of other mainland garrisons.

On 18 July the nationalist General Queipo de Llano marched into the city and standing in the Plaza de la Gavidia proclaimed a state of war. A crowd meanwhile ran to the barracks of the Assault Guard in the Alameda de Hércules, hoping to stock up with weapons. They set up barricades in various parts of the city, including the Macarena and Triana. Queipo de Llano went on to depose the civil governor – the sixteenth in five years and three months – and the mayor. To the dismay of many the resistance seemed to fade away, as people went back home to their districts rather than defending the centre. The rapidity with which Seville was taken amazed even Queipo de Llano: 'From time to time I had to rub my eyes to convince myself I wasn't dreaming,' he wrote later. He had achieved it with just 130 soldiers, because the remaining soldiers and officers were away on leave. To finish off the task he was sent a detachment of legionaries from the Third Brigade in Morocco, who landed on 20 July. They were flown in to La Tablada, beyond Triana, by Fokker aircraft supplied by Hitler, in the first airlift in modern warfare. Queipo de Llano had them driven back and forth through the city to look as if there were more of them than there really were.

Once again, Seville had been conquered by North Africans. And, as so often before, Seville had succumbed to a new ruler, but faster than anyone could have expected. Ronald Fraser, in his oral history of the war, *Blood of Spain*, says that the left credited the general's easy seizure of the city in large part to the false sense of security General Sanjurjo's defeat in the *pronunciamiento* of 1932 had created among them.

On both sides there was bloodshed and bravery; there were also unspeakable atrocities. The Moroccan soldiers attacked the people of Triana with horrible brutality, knifing them in the streets and destroying buildings. In the uproar a number of churches were set fire to: San Gil, San Julián, San Marcos, Santa Marina, Omnium Sanctorum. However, the Virgen de la Esperanza Macarena, the heroine of Holy Week, had been rescued from her church and safely hidden a few days before the nationalists entered the city.

Reprisals were swift and savage: many leading figures were shot by the nationalists, including Blas Infante, Andalusia's ideologue. Seville's surrounding towns and villages were not spared. In El Arahal, Ronald Fraser records, 'a township of 12,000 with a long anarchist tradition near Seville, twenty-three right-wingers were burned alive in the jail shortly before the place was taken by the insurgents. In return, legionaries "inflicted an exemplary punishment", the *Correo de Andalucía* of Seville reported on 25 July 1936, killing some "seventy to eighty people".'

But though Seville was so easily caught, it took Franco's

nationalists another three years to defeat the republicans nationally. Nor was there any let-up in the resistance in the city and the ensuing repression. In November 1936, on the eve of the onslaught on Madrid, army activity intensified in Seville. One of those captured was the young Francisca de León, niece of José Diaz, the secretary-general of the communist party. She was taken to the Jáuregui Cinema, which had been converted into a prison. All the seats had been removed, but with some 2,000 people inside there was no room to lie down. She saw many of her friends taken out to be shot. She remembered later:

In the first days they shaved women's heads, forced castor oil down them and led them in their underclothes through the streets to sow terror in the working-class districts. In the mornings you could see mothers crying for sons or husbands who had been shot. Bodies were left lying in the streets without burial. The working class was completely terrorized by the repression.

Queipo de Llano became the Lord Haw-Haw of the Civil War. He made his first broadcast half an hour after the radio station was taken:

Sevillanos: To arms! The fatherland is in danger and, in order to save it, some men of spirit, some generals, have assumed the responsibility of placing themselves at the forefront of a movement of salvation which is triumphant everywhere.

The Army of Africa is preparing to cross Spain to take part in the task of crushing this unworthy government which has resolved to destroy Spain in order to convert the country into a colony of Moscow.

Sevillanos: The die is cast, it is useless for the scum to resist. Legionaries and Moroccan troups are en route for Seville, and when they arrive they will hunt down these trouble-makers like wild animals. ¡*Viva España!* ¡*Viva la República!*

Many listened to his broadcasts more with amusement than apprehension, but for all that they were crudely violent. This extract from his broadcast on 25 July 1936 is typical:

> In various villages of which I have heard, right-wing people are being held prisoner and threatened with barbarous fates. I want to make known my system with regard to this. For every person killed I shall kill ten and perhaps even exceed this proportion.
>
> The leaders of these village movements may believe they can flee; they are wrong. Even if they hide beneath the earth, I shall dig them out; even if they're already dead, I shall kill them again.

Queipo de Llano instituted a rigid and repressive regime in the city. But he also made some attempt to tackle the miserable housing conditions of the working class, many of whom were still packed into the overcrowded *corrales*. To the satisfaction of the employers who had detested the regular strikes during the period of the republic, trade unions were abolished. On the other hand, in a city already impoverished by Expo 29, there was not all that much employment about from which to strike. On the prompting of a lawyer, Prudencio Pumar, Queipo de Llano successfully found the backing for a processing plant for the cotton grown in Andalusia. Was not Seville the 'birthplace and heart of the nationalist movement'? Then why should not Seville have an industry beyond agriculture, and that mainly olives? Hytasa, one of the big industrial names of post-war Spain, was launched in 1937 and was immediately successful, given the shortage of textiles in the nationalist areas.

The nationalists finally won the war in 1939, and Franco became head of state, just when the rest of Europe was plunging into the Second World War. Spain kept out of it, just as it had of the First World War, but it prospered little. Elderly members of the right-wing bourgeoisie will say that 'life wasn't that bad'. But for the rest, the six years of the Second World War were known as one long 'year of hunger'. Thousands died of tuberculosis and typhus. Nevertheless, in such times of strife, as José María de Mena so delightfully puts it, 'the fury of Mars breeds the fury of Venus'. Births boomed, while medicine reduced the rate of deaths. Seville had a population problem once more. The new births combined with the influx of people from the countryside meant that it had 250,000 citizens, but accommodation only for 150,000.

Seville's remarkable post-war recovery was slow and uncomfortable. The Civil War had left deep divisions and the economy was shaky. There were no easy solutions to the agrarian problem. Evidence of this were the *jornaleros* who would collect in town squares each day for work, but who spent much of the year unemployed. There were still three-quarters of a million of them in Andalusia well into the 1960s.

Many commentators have stressed that the Franco regime was not strictly fascist. The fascist crown, after all, goes to José Antonio Primo de Rivera, a son of the dictator. He led the Falange, which was subsumed into Franco's nationalists, and he was conveniently (for General Franco) executed by the republicans in 1936. José Antonio was the charismatic hero, the complete antithesis of the squat Franco. People still speculate on what would have happened if he had not died such a timely death. Once dead, he was just the hero that the dictatorship needed, and full use was made of him. His name was everywhere. That was one of the things that struck me on my first visit to Franco's Spain – the seeming desecration of churches by graffiti proclaiming *¡José Antonio presente!* ('José Antonio is with us'). The calligraphy was elegant but the concept of such holy propaganda abhorrent. (It is interesting to note that the only other politician who is universally addressed by his first name in this way is Felipe – González – the socialist leader and prime minister, who has, or had, a public appeal way beyond those who voted for him.)

Fascism had to be quietly forgotten after the defeats of Mussolini and Hitler, though it still had its uses for Franco. What took its place was an ultra-conservative, ultimately monarchist dictatorship, based on the cornerstones of the Church, the army and the Falange, supported with notable exceptions by the aristocracy and the middle class. It took Franco eleven years to declare Spain a monarchy, and it was 1969 before he nominated Juan Carlos his heir. Alfonso XIII, the last king, had died in 1941, soon after he abdicated. His eldest son, Alfonso, renounced the throne to marry a Cuban woman (Edward VIII was not alone in those years), and died soon after in a car crash. His brother Jaime was thought unfit to rule, on account of being deaf, and he too renounced the throne, and later had two sons, Alfonso and Gonzalo. Alfonso XIII's apparent heir was therefore his son Juan ('Don Juan'), Conde de Barcelona, a Bourbon who had also married a Bourbon.

Two weeks after the Civil War began, Don Juan crossed over into Spain to join the nationalists, but the republicans threw him out. Franco resisted all pressures to have him put on the throne when the war was over, and the relationship between the two men was cold. Don Juan finally handed over his son Juan Carlos, who had been born in Rome in 1938, to Franco to be educated in Spain, in preparation for the ultimate restoration of the monarchy. But he was not easily reconciled to Franco's choice of his son in preference to himself as heir to the throne. Not until 1977 did he give his blessing.

There remained a couple of Carlist pretenders to the throne, but by this time Juan Carlos' claim to the throne was clearly strongest. In Franco's later years, his granddaughter María del Carmen Martínez Bordiú married Alfonso de Borbón-Dampierre (Alfonso XIII's grandson, and Jaime's son), and there was a last-ditch lobby, urged on by Franco's wife, to crown the dictatorship by making Alfonso king. Juan Carlos stepped smartly on that idea. The happy couple are now divorced and remain popular figures in *¡Hola!* and the other *revistas del corazón*, or gossip magazines, along with the rest of the extensive royal family, the distant Carlist pretenders and royalty in general, wherever it is to be found, whether ruling or aspirant.

Fundamental to any dictatorship is indoctrination, and the Franco regime knew how to catch 'em young. In a small village

outside Seville, the children would practise their handwriting
with the following phrases:

*El Generalísimo Franco es nuestro Caudillo. Franco,
Franco. ¡Arriba España!*

('General Franco is our leader. Franco, Franco. Long
live Spain!' The word *caudillo* has connotations of the
great heroic leaders of centuries past.)

The contrast with the schooling of these children compared
with that of their older brothers and sisters could not have
been greater. The Franco regime quickly reversed the radical
reforms of the Second Republic, which had emphasised
primary education, lowering the high illiteracy rates and providing a secular education. Under Franco, the Church
regained and strengthened its hold over education. In 1931,
twenty-nine per cent of secondary school children were in
Church schools. By 1943, the proportion had risen to seventy-
nine per cent. The children of post-war Seville followed a
timetable that began with prayer and was heavily weighted
towards religion and nationalism. The curriculum returned to
the stress on national unity which the Catholic Monarchs had
never actually achieved, but which Francoism wished on
them. Co-education was banned, textbooks were censored and
teachers had to be approved by both the Church and the
Falange. In universities, the same requirements were laid
down, and the rectors had to be active members of the Falange. Even as recently as 1972 lecturers had to produce a
certificate of loyalty to the National Movement. In 1991 a
retired doctor recollected for the newspaper *ABC* his medical
training of the post-Civil War years: 'They used to set what
were informally known as "patriotic exams". You could be sure
of succeeding in the exams if you were wearing the uniform of
the victorious army and were covered in decorations.'

Schools were under heavy pressure from the growth in numbers of school students and the increased demand for post-compulsory secondary education – schooling was compulsory only between the ages of six and twelve until reforms in the 1970s and 1980s, when the school-leaving age was raised to fourteen and then to sixteen. Spain joined UNESCO in 1952 and was accepted by the UN in 1955 (to the great irritation of the republicans; but it was the height of the Cold War and the West was looking for allies). The demands of the economy and the influence of UNESCO eventually led to educational reforms and a major Education Act in 1970. The system was in desperate need of complete reform by the end of the 1970s, particularly because of the relatively high failure rates. It has taken the socialist government ten years of work to begin to introduce reforms to a system that was still labouring in the nineteenth century. Much remains to be done. Andalusia, for instance, still has almost the highest rate of illiteracy in Spain, coming a close second to the historically impoverished region of Extremadura.

One of the moneyspinners of the Franco years was tourism, and in this Seville was protected from the ravages of cheap tourism for Britons. Yet in Seville, as elsewhere in Spain, everything came to have its price, especially the cathedral, which would charge separately for visits to its cloisters and its treasures. Still, Seville did not suffer the fate of so many historic cities of Spain. Not for nothing is the old centre of such cities known as the *casco antiguo. Casco* may mean 'centre' or 'quarter', but it also means an empty bottle, or the hull of a ship. There was nothing more empty than the sanitised antiquities of Franco's Spain. The *casco antiguo* of Cáceres became a picturesque but empty shell, with the city bustling below.

Seville, however, is a more integrated city. The historic churches and palaces are spread across it, rather than packed on to one historic desert island. The one exception is the Barrio de Santa Cruz, extensively gentrified in the 1920s. Some people do still live in the *barrio*, even though it does seem at times to have surrendered to ceramic and souvenir shops. What gives it its continued vibrancy is that *sevillanos*

76

find it quicker to walk through it than round it, that *sevillanos* work in it and that it has sufficient bars that they are not all stuffed with tourists.

If the city did not succumb to the dead hand of the heritage industry, town planning took its toll. The journalist David Gilmour, in his book on Spain's transition to democracy, is vituperative about the man he calls the 'biggest vandal in the city': José Hernández Díaz, former President of the Historic and Artistic Monuments Commission of Seville Province, and co-author of a mighty four-volume work on Seville province's monuments. Yet:

> . . . during his term as mayor he presided over acts of official barbarism such as the demolition of the beautiful palace of the Medina Sidonia family and its replacement by one of the ugliest department stores it is possible to conceive. Once Hernández Díaz had set such an example, Seville naturally acted as a magnet for anyone who felt like picking up some easy money by obliterating a piece of its history. Old Seville might have disappeared altogether had not a young aristocrat, the Duke of Segorbe, formed a pressure group called *Pro Sevilla* which effectively put an end to speculation in the city.

The archaeologist Reyes Ojeda took me through a huge book of black and white photographs, *Arquitectura Civil Sevillana*, published by the city council in 1984. Again and again she pointed out lost palaces and historic buildings. If Seville is a remarkable city now, how much more striking it was only a generation ago. Even making allowances for the natural preferences of an archaeologist for the old as against the new, it was a depressing survey. Talk to a former mayor of Seville, though, and you will find a different view.

*   *   *

Félix Moreno de la Cova was born in 1911 in Palma del Río ('it's actually in the province of Córdoba, but to all intents and purposes, it's in Seville'). His life illustrates exactly that of the Andalusian landowner in the twentieth century. Alfonso XI first gave Simon Boccanegra's brother the *señorio* de Palma. El Gran Capitán ('the great captain', Gonsalvo Fernández de Córdoba, the conqueror of the kingdom of Naples for the Catholic Monarchs) was married in the palace in which Félix Moreno was born. Félix Moreno's father was a *latifundista*, the biggest landowner in Andalusia after the Duque de Medina Sidonia (the descendant of the ill-fated, sea-sickness-prone leader of the Armada). He was also president of the *ganaderos*, or stockbreeders, and in 1930 had 6,366 head of cattle, and a Cadillac 30 hp, the flashest car in town. The pattern of land-holding in the province was typical of Andalusia: in 1930, less than half of one per cent of the landowners in Córdoba province owned almost half of the properties over 250 hectares; and almost the same proportion owned more than two-thirds of the property between 100 and 250 hectares. To put this in perspective, Félix Moreno says, only a handful of estates today are more than 500 hectares; 'only Cayetana [the Duchess of Alba, who shares the honour with José Antonio and Felipe of being known by her first name] owns more than a thousand hectares'. Cayetana's status is such that this is like saying, 'The only really big landowner is the queen.'

The young Félix Moreno trained as an agricultural engineer in Madrid. He was in the capital in July 1936 and heard the news that the rising was about to take place. As it happened, everything started a day early, and he vividly describes the excitement of his journey back to Seville on the 18th. In the end he never reached the city; the train was stopped at Córdoba, because of the news of the rising in Seville. He was as surprised by the events in Seville as anyone: 'I really thought that the left had won in Seville, that the rising in Seville was by those we then called the reds, and who called themselves republicans after the war.' He joined an artillery regiment and fought on the nationalist front at Madrid. The town of Palma del Río was strongly left wing. When the coup came, the left shot some of the right in the town. Most of the right made off, but returned later with the local landowners. The men of the left were rounded up and executed, many on Moreno land.

After the war he became 'a modest farmer', so he likes to say, though he also became president of the major tractor company in Spain, as well as president or director of an array of agricultural and commercial organisations. He was mayor of Seville in the 1960s and enthusiastically produces a sheaf of papers outlining his achievements – and, with honesty, his failures. The biggest of these is the failure to build the metro, but this is a saga that will receive more space later, and he is not the only one to have failed in this. Socialist MPs in the Andalusian parliament will grudgingly say he was one of the city's better Francoist mayors.

Today he is in his eighties, still ready to expound his views on Spain in the past, and the transition. Amongst his achievements, he is proud to point out that he was the first *sevillano* to buy a flat, fifty years ago. There is a very ornate piece of calligraphy framed on the wall of his present flat to prove it, though one would hesitate to call such an extensive property, which also houses some of his children and grandchildren, and his records, decorations and photographs, a flat. Still, he started a trend. Whether he foresaw the agglomerations of scrubby flats jumbled amidst rubbish-strewn wasteland on the outskirts of Seville is another matter. He is recorded as having predicted that Seville would have two million inhabitants in 1990; perhaps the population has peaked at 700,000 because none of them can stand the pressures of city life or afford the soaring cost of property.

In his reflections on 'Franco and the Spanish revolution', he sums up the views of staunch Francoists:

We are part of a generation which, led and governed by an exceptional man, Francisco Franco, not only won a war, and moreover one which was inevitable and justified, but also in forty years of peace utterly transformed the political and social face of Spain.

Our war has been the basis of what we can call the national revolution of Spain.

England began its national revolution in the middle of the seventeenth century and, after a long, cruel and violent civil war which lasted eight years and which culminated in the decapitation of a king, created a political situation in which there could be economic growth during the subsequent decades and, as a continuation of that, great social improvements . . .

Spain had had no revolution. It had had dynastic wars, military *pronunciamientos*, popular uprisings, etc., but all of that had been without a clearly defined political goal.

Well, in my opinion, the Spanish Revolution began in 1931 with a movement which, under the cloak of republican-socialist unity, was in fact a muddled group of Marxist, anarchist, separatist and revolutionary acts of all types; if in the beginning the originators of the republican movement thought that they would control it and lead it, it soon escaped them and left its initiators standing. . . .

As for the revolution in politics, . . . it has got the Spanish to a point where they can attempt to govern themselves and, above all, it has created a climate of coexistence which would have been impossible before our national revolution.

Spain today is not the old Spain of Franco. We have problems, many of them, comparable to those of the developed countries of the West.

Franco, with our assistance, pulled Spain out of underdevelopment and put us on a level with industrialised Europe.

In conversation he wears his politics lightly, and it comes as a shock to hear this redoubtable member of the *alta burguesía* using the vocabulary of the nationalists all these years later. He likes to stress that relatively more people died in the English Civil War than in the Spanish, and that the numbers of dead in the Spanish Civil War were not as high as they were reputed to be.

While Félix Moreno and his colleagues were governing Spain for Franco, beyond its borders the republicans continued their political partics in exile. Their activities seemed an increasing irrelevance, as Spain was gradually accepted by the governments of the West, even if most of them found Franco's politics hard to stomach. The opposition, stranded, could do nothing but wait for somebody else to overthrow Franco. Yet Franco had kept sufficiently on the right side of the allies, despite his reliance on Hitler and Mussolini, to prevent them deposing him. The changes, when they occurred, would have to come from inside – from the workers, the intellectuals and the students. One such was the young *sevillano* labour lawyer Felipe González, who took as his codename, in the underground movement Isidoro, the name of the sainted bishop of Seville.

After bitter arguments between the old guard in exile and the young activists and professional people, Felipe González was elected as secretary-general of the socialist party in 1974 at Suresnes in France, at the party's last conference in exile. The party organisation within Spain was revamped and revived. As Franco's life ticked away, political activity in Spain became more overt, and even the communist leaders were eventually able to live openly in the country without fear of reprisals. The government oscillated between repressing the opposition and inactivity, tending ever more to the latter.

In 1977, in the first democratic elections since 1936, the prime minister's party, the Unión de Centro Democrático, won, but González's socialist PSOE came a strong second. As the votes started to come in, it had seemed that the socialists might even win, to their great consternation, since they felt themselves unready for government and the country unready for them. In 1978 the constitution was passed. It had taken fifteen months to get agreement, but it has already outlasted the constitutions of 1812 and of the Second Republic. In many ways it is one of the most liberal in Europe; amongst other elements, it did away with the death penalty.

In the 1979 elections PSOE was again runner-up. Die-hard socialists put its failure to win down to PSOE's increasing moderation. Felipe González had resigned as secretary-general of the party earlier that year because of the continued use of the word 'Marxist' in the party's policy-making. After some uproar and confusion, he was re-elected and Marxism more or less disappeared from their political vocabulary. In the next elections, in 1982, PSOE finally won a decisive victory. I vividly remember old people saying in amazement the day after the elections that they had never believed they would see a socialist government, while a young man laughed and said even the dogs looked socialist now. The celebrations were understated, at PSOE's request. Certainly many activists remained anxious about the threat of a run on the *peseta* and a military coup, followed by enforced exile – the historic pattern. Already on 23 February 1981, commonly referred to as '23F', one Lieutenant-Colonel Antonio Tejero of the Civil Guard marched into the *Cortes*, the parliament, and held it to ransom for a day. The king's cool head prevented a coup. He managed to ensure most of the generals stayed loyal, and made a television broadcast to the nation. But for a time, it was finely balanced. Many socialists and communists had their escapes planned; some in the south had boats ready to flee to North Africa. As it happens, the fragile democracy survived and survives still, and those plans remain in cold storage until the need should ever arise for them again.

According to the newspaper *El País*, there have been at least four attempts to murder the king and overthrow the government since 1981. The latest effort was in 1985, when members of the military failed in a plot to blow up the king and queen, prime minister Felipe González and his defence minister Narcís Serra, as they took the salute in La Coruña – Franco's home ground – on Armed Forces Day, 1 June 1985, just before Spain joined the European Community. The murder would have been blamed on the Basque terrorist group ETA, who in 1973 had murdered prime minister Admiral Carrero Blanco with a car bomb in Madrid.

The Tejero episode came to a bizarre conclusion in 1982, when he formed his own political party and stood in Madrid in the general elections. His daughter headed the party's list of candidates in Seville.

And there the story of Felipe González might have faded out to the traditionally happy ending. But the handsome prince who rescued Spain from the wicked dictator has had to endure ten years of married life. He has become middle-aged, slightly stooped and more rotund, and his eyesight is failing. His politics have moved from red to pink, as Spain has joined Europe and played an increasingly international role. There are times when he looks as if what he really wants is a divorce, but there are no serious pretenders. His vote decreases at each election, but as yet the opposition cannot muster enough votes to unseat him.

Without doubt, Felipe González's open, honest personality was immensely important in the socialists' victory. But from his earliest days as an activist, he has had two valuable companions, both *sevillanos*. The first is Alfonso Guerra, the Machiavelli behind the throne or a subtle politician, depending on how you choose to look at it. Alfonso Guerra has been the hard man of the two, protecting his master's clean image amid the inevitable carnage of government. It was, perhaps, inevitable that it was Alfonso Guerra who should have been brought down in the end. As the years of socialist rule passed, there had been increasing criticism of nepotism within the party. The party's reply was that it had come into government and had introduced devolution. Suddenly it had to fill thousands of jobs. Like-minded people had to be found quickly, and inevitably some mistakes were made.

Near the end of the 1980s, critics found a specially juicy target, Alfonso Guerra's brother Juan. The stories about his misdemeanours mushroomed and have occupied the press for several years. It was alleged that Juan Guerra had been involved in corrupt dealing over a property development at the resort on the coastal edge of the National Park of Coto Doñana, which lies between Seville and the sea. It was alleged, too, that he had been given a free office in a government building in Seville and that he had used it for years without paying for the rent, the electricity or the telephone. The press went to town. Alfonso and Juan Guerra's personal lives were investigated as only today's popular press in Spain can investigate, having been restrained from publishing juicy details and salacious photographs for so long under Franco.

The real intention was to hit Felipe González through his deputy. Eventually Alfonso Guerra offered his resignation, but Felipe González refused to accept it for a year. In that time the government was damaged by continued criticism and speculation, and the 'Juan Guerra affair' gave rise to fresh allegations of corruption in government in other spheres. As I write, Juan Guerra is still under investigation, while Alfonso is a deputy in the *Cortes* and works for the PSOE organisation. Felipe González is discovering the perils of losing his right-hand man. As for the Juan Guerra affair, socialist parliamentarians in Seville I have spoken to shrug the matter off: Juan Guerra has done nothing, maybe he has been a little stupid, perhaps there has been a minor problem with his taxes, who knows? Yet the prime minister and his deputy have to be (reasonably) above reproach. In many ways the Spanish electorate is much more forgiving than the British and American ones when it comes to peccadillos. But after forty years of dictatorship they can be forgiven for being particularly sensitive to allegations of misdemeanours in government.

Felipe González's other companion since his early days in Seville has been his wife, Carmen Romero. Before 1982 she worked as a teacher, and she kept on her profession for some years after the family moved into the Moncloa Palace. She also managed to keep her own life and that of her two small children (now teenagers) relatively private. Ten years on, things have changed. First, there was the Don Juan affair. This was a subject swooped on by the *revistas de corazón*, the gossip papers, and the illustrated serious weeklies. What happened was that Carmen Romero acquired a particular interest in Italy, and after she gave up teaching she was able to devote more time to studying the language. In addition, she was studying the myth of Don Juan, reasonably enough, since he is one of the great stereotypes of Seville and of Spain, and this involved trips to Italy. Her visits were soon interpreted as the cover for a love affair, and learned professors were interviewed to give testimony to the real quality of her studies. Inevitably her marriage has had its bad moments and the press has revelled in them.

The second change in Carmen Romero's life as consort came in 1990, when she was elected a deputy for Cádiz province in the national parliament. Since Spain uses proportional representation, where regional lists of candidates are compiled by each party, the socialists were criticised for pandering to the prime minister by putting his wife at the top of the Cádiz list. It was difficult at the beginning, but Carmen Romero has begun to establish some sort of independence from her husband. She has certainly managed the task of being a socialist prime minister's wife in a constitutional monarchy with great skill. When the occasion demands she will put on her finery, but is happy to confide to the journalists of *¡Hola!* that she buys most of her clothes off the peg, and is not worried about being seen wearing them more than once in public. In this she has much in common with the queen, Sofia, the elder sister of Constantine, ex-king of Greece. Both of them show far less concern with their appearances than the majority of their compatriots.

The most important political change for Seville since the arrival of democracy has been the granting of regional autonomy to Andalusia. The question of devolution and autonomy was one of the first items on the agenda of the first post-Franco government of Adolfo Suárez. The Cataláns and the Basques, like the Galicians, were distinct nationalities with their own languages and with their own histories of rebellion or separatism from Castilla. The government had to act quickly to appease the Cataláns. But with the recognition of nations such as Catalonia, other regions with less of a claim started to rediscover their own nationalism. Many of them could not make a strong case for home rule, but Andalusia was a little different. Yet, for all that outsiders saw Andalusia as a distinct region, it was by no means united. Western Andalusia differs from eastern Andalusia, in history as in agriculture. Still the two halves of the region have more recently shared a common campaign against poverty, as the rest of Spain has grown richer around them. Blas Infante created the concept of Andalusia about a century ago, and his ideas have been revived. Andalusia now has its own ubiquitous green and white flag (Franco introduced the red and yellow national flag; and for many years its use was seen as a nationalist symbol). After prevarications by the government, elections for the Andalusian parliament were held in May 1982.

Seven years later, an academic in Granada surveyed the opinions of a sample of these newly united people. The most important event in Andalusia's history, after the statute of autonomy, the respondents said, was the period of Muslim rule, more important than the discovery of America, the Civil War, Expo 92, or the *cortes* of Cádiz with its constitution of 1812. Who was the most important person in Spanish history? King Juan Carlos, followed by Felipe González, Franco and Columbus. Whom did they trust most? The Swiss and the Japanese. And the least? The Chinese and, least of all, the Moroccans. In the EC, the *andaluces* had most confidence in the Italians, and least in the French and the British. They saw the most typical feature of their region as the climate, followed by their way of speaking (notably, 'swallowing' the ends of their words) and their folklore. The survey also revealed that Andalusians felt they differed from the rest of Spain by their personalities, and in the food they ate. Three-quarters of the sample felt that the province of Seville was getting most of the benefits from autonomy, but half felt that with the Expo and the Quincentenary celebrations Seville was getting the attention it deserved.

Certainly, Seville's fortunes began to revive when it became the capital of the autonomous community. The community is headed by a president and administered by a governing council, a legislative assembly, and a supreme court. It received devolved powers from the government over agriculture, forestry, freshwater fishing, housing, town and country planning, tourism and sport. Health and social services were also handed over, though they had to fit into the national structure. Central government kept direct control of civil aviation, defence, external trade, foreign affairs, justice and criminal, commercial and labour law, merchant shipping and offshore fishing. In certain areas like education there has been a sharing of powers.

For Seville, the outcome was another influx of people, many of them intellectuals, with comfortable middle-class lifestyles – yuppies, in effect. This has had its repercussions on Seville society. All of them needed offices. Local and autonomous government together have taken over a number of derelict palaces and in the process have acquired desirable addresses. The parliament itself is yet to move into its new home, the former Hospedal de las Cinco Llagas (Hospital of the Five Wounds), opposite the Basilica of the Macarena, just outside the city walls. The building was started in 1545 and used as a hospital until the 1960s. Its chapel will become the debating chamber; during parliamentary sessions the altar and sculptures will be covered up.

The autonomous community is now a fair-sized publisher, with a programme that includes many books that would be too expensive, for reasons of the shortness of the print-run or the large numbers of illustrations, to publish commercially. It publishes materials for schools, since all schoolchildren in the autonomous communities are taught about their own community – and for some or all of the day in their community language, if there is one (though the *andaluces* have the distinctive habit of contracting their words, for instance by shortening words ending in -*ado* to -*ao*, they are basically speaking

Castilian). The Andalusian government has become very active in sponsoring the arts across Andalusia – everything from painting and theatre to flamenco. This political enthusiasm for the arts is strongly reminiscent of London in the early 1980s, when Ken Livingstone's Greater London Council was pouring funds into all kinds of popular arts. As it was in London so it is in Seville: not everything that is sponsored is worthy of the attention, but it certainly brings the city alive.

Andalusia's economy in the second half of the 1980s grew faster than Spain's and faster than the EC average. There was a general recession with the Gulf War, but Seville was cushioned more than most by the fact of its being the community capital, and by the massive spending on infrastructure occasioned by Expo 92. Not surprisingly, construction was the fastest-growing sector, averaging growth rates of more than twelve per cent in the years since 1987. Agriculture still employs more people across the region than construction, but it is now sharply divided between the traditional, still fairly primitive farming of the rural centre, and the high-tech intensive agriculture on the coasts, especially in eastern Andalusia. In the finance sector, there is, as anyone who has ever tried to change a traveller's cheque in the province or the city will know, a relative shortage of banks: Seville province has a third fewer banks and building societies per head of population than the national average. In industry, the largest sector is food, drinks and tobacco. The city recently suffered something of a tragedy, when the manufacturers of its favourite beer, Cruzcampo, as much a symbol of the city as the Giralda, was taken over by foreign capital. And the scandalous new owners? Guinness, manufacturers of beers for the British, a people who, as thirty years of British tourism have taught the Spaniards, know not a thing about beer.

In the Andalusian parliament the socialists are currently in power, led by the president Manuel Chaves. In the city council things are more complicated. In the first municipal elections after the restoration of democracy, the Andalusian nationalist party, the Partido Andalucista (PA), came top. PA subsequently lost to PSOE, in the great wave of pro-socialist euphoria. Then in May 1991, PSOE was shaken in a number of its strongholds. It lost Madrid and Valencia. In a number of towns and cities the votes were very evenly balanced and parties of all sides entered into pacts, to the anger of many politicians, especially the socialists. In Seville, PSOE had the most councillors, but the PA and the right-wing Partido Popular together created a pact to put PSOE into the minority. The negotiations took a number of days to complete, for Seville was a particularly important prize. Not only was it the home town of the prime minister and his former deputy, but the party leaders were fighting for the prestige of being *alcalde*, or mayor, in Expo year. The PA and PP were anxious to exclude PSOE from this moment of glory in their stronghold and PSOE briefly considered bartering the mayoralty of Seville for one of the other cities of Spain that it still held.

In the end, the pact produced the most unwieldy solution of all. To the gratification of the opposition PSOE *was* squeezed out. The PA and PP then had to negotiate over the share-out of responsibilities. After several days of brinkmanship, Alejandro Rojas Marcos of the PA came out on top as mayor, with Soledad Becerril of the PP as his runner-up and deputy. Rojas Marcos was only too pleased to be able to underscore his success soon after, when he welcomed the royal family, who came to stay in Seville a few days later.

The members of the new Ayuntamiento or city council are typical of the new politicians of Spain. Of the thirty-one councillors, nine are women, their average age is forty-one, and they are nearly all professionals, many of them lawyers, most of them married with children. Many observers doubted at the time of the pact whether the unwieldy council thus created would even last the year until the Expo. But survive it has, with the PP and PA remaining united in their political opposition to PSOE. Both left and right condemn the PA for being a party without any real idology of its own. Furthermore, Alejandro Rojas Marcos is seen as having a 'past'. He was a councillor in Seville while Franco was still alive. One right-winger spoke for many when he said, 'Alejandro's very well-connected, he comes from a very good family. He shouldn't be messing about with something like the PA, which was just cobbled together.' Some on the left are equally critical. One PSOE member, a *sevillano* with close connections with Felipe González, chose to call Rojas Marcos a cynic and a demagogue. 'He may be a populist, but his family own whole streets in Seville. What gets him the support now is the youth votes; he's got them taped.' There is no love lost between the PA and PSOE. The PA was formerly the Partido Socialista de Andalucía, much to the irritation of the Andalusian socialists González and Guerra.

The PP leader Soledad Becerril, like Rojas Marcos, is also well-connected, and the right – and the left – feel that she, unlike Rojas-Marcos, is in her proper place in the right-wing PP. As one of the few women at the top of politics in Spain, she is the focus of chauvinist doubt as to whether a woman, even when deputy mayor, will ever manage to carry the day in the council, when the mayor is a man. Soledad Becerril has had to tread a fine line in her role as a politician, while still keeping up the fictions of clothes-horse, mother and home-maker required by her party. The last days of campaigning for the municipal elections, for instance, coincided with the *feria*, the spring fair. Nothing could have been better for campaigning than the *feria*, where everyone goes to see and be seen. I watched Alejandro Rojas Marcos, and Luis Yañez, the PSOE candidate for mayor, strolling the avenues of the *feria* in their regulation dark suits. Neither was dressed up as a *caballero*, with cummerbund and short jacket. Yet Soledad Becerril – like the other women candidates in the election – had to appear in full flamenco dress and was clearly disadvantaged. She looked to be no more than just another politician's wife in the crowd, rather than the politician herself. The *feriantes*, the people at the *feria*, simply gossiped about how well, or not, she and the other women candidates passed themselves off as *gitanas*, gypsies, how authentic their costumes were, and whether they looked good in them.

The three parties differ little in their analyses of Seville's problems. The first comes broadly under the umbrella of 'quality of life'. The concern for the 'environment', so lavishly expressed in Britain and North America in the search for votes, is only just beginning to catch on in Spain. But though the words *medio ambiente* may seem new to the political vocabulary, their meaning is not. *Sevillanos* are rightly very critical of their dirty city – though they don't seem to make the connection between their own behaviour, when it comes to litter and cigarette ends, and the rubbish they dislike in the streets. The cathedral is symbolic of the dirty city. Seville may be sprouting railway stations, airports and offices of shiny marble, but one of its most historic monuments is black with grime, especially on the west side facing the Avenida de la Constitución. Still, there are many houseproud housewives continuing to fight the unwinnable battle against the dirt, washing down their doorsteps daily. The streets, too, are regularly sprayed with water to dampen the dust, and the street cleaners who appear on special occasions like Holy Week perform a remarkable task in the depths of night.

Sevillanos are sick to death of the traffic in the city, especially since no lasting solution has been found. Seville is Andalusia's largest city, and Spain's fourth largest, after Madrid, Barcelona and Valencia. The population of the province stands at over one and a half million, while the city has some 685,000 residents. However, observers believe the city population is levelling off and possibly beginning to fall as increasing numbers of *sevillanos* find the overcrowding unbearable. In support of this contention are the growing populations of the outlying towns. Dos Hermanas has a population of 70,000 and Alcalà de Guadaira 51,000 (the latter is also known as Alcalà de los Panaderos because it has been famed for its bread since its Arab days). Camas, Coria del Río, Mairena del Aljarafe, San Juan de Aznalfarache and La Rinconada all have populations of 20,000 or more. Dos Hermanas continues to be the most popular town, receiving the most immigrants of any town in the province in 1990.

Many of the people who live in these suburbs work in Seville, but prefer the newer, slightly greener conurbations that have sprung up everywhere in recent years. Yet these commuters who have to travel in to Seville at rush hour, whether by bus, car or train, face a crowded and uncomfortable journey. Seville has more lorries, buses, cars, motorbikes – and tractors – than any other province of Andalusia, and it sometimes seems as if they are all converging on the city at once, polluting the air with their noxious fumes. No wonder the orange trees on the Avenida de la Constitución alongside the cathedral look so seedy. Their *medio ambiente* is poisoning them.

Another aspect of the polluted environment is noise. Stop for a minute. You may be in the gardens of the Casa de Pilatos, sitting on a stone seat contemplating the blowsy flowers. What can you hear? Ignore the loud-mouthed tourists, a hazard of any great city. There is bird song, and the rustling of the leaves in the breeze. There are, irregularly, cars in the street beyond, and the more distant noise of persistent traffic on the ring road a short distance away. Inevitably a child will be crying. And there will be the noise of roadworks or builders – but this, though irritating, is only temporary. A reasonable array of sound in fact, and bearable, for a house in a quieter section of the old city. Go now to the Avenida de la Constitución or the Plaza Nueva. What is the noise level like there? Roaring cars, buses, lorries and motorbikes. Drivers shouting at each other in the traffic jams. Children crying, everyone shouting at everyone else above the noise. A wall of noise, with not a bird, not even a foreign tourist who might seem supportable here, to be heard. And do not dream of dropping into a bar for relief and a peaceful drink. The *sevillanos* have come to talk, to slap each other on the back, to shout at the waiter down the other end, to sing a snatch of a *copla*, to watch the television which will be yelling hoarsely in the corner, to add their individual bit to the convivial hubbub. Most times of the day the *sevillano* abhors a silence.

One of the sure topics of conversation in the bar, along with last night's match, will be the traffic. As with the weather, *sevillanos* enjoy complaining about the jams. The obvious answer to the problem is a metro, and this was under discussion thirty years ago – Félix Moreno de la Cova had it on his agenda as *alcalde*. The first studies were made in 1972 and the plans were approved in 1975. The construction of the Seville metro was the last piece of legislation that Franco signed before he died in November the same year. Work began the following year, but the *alcalde* (a PA mayor heading a left coalition council) stopped it abruptly in 1983. Bits of the city had started to collapse into the tunnels that were being sunk for the metro.

The digging had started below the Avenida de Eduardo Dato, one of the main arterial roads to the east of the city. The avenue started to subside, and the undulations remain obvious today. As the metro tunnel came nearer into the city the problems multiplied. When it arrived at the Puerta de Jerez, the former gate to the city and now a busy roundabout by the Alfonso XIII hotel, the calamity occurred. The old buildings on three of the four corners of the Puerta de Jerez started to fall down. Only the Alfonso XIII survived. There was uproar. If there were buildings falling already, the Giralda would surely be the next to go. *'O Sevilla o el metro'* ('either Seville, or the metro') was the cry of the conservative press.

For three years there was deadlock, while the problems of the traffic above ground increased. Then the socialists, who were by this time in power, promised to look at fresh proposals. The metro became a symbol of political backbiting, as each party accused the other of incompetence and everyone blamed the socialists. In the 1991 municipal elections, the metro was at the top of everyone's manifesto. The PP candidate for *alcalde*, Soledad Becerril, was asked why her socialist opponent Luis Yañez was campaigning in favour of a metro, when he had opposed it during his past eight years in the Ayuntamiento. Her reply was brisk: 'If he says "no to the metro", he won't get out of the campaign alive.' Guillermo Gutiérrez, a former architect and now a socialist member for Seville of the Andalusian parliament, believes the solution lies in one of the new, above-ground, 'light' railways. Nothing, however, will happen before the mid-1990s, too late for Expo year.

Guillermo Gutiérrez was a socialist councillor in the Ayuntamiento for eight years, where his responsibilities included traffic. He is not the first to have worried about

Seville's congestion. Ever since 1929, councils have been try-ing and failing to implement urban plans. Added to this, the boom in personal affluence in the last decade has increased the numbers of cars flooding in. To cope with the crisis, an enterprising company set itself up in March 1991, hiring out motorbikes to people who wanted to get round the city quickly: people working for the Expo, businessmen, doctors on emergency calls, architects on site visits – and tourists. (There used to be a company doing a similar thing with motor-scooters in the 1950s. Why had the idea not been copied before? 'Because,' said the company's managing director, '*sev-illanos* aren't very keen on becoming businessmen.')

Guillermo Gutiérrez's enthusiasm shines as he expounds his theories for ridding Seville centre of the tortures of the traffic jams. (Anyone who has not sat in a Seville traffic jam in a non-airconditioned car or taxi in the heat of the day, with the exhaust fumes mounting, the sun pounding down, tempers rising and horns blaring, has not suffered.) His goal was to close off the centre of the old city to through traffic, except buses and taxis, but it was thought to be too sensitive politi-cally. He points out that Seville has one of the largest old centres in Europe, with streets that were designed to keep out the sun, not provide space for modern traffic. The city's roads were originally radial, which meant traffic had to come into the city to get out of it again. His intention was that cars would be able to enter by one of four arterial roads and then park. Nowhere in old Seville is more than twenty minutes' walk away, and internal connections would be much faster when the buses were running freely. The scheme was shouted down: '*ABC* [the right-wing newspaper] called for demonstrations, and said I was a red.' The difficulty remains that '*la gente no tiene cultura de circulación*', 'people don't know how to behave in traffic', and 'they'd never wait half an hour for a bus, like you might do in London'.

Few have a good word for the buses. For a visitor, though, they are ideal. Every stop has simple plans of the routes of the buses that stop there, so strangers can plan their journeys on their maps. The *bonobus* ticket available throughout the city gives cut-price rides and if you take another ride within the same hour you travel free. Guillermo Gutiérrez is proud to point out that he also introduced air-conditioning on the buses. Still, the people sweltering on the crowded buses to Santiponce at lunchtime continue to open the windows, even though the sign says, 'This bus is air-conditioned, please do not open the windows'. (Is this another example of the much-vaunted independence of the *andaluz*, who will not follow other people's orders?) During the *feria*, extra buses are laid on to transport the world from the Prado de San Sebastián to the *feria* and back again. This is the one time of year when the buses become really democratic. Since it is impossible to catch a taxi back from the fair site in the early morning because of the hundreds of thousands of people, those who are too tired to walk, however rich or poor, young or old, catch a bus. Nor, despite the queues, are the buses too crowded. This is because of a piece of complicated arithmetic that only Seville could set: How many giggling girls can you pack on a municipal bus, if each is wearing a flamenco dress with three full flounces, and four of them are carrying giant cuddly toys they have just won in the fair?

Guillermo Gutiérrez was also in charge of the police, and gives the local force a reasonably clean bill of health. He saw his job as helping to transform the police, which had suffered politically and professionally under Franco. The one advantage of their experience of dictatorship was that they were already well disciplined. The problem was that, like all civil servants, they had tenure, and they had a vested interest in keeping the status quo. The task has been to winkle out corruption and gradually supplant the former practice of suppression of citizens' rights with the democratic spirit of the day. Today, Guillermo Gutiérrez reckons, the police are no longer feared – though they are not yet respected. They have yet to be tested over the handling of Basque terrorism, for Andalusia has so far escaped the attentions of ETA. But as Seville's profile rises, especially with the Expo, so the risks increase, as the bomb planted on the high-speed rail line between Madrid and Seville in August 1991 showed. Instead the police have been much more exercised about theft. The new democracy suffered almost a decade of what he calls 'psychic insecurity', where people's real insecurity increased, but their fear of it was further exaggerated. This, he says, was used by the media to attack the government, linking the idea of personal insecurity to the arrival of democracy. As he is well aware, it made headlines around the world.

Seville had the worst press of all, surpassing even that of the Costa del Sol. Every foreign tourist knows that you have to look after your bag in snatch-happy Seville, that there are robbers in every crowd and youths on motorbikes who will snatch your bag off your arm. These reports are no different from the highly coloured warnings given by the tourists who visited Spain in the last century and were waylaid by bandits. The organised groups of brigands who were involved in smuggling contraband and the small-timers on the make were both a risk, especially crossing the Sierra Morena on the Madrid–Seville route. Benjamin Disraeli travelled in Spain as a young man in 1830, returning to the country of his Sephardic ancestors, and reported of the bandits in the Serranía de Ronda, 'If you have less than sixteen dollars, they shoot you.' Richard Ford took a different view. You would meet the real brigands, he said, 'not on the road, but in confessional boxes, lawyers' offices, and still more in the bureaux of government'.

Seville continues to be popularly viewed as the Naples of Spain, where tourists who come from the crime capitals of London and New York go in fear of the petty criminal. Far better, surely, if you are going to lose your handbag, to have it stolen in Seville, than in either of those cities, where the risk of getting beaten up in the process is so much greater. In any case, popular opinion internationally has not caught up with the reality of Seville today. While tourists' casually worn handbags are a great temptation and Seville thieves are very quick at robbing hire cars of their luggage, the police have also become more effective.

One of the reasons for the increase in petty crime was drugs; tourists' handbags were a good source of cash to feed the habit. Seville is one of several cities in Spain which have been important distribution centres for drugs coming into Europe from North Africa. In 1990, the police caught 886 kilogrammes of heroin, 5,252 of cocaine and 70,075 of hashish, and 24,812 people were detained as a result. There are different methods of handling the drugs issue. Across Spain there have been angry anti-drug demonstrations in recent months. A group of lawyers in Seville supports the legalisation of all drugs, whereas the *alcalde*, Alejandro Rojas-Marcos, declared at the time of his election in 1991 that he would ban the consumption of any drug in public. The high proportion of young people who take drugs is a matter of concern in Seville and throughout Andalusia. It is seen as being closely associated with the high levels of unemployment in the region. For all that, there are many who take *un porro*, a joint, *de chocolate*, of marijuana, at the end of a hard day. My taxi-driver, seeing me yawning in the back seat after a lengthy session following virgins round the streets in Holy Week, chided me for being so feeble. How did he keep going on these never-ending days and nights? 'Easy,' he said, 'I smoke a joint. Nothing excessive, you understand, just one or two in Holy Week, and maybe another on New Year's Eve – they give me just the charge I need.'

Despite the high levels of the intravenous use of drugs, Seville does not have the highest incidence of SIDA (AIDS) in Spain. But Spain was tenth in the ranking of countries with confirmed cases of AIDS in 1990, and the only European countries ahead of her were France and Italy. On the public health tables, the province of Seville is neither particularly healthy nor unhealthy, compared with its Andalusian neighbours. Except, that is, for two diseases. The first is chicken-pox, where Seville in 1990 had almost twice as many cases as any other province except Cádiz. The second is syphilis; Seville had the highest incidence of the disease in Andalusia in 1990, and was beaten only by the larger conurbations of Barcelona and Madrid in the national syphilis stakes. This may be because Seville's authorities do not yet have an especially enlightened approach to its prostitutes. Acknowledging Seville's oldest professionals is too sensitive politically. Not so long ago, a politican in Jerez de la Frontera, down towards Cádiz, tried to liberalise his council's policies on its prostitutes, but soon found it was not a vote-catcher.

Housing remains a hot potato. Since the late nineteenth century, when increasing numbers of *sevillanos* were crowded into the *corrales de vecinos*, the poor quality and small quantity of the housing in Seville, especially for the working classes, has been an issue. The arrival of Expo 92 only exacerbated it. The Expo, like the Junta de Andalucía before it, brought a new group of people into the city who were able to pay whatever landlords chose to demand. *Sevillanos* screamed as they were squeezed out, as flats became simply too expensive to rent. Everyone had stories of somebody's mother who had managed to get hold of some flats years back and was now turning herself into a mini estate agent and raking it in.

For many the only solution was to move out of the city altogether, to one of the burgeoning suburbs. Others put up with the overcrowding and spent the money on second homes in the countryside. The depopulation of the countryside in recent years has left many homes empty for those who go beyond the suburbs to buy cheaply. The critics of the *nueva jet*, the young professionals and politicians, point to this rash of second home buying as a yuppy disease. Yet many of these same critics come from the upper classes and have long had second homes themselves. What agitates them is that these new owners of two homes are perfectly ordinary, middle-class members of Seville society, who have bought these properties out of their own fairly average earnings, and have not inherited them. The effect of second home fever is that Seville becomes emptier at the weekends as each year passes.

For the tourists, at least, this brings relief from the constant roar of people and traffic. At the weekend, the monuments are accessible, the roads can be crossed with reasonable impunity, parking is possible. The *sevillanos* are long-suffering with the year-round invasion of tourists. But don't be deceived that this is because of any warm-heartedness for the foreign hordes. While *sevillanos* are generous to any who show a real interest in their city, they ignore tourists as best they can. They know, however, that the city, and its bars, hotels, shops and service industries, rely on the visitors. Tourism is the largest part of the service sector, and the service sector in turn is the largest part of Seville's economy, accounting for almost two-thirds of it, and faster-growing than either Andalusia's or Spain's services. During Holy Week, the *feria* and other festivals, prices are allowed to go up in the bars and hotels of the city. You will suddenly find that your *bocadillo de queso* costs you twice as much. It is easy to think the bar in question is ripping you off because you are just another tourist. Many misunderstandings have arisen this way. But be assured; the *sevillanos* are being ripped off too. They complain about it more loudly than anyone.

Spain's income from tourism is dropping. The old beach holiday has lost its appeal and the government is working to raise the standards of its provision to tempt the holiday-makers back. For cities like Seville it is a different story, for they are only beginning to exploit their appeal to independent travellers who want to see more than beaches. While almost a million visitors stayed in hotels in the province of Seville in 1990, there were twice as many in the province of Málaga. Servicing the visitors to Seville still does not provide enough jobs. Seville is the unemployment capital of Europe with a third of its population of working age out of work. Expo 92, whose construction was supposed to bring a quantity of – admittedly short-term – employment to the city, has been a disappointment. Some exhibiting countries simply cut corners by importing their pavilions in pre-fabricated sections; others employed cheaper Portuguese or African labour. The journalist Nicolás Salas in 1991 predicts an unemployment boom after the Expo: 'There's always a crisis after every Expo.'

Expo 92 was popularly viewed as another sign of Felipe González's favouritism. How could it be otherwise when Felipe's home town won the Expo, when Seville had already had the opportunity – even if the financially disastrous one – of hosting Expo 29? Yet, the organisers stress, this is not the case. When the decision was made, Felipe was not around. As it happens, though, his home town has benefited. Expo has given Seville ten new bridges, two of them pedestrian, several of them particularly interesting structures. This has the great advantage of breaking the psychological divide between the centre of old Seville on the east bank, and the suburbs of Triana and Los Remedios on the west. They should also do something to ease the traffic, since crossing the Triana, San Telmo and Generalísimo bridges in the lunchtime rush is like crossing the centre of Istanbul. Yet there is one of the new bridges, the most southerly crossing of the Guadalquivir, which at 140 metres towers over the next highest at 98 metres and looks completely out of place in the flat lands around it. Admittedly, it is on the outskirts of the city. But it far outdoes the Giralda, the one tall building that for seven centuries had dominated the city. For the modernists, the bridge emphasises Seville's entry into the twenty-first century. For my part, I regret that having held off skyscraper fever for so long, Seville had to start now.

In the run-up to the Expo, Seville, and not just the Expo at La Cartuja, was one large building site. Standing on the roof of a building in the centre of the Barrio de Santa Cruz in spring 1991, I counted the expected fifteen church towers, including the Giralda, a sight so often praised by early travellers. But I also counted an even greater number of cranes swinging over the roofs of the city. Roads were up everywhere, old buildings demolished, palaces restored. The airport was rebuilt in architecture that echoed Andalusia's Islamic past, but in a design that disloyally had more of the mosque at Córdoba in it than of the local masterpiece, the Alcázar.

The two railway stations were replaced by one post-modern marble cathedral, named after one half of the martyred saint-sister team: Justa. In its vast central hall passengers shrink away to nothing. The lines were laid for the high-speed train, the AVE, which by the time it arrived was, like Concorde, a white elephant. The idea had been to link it with the French high-speed train, and there had been initial plans to join up a number of cities across Spain. Costs rose and projects shrank, until only the Madrid–Seville section was completed. The river between La Cartuja and the city was closed off, creating the Meandro de San Jeronimo, a stretch of still water for international rowing competitions (that's why the bridges here were designed without central struts – to enable scullers to pass freely). Ten hotels were built, providing a surfeit of beds in an average year, even with the programme to increase its popularity as a conference centre, though there were plans to convert some into flats and offices after the event. The Expo site at La Cartuja was an obvious place for expansion for city businesses, but it needed the international investment in the Expo to make it possible, and to dissipate the centuries of psychic distance from the west bank.

For anyone who remembers the Seville of Franco's days the transformation has been extraordinary. Seville enters the twenty-first century with good reason to be ebullient. However, beyond Expo lies the Single European Market. For a province that is heavily reliant on foodstuffs and primary products, many still produced by outdated machinery, free trade is a great concern. By the time Seville catches up with the rest of Europe, or manages to corner the market in a few high-value goods, it may be too late.

PART 2

5. Behind closed doors

Magdalena Hernández starts the day with a cup of coffee and a slice of Bimbo bread. Bimbo is the ubiquitous slightly sweet, pappy, *ersatz* sliced white loaf of Spain, nastier even than anything the British bakers have so far produced. On the other hand, it is possible, as I have discovered, to acquire a taste for it. It just takes time. Magdalena toasts the bread on a grill on top of the gas burner on the cooker, but she has to stand over it – being so synthetic the bread burns easily. She covers it lavishly with Flora margarine, since she has recently learnt that she has heart trouble and is just coming to grips with cholesterol. (Inconsistently: she eats eggs and hard cheese but has banned chocolate.) She takes the breakfast on a tray through to her little dining room, which has a small round table covered with a deep red, velvet-effect tablecloth which she lifts over her knees for warmth. Under the table there is a small electric heater, which builds up a cosy warmth round her arthritic legs. In the summer she appreciates the cool of the marble floors of her flat, but for the rest of the year they can be chilly. The television dominates the little room; she spends much of the day with her knees tucked under the tablecloth watching the television and snoozes the evening through in her rocking chair. Television is important to her;

her daughter lives some distance away in Granada, and her son is working abroad.

In Franco's time television was dire, a propaganda tool for the masses, with all the output censored. It worked on a bread and circuses policy, except that what the people were fed were endless football matches. Even the news appeared at times to be nothing but football and goals. Today, things have improved slightly. There are two state stations, two private stations, a subscription service and a regional station. The state service in the early years of socialist government was regularly accused of incompetence and corruption. Its programming is still uneven, with an excess of soap operas, cartoons and seriously trivial game shows. Magdalena enjoys watching Canal Sur, the regional station, which provides local news, romanticised amateurish features about Andalusia and village choirs singing local songs in regional costumes in unconvincing studios. It is a station with an identity and can be relied upon to cover major events in Seville like Holy Week for those, like Magdalena, who prefer to stay indoors.

The flat is comfortable, with three bedrooms, the dining room, a sitting room, a kitchen and a bathroom. The large sitting room is furnished with dark wood pieces and is only used for 'best'. The kitchen has a fridge, a sink, a small table, a few cupboards and a bottled gas cooker, and hot water comes from a gas heater on the wall. Magdalena's home is on the first floor of a four-storey block of flats in the Barrio Tartessos, a small district named after Seville's mythical founders. She keeps the shutters on the windows two-thirds closed for much of the day, to keep out the bright sunlight. The only disadvantage is that she has to move about in semi-darkness all the time. Alone in her flat, she has no one to call in to say hello. But she and her neighbour upstairs keep in close touch by shouting up and down the block's central well. Since many of the other neighbours do the same thing, there is plenty of opportunity to listen in to other people's business and follow the family arguments of 'her on the top floor'.

Magdalena goes out to put her rubbish into the street bins, which are emptied nightly, and to visit her pensioners' club.

Justa and Rufina were Seville's first Christian martyrs, and were painted in 1682 by the *sevillano* Murillo, a typical example of his sickly virgins. They carry the martyr's palms and the Giralda, the icon of Seville. As well as representing the city, the sisters also became the patrons of Spain's potters – at their feet are the symbols of their trade.

Velázquez painted several atmospheric pictures of everyday life in Seville before he left the city to go to the court in Madrid. One of the most famous, *The Water-Seller of Seville* (1622) is said to portray a contemporary *sevillano*. The fruit in the bottom of the glass helped sweeten the possibly polluted water. The water-seller has his left hand on a large container of a type which the potters of the city had been making for centuries.

Caspar de Guzmán, Count-Duke of Olivares (a village just outside Seville). Felipe IV's prime minister for over twenty years, he is variously described as a radical and an authoritarian. He sanctioned Spain's involvement in the costly adventure that became the Thirty Years' War.

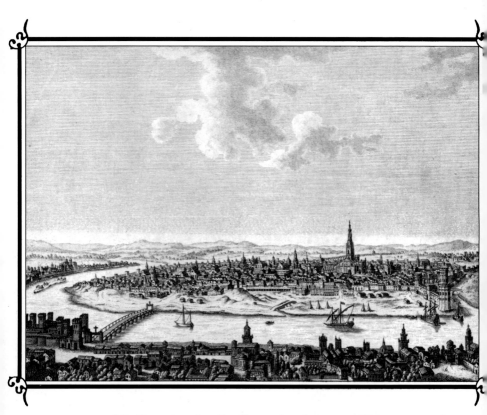

'*Quién no ha visto Sevilla, no ha visto maravilla*' –
'If you haven't seen Seville, you haven't seen
anything' – runs the old cliché. The Triana district
is in the foreground. Bottom left is the Castle of
the Inquisition, until recently the site of a popular
market. Stretching behind the city is the aqueduct;
a few insignificant arches linger today (see map).

A Protestant view of the Inquisition:

'Yet there at ease with his whole court around him
King Ferdinand sits "in his GLORY" – confound him! –
    . . . His pouncet box goes to and fro at his nose
As somewhat misliking the smell of old clothes,
And seeming to hint, by this action emphatic,
That Jews e'en when roasted are not aromatic.'

From 'The Auto-da-fé', *The Ingoldsby Legends.*

The writer and cleric José Maria Blanco Crespo, the only Spaniard to have an entry in the *Dictionary of National Biography*. During the War of Independence he left Seville and emigrated to England, where he became known as Blanco White. Robert Southey called his poem 'Night and Day' 'the finest and most grandly conceived sonnet in our language'.

The *feria,* the spring fair, in its original form of cattle fair. The market aspect of the fair did not last long, but the *feria* continued to be held on the Prado de San Sebastián until relatively recently. Today the 'meadow' is a dusty bus station.

(Above) The *café cantante,* a familiar feature of turn-of-the-century city life. Flamenco is a fleeting art, but early photography required poses – hence the picture's rather stilted air.

(Below) The Torre del Oro once watched over the gold from the New World being unloaded. Today only pleasure boats anchor alongside.

Seville's Coat of Arms

In the centre is San Fernando, flanked by the brother saint-bishops Leandro and Isidoro. The crest proudly bears five epithets. *'Muy noble'* – 'very noble' – granted in 1248 at the Reconquista; *'muy leal'* – 'very loyal' – granted by Juan II in 1444; *'muy heroica'* – 'very brave' – granted by Fernando VII for the city's support during the War of Independence; *'invicta'* – 'unconquered' – granted by Isabel II for standing out against General Espartero; and *'mariana'* – 'Marian' – granted by Franco in 1946 because of the city's special dedication to the Virgin Mary.

The symbol of the letters NO and DO enclosing a *madeja* or skein can be seen all over the city, on everything from drain covers to the paper wrappings of *confiterías*. It is a play on the words 'no *me* ha *deja*do' – 'she has not abandoned me' – and dates from the time of Alfonso X, *el Sabio*. Alfonso's son Sancho fought his father and acquired extensive territory. But Seville held out against him and for this it was rewarded with the punning motto. The romantic also interpret it as suggesting that the memory of Seville will not die.

The Puerta del Aceite (the Gate of Oil), just west of the cathedral, is one of the few remaining gates of the city. The stalls may have been supplanted by a crush of cars, and several of the shops converted into bars, but the bustle of the photograph remains.

Seville, August 1932: General Sanjurjo tried, with a
nineteenth-century-style *pronunciamiento,* to install a
right-wing republican government. Like most of its
predecessors, the *pronunciamiento* failed miserably. But
the event was a foretaste of civil war, which came just
four years later.

(Above) 20 July 1936: Seville fell to General Queipo de Llano within twenty-four hours of Franco's uprising in Africa. Resistance was brutally crushed in the Triana district, where men were knifed to death in the streets.

(Right) February 1937: Bread and circuses. Within six months the fascist slogan *¡Arriba España!* and the accompanying symbol of the bundle of arrows had been emblazoned on the sand of the bull-ring, and the standard was passed round to collect donations for Franco's war effort.

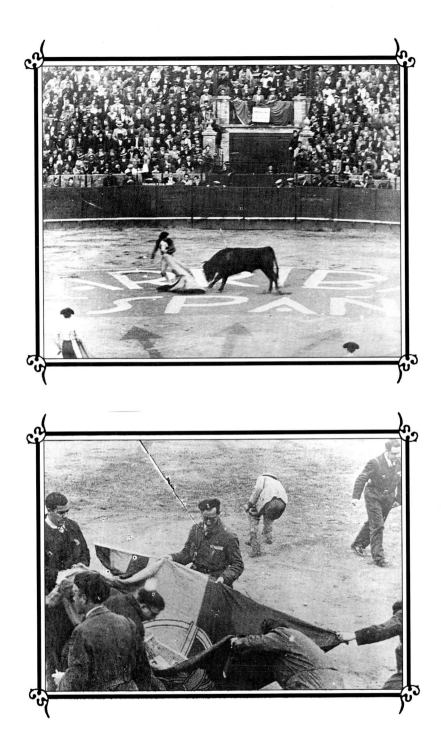

(Above) At Castilleja de la Cuesta, in the hills just outside Seville, they still follow the traditional recipes. Here, the lard is about to be mixed with flour and sugar to make crumbly *polvorones*. In a region that relies so heavily on olive oil, this is one of the infrequent uses of animal fat.

(Right) Several convents in the city make cakes, sweets and biscuits. The sisters of Santa Paula make 2,000 kilos of *membrillo*, quince paste, a year. When the season comes, all the sisters have to join in. For the rest of the year they make jams and preserves which can be bought at the convent.

April 1990: *feria* as it is today – almost. In 1990 Spain was swept by an equine fever. No horses were allowed out in public, which meant that the traditional horse-drawn carriages and *caballeros* on horseback, so characteristic of the *feria,* disappeared. The *feriantes* were obliged to resort to less picturesque means of transport to ferry them to their *casetas.*

And she goes out to shop. All the shops that she needs are in the ground floors of the blocks of flats: knickers and tee-shirts are immediately below; flowers round the corner; and screws and widgets over the main road. Small, characterless bars on most corners compete at night over which has the most garishly lit advertisement for beer. The children can only play in the scrubby open spaces between the low-rise blocks, and in a small playground at the end of the street, surrounded by double-parked cars.

Magdalena is immensely house-proud, like all women of her generation, reared to keep home for their husbands and children. Her world was turned topsy-turvy by the Civil War. She was fourteen when the war broke out, and both her parents were killed by 'the reds' soon after. She therefore came to live with her grandparents in Seville, where she subsequently met and married her husband. But he died when her children were young, so she had to bring them up alone, seeing them through school and then university, the first of their family to go on to higher education. Now she is an exceptionally proud grandmother. Magdalena represents the classic image of the Andalusian woman typified in the emotional worship of the Virgin Mary, with whom this city identifies itself so closely. The adjectives run away with themselves – such women are devoted, long-suffering, faithful, ever-present, caring. The reverse of the same image is the other heroine of *andaluz machismo* – seductress and whore. The nineteenth-century Italian traveller Edmondo de Amicis was much taken with the women:

> I do not believe that there exist in any country women who are so thoroughly fitted to suggest the idea of abduction as the Andalusians, not only because they arouse the desire to commit all sorts of devilries, but because they really seem created on purpose to be seized, bundled up and hidden away, so small, light, plump, elastic and soft are they. Their little feet can easily be got into your coat-pocket . . . They slide, glide and float along, and in a single moment, while passing you, they show you their

foot, make you admire their arm or waist, display two rows of white teeth, shoot a long, veiled glance at you which is transfixed and dies in yours, and then go on their way, confident of having raised a tumult in your breast.

Today, as the writer Tom Burns has remarked, Spain has ceased to be a Byzantine bolt-hole for sensation-seekers such as Amicis. The modern-day Carmens are a more independent breed, and the daughters of the 'haughty *hidalgos*' have MBAs from American universities.

One of the younger generation escaping from the chauvinist vision of Andalusian womanhood is archaeologist Reyes Ojeda, who lives with her sister in a newish block of flats in the centre of town. By day she works for the Junta de Andalucía, the Andalusian government; by night she likes to go out with her boyfriend. Housework is not a vocation, nor even a priority. Her neighbours are inclined to let bits of rubbish drop down the central well, which then collects at the bottom, outside her window. When the pile gets sufficiently large, she climbs out to sweep it up. Until then, it has to wait. The flat belongs to her parents and when her mother visits she complains about the dust and the dog hairs from the friendly but hairy red setter. She is thinking about getting a girl in to clean the flat once a fortnight, but has not got round to it yet.

Reyes shops once a week at the central El Corte Inglés in the Plaza del Duque de la Victoria. (This was for centuries the plaza of the Dukes of Medina-Sidonia, whose palace was sold in the nineteenth century, and over the houses built in its stead El Corte Inglés was built. It is now named after the Duque de la Victoria de Tetuán, General Espartero, Isabella II's regent.) It may be more expensive than the edge-of-town hypermarkets, but it has everything she wants and she can walk home with her shopping. She enjoys cooking, but does not have time to prepare a main meal in the middle of the day, as is traditional. She finds that she and her contemporaries are caught in the trap between independence and traditionalism.

'The Andalusian woman is still traditional at heart. She may be studying now, but she wants to marry.' One day, she supposes, she will have to make the choice between children and career. She imagines that she will ultimately choose children. But for the present it is not a decision she wants to have to think about. It doesn't help relationships that 'men don't do a thing in the house, not even make a cup of tea. Most mothers still don't ask their sons to help in the house, and until they do things will change very slowly.' Certainly, Andalusian man needs to adapt: the region has one of the highest rates of wife-beating in Spain.

'Living in the centre of Seville is like living in a village,' says Reyes, which is why she likes it so much. But like many of her generation, she wants to buy herself a house in the mountains, in the Sierra, since they can still be found quite cheaply. Reyes lives in the south-eastern part of the old city, in the 04 postal district. The former *alcalde* Félix Moreno also lived there in his bachelor days. His sister now looks after the Moreno home in the Barrio de Santa Cruz, in calle Guzmán el Bueno, a street which contains several grand houses, though one of them has already been gutted and turned into flats. The ownership of the house has changed down the centuries, and the Morenos bought it from an English family in 1943. It was built in 1584 around the classic patio. Around the edges of the patio there are Roman statues, and in one corner a group of comfortable chairs. In the summer, when the open space above is covered over, the patio is cool and fresh. The rooms on one side of the patio are used by the family as offices, on another side is the family chapel. A grand staircase, with a huge tapestry on the half-landing, leads to the first floor, which has a mixture of public and private rooms. There are collections of all kinds, most notably in the dining room a glass-fronted cabinet of ornate silver cruet sets. One corner ends in an airy balcony, another in a pleasant sitting-out area, overlooking the garden and the swimming pool. It is a reminder that as you toil round the streets, desperately seeking a respite from the sun and the heat, over the high walls someone will privately be enjoying just the cool you desire. Hans Christian Andersen, who visited Seville in 1862, said the houses were like human beings: 'Outside one looks very like another, but inside there lies the difference.'

Looking after such houses is an immense task: so much to be cleaned and so few staff available. In the old days there were plenty of young girls who used to come into service. Félix Moreno remembers that his parents would treat the country girls who came to the big city from their Palma de Río estate like members of their own families. They would go to their weddings and be godparents to their first children. Today, though, young girls seem to want to be independent. . . .

As the population statistics suggest, increasing numbers of people are moving out, finding the overcrowding and lack of green space in Seville unbearable, while the cost of housing is beyond their reach. One such couple are Antonio Lara and his wife Susi. Antonio is a secondary school English teacher and his wife is an authentic *sevillana* who lives for flamenco and gives lessons in it. They have two teenage sons and decided some years back, like so many others, to move to the largest of Seville's dormitory towns, Dos Hermanas. Today it has an old-ish centre around the railway station, and from it have mushroomed new developments for its growing populations. Antonio's conurbation is one of the furthest, separated from the centre of Dos Hermanas itself by the busy dual carriageway from Seville which links up with the nearby motorway to Cádiz.

Nothing could be more different from the Laras' former existence in the city. Their house is on the very edge of the development, looking out over fields; in the evenings cows and goats amble past, their bells tinkling, and a farmer trots by on horseback. Inside the houses are shady, more northern European than Spanish in style; there is no patio, but the floors are marble. Antonio is good at DIY and has made nearly all of the pine furniture. Most of the houses have large front gardens with 'English' lawns and climbing roses. What makes them instantly Mediterranean is their lemon trees and medlar trees, and the bougainvillaea tumbling everywhere like a particularly vigorous bindweed. One or two neighbours have installed car ports; one has even taken over half his garden with a DIY swimming pool. It's an artificial, 'instant' community, which is gaining an identity as it gets older. Round the corner there's a small supermarket, a greengrocer and a couple of bars; a few blocks down in the still unfinished *plaza* is the newspaper kiosk – and the bus stop. In one sense it's like Seville without the aggravation – the city's just near enough if you have a car. In another, it's like being at the end of the world, if you have to get to Seville on public transport.

Sevillanos in the suburbs have reason to complain about the public transport. Buses between Antonio's conurbation and the centre of Dos Hermanas come only every hour and a half, though once the bus comes the journey only takes fifteen to twenty minutes. If you want to go to Seville, you can catch a bus to Dos Hermanas to catch a train. The train only takes fourteen minutes, but it runs irregularly and the bus and train timetables do not coincide. Alternatively, you can catch the bus to Seville from the dual carriageway. This bus stop is twenty minutes' walk from Antonio's door. Or you can wait for the once-every-hour-and-a-half bus to drop you at the stop. (If you do not fancy walking back home across a stretch of open wasteland from the bus stop in the evening, you will have to come home early, for the last once-every-hour-and-a-half bus leaves at the scandalously early hour of 9 p.m.) The bus to Seville runs every twenty minutes to half an hour, and the journey is fairly quick – until you hit the traffic on the outskirts of the city. The buses are pretty ancient and some of them leak in the rain. What with wet plastic seats, mud on the floor and condensation on the windows, it detracts from the benefits of the green environment they have chosen. All in all, Susi's average journey time into Seville, if she takes the bus, is about an hour. If she goes by car it may take her only twenty minutes, but then she will have the usual problem parking.

So how do the *sevillanos* who prefer the aggravations of the city to the irritations of the suburbs decide where to live? The old city is divided up into four postal districts, which are shown on some of the better street maps. District 01 is Arenal, which stretches down from the cathedral to the old port district and along to the bull-ring, taking in the Plaza Nueva and some of the most popular shopping streets. District 02 contains what used to be one of the most run-down parts of the city, housing the red-light area. It still does, as well as several gay bars, but it is also being taken over by young professionals. District 03 is crossed by calles San Luis/Bustos Tavera and Castellar. Here were the largest concentration of *corrales de vecinos*, rooming houses set round a courtyard. Much of the housing is still in very poor condition, occupied by an elderly population, mainly female, who do not wish to move from their neighbourhoods. The city council has built some public housing for them nearby, so that they are not uprooted, but there is not nearly enough of it. The nuns of the Santa Paula convent off calle del Sol will warn you to look after your belongings as you leave. They may love and nourish the people of the district, but they have a shrewd understanding of the attractions of a stranger's handbag.

District 04 runs down from 03 to the river and contains the historic red light district of the city. It is also becoming increasingly popular with young professionals. North beyond the Macarena wall, districts 08 and 09 are working-class zones where people are in jobs and reasonably prosperous. Round to the east in districts 07 and 06, the standard of living is lower, with increasing levels of unemployment. Closer in to the centre, the *barrios* of Los Pájaros, La Candelaria and Madre de Dios were built some twenty years ago as state housing for those who had to be decanted from the low-lying centre because of the continued risk of floods. District 05, closer in still, takes in the immediate contrast of the expensive district of Nervión, the highest part of the city, where the residents relish the (relatively) cool breezes. A recent acknowledgement of the affluence of the neighbourhood is the siting of the new El Corte Inglés in the *barrio*. On the far eastern edge of 06 is the *barrio* of Padre Pio and the Barriada de Palmete, two of Seville's most depressed and depressing sectors. These were started up by immigrants who built their own homes out of anything they could find when the city provided them with nothing. Eventually the socialist Ayuntamiento laid on buses, water, and electricity. The Poligono Sur in district 13 is equally depressed. The centre-right UCD created this urban ghetto; it was built for the poor and has become a dispiriting dump. Those who can, leave. Those who can't, stay, most of them unemployed and many on hard drugs. It is one of the few places in Seville taxi-drivers will not enter.

On the other side of the river the Triana district has a long, colourful history. This was the zone of the potteries and soap factories, and it was also a haunt of sailors and gypsies in particular and the working class in general. Over the centuries, Triana has grown further away from the river. As it was extended once more in the late 1950s officials chose to name the new streets with a misplaced piety. *Virtud, Prosperidad, Voluntad, Constancia, Consuelo* (Virtue, Work, Prosperity, (Good) Will, Constancy and Solace) were wished upon the worldly citizens of Triana in a last-ditch attempt to reform them. An immense wall of public housing running down the side of the Avenida de Alvar Nuñez was also erected at the time. This undistinguished development earned the nickname *'El Tardón'*, 'slowcoach', because it was so long in the building. The district peters out in an unpleasant muddle of tower blocks, bounded by the noisy and busy ring road. Not that the unpleasant tower blocks fringing Triana are anything uncommon. Most of the approaches to Seville are equally unappealing. Short of arriving by parachute and landing in the Alcázar, it is probably best to arrive by the Cádiz road. This way at least you get the chance to drive along the Avenida de Manuel Suirot, past some very elegant turn-of-the-century housing, and down the Avenida de Borbolla past the Parque María Luisa, ending up in the hair-raising roundabout of Plaza Don Juan de Austria, where the independent spirit of the *andaluz*, especially when driving a car, becomes terrifyingly apparent.

Life has changed in Triana. It is common to be sentimental about the salt of the earth who live there, setting them up as an anthropological curiosity, 'real Seville'. But Triana has become as popular with young professionals as the red-light district on the east bank of the river. It becomes even more up-market the closer you get to Los Remedios, a *barrio* in district 11. The two *barrios* are divided by the dead straight Avenida de la República Argentina, which is constantly jammed with traffic and resounds with tooting car horns. Los Remedios was designed as a very smart *barrio* of blocks of flats. There is certainly the requisite selection of expensive dress shops and patisseries. However, the flats were placed too close together with too little parking space between to cope with the boom in car-owning since it was built. It is a warren of narrow streets, none of the east–west ones open to the river, and has gradually lost its sparkle. The only bonus for residents of Los Remedios is that the *feria* is currently held on the adjoining open space. Eleven and three-quarter months of the year it is a scrubby stretch of open ground beloved of learner drivers. In May each year it hosts a week-long twenty-four hour party. During the *feria*, the fortunate residents of Los Remedios can go home during the day and take a shower and a nap. They soon discover they are mysteriously almost as popular as the people who have a *caseta*, or small marquee, on the *feria* site. The really lucky ones, including the popular singer Isabel Pantoja, have flats overlooking the ground and can enjoy the fireworks and the bright lights from a distance. There are plans, however, to move the *feria* to a larger site a little further away at La Tablada, where the Moroccan troops landed in 1936, or, some say, to the Expo site. 'If the *feria* goes, then I'm not staying,' was the typical comment of a local resident disenchanted with the less-than-sparkling *barrio*.

If Seville's districts are carefully ranked, so is Seville society. *Sevillanos* will appear friendly and open-handed with any foreign visitors who take an interest in their city; they will be much more cautious with Spaniards. 'They're a load of snobs in Seville,' declared a friend from Cádiz. '*Gaditanos?* [people from Cádiz] They're all poofters,' was the response. Whatever the rights of the case, and one observer has noted that both sides believe there are only two cities in the world, Seville and Cádiz, *sevillanos* have a very strong sense of their city's social structure. Top of the heap comes the aristocracy, and top of that particular heap is Cayetana Fitz-James Stuart, Duchess of Alba.

Cayetana is a kind of national treasure and has the most titles (fifty-three) of any aristocrat in Spain. She is as remarkable for her individualism as for her curly blonde hair. Her hair gives her the air of a literary lion, or the painter that she is. She is also popular because she likes to take part in Seville's festivities, and can be sure to be seen in her mantilla on Maundy Thursday, and in her *traje de gitana* a few weeks later for the *feria*.

She caused a storm in early 1991 when she failed to appear at the first official meeting between the king and the *Grandeza de España*, the leading grandees of Spain created by Charles V, since the restoration of the monarchy. Everybody had turned up except the Duchess of Alba. Surely this was a slight on the other grandees? Not at all, she said, her husband had been ill. And she was not being rude to the king. She said, perfectly reasonably, that since she already saw him on numerous occasions, neither of them needed to see each other again at this point. The affair died down, but the feeling remained that the Duchess of Alba had taken a bit of shine off the day for those lesser grandees who did not regularly move in exalted circles.

The next most important of the titled families are the Dukes of Medinaceli, who live in the gorgeous Casa de Pilatos, and the Dukes of Medina-Sidonia. The Duchess of Medina-Sidonia is popularly known as the 'red' duchess, on account of her political sympathies. Also in the top rank of society are the members of the Real Maestranza de la Caballería. This royal order of chivalry dates back to the Reconquista, to 1248 when Fernando III, *el santo*, conquered Seville for the Christians. He founded a brotherhood of knights who practised their equestrian arts outside the city walls. Then in 1670

Felipe II set up Real (or Royal) Maestranzas in five cities, including Seville and Madrid. The intention was to keep his nobles fit and ready for cavalry action in war at a time when there was no regular army. The Real Maestranza was open only to nobles, and they were prevented from taking part in commerce. This excluded such grand families as the Ybarras, who were tainted with trade. The side effect of this was to increase Spanish disdain for commerce, on the basis that what's not good enough for the Real Maestranza is not good enough for me. This only weakened Spanish trading power at a time when competition was increasing abroad.

There are some 250 *maestrantes* in Spain, who have to be descendants on both sides from *maestrantes*. Thus what matters is not so much whether you have a title or what type it is, but what your parents' names are. Here again the obsession with surnames and lineage emerges, with *sevillanos* inspecting each others' surnames as monkeys examine each others' fleas.

The qualifying age is twenty-three, and the *maestrante* is expected to be well-educated, almost certainly with a university degree. He must be well-mannered and able to support himself in the position in society to which he should be accustomed. In effect, *'un maestrante debe de ser todo un señor'*, 'he should be a complete gentleman'.

The *Hermano Mayor*, or president, of the Maestranza is the king's father, Don Juan de Borbón, Conde de Barcelona. His deputy, and therefore effectively the head of the organisation, is the very model of a modern *maestrante*. Luis Manuel Halcón de la Lastra, Conde de Peñaflor de la Argamasilla, Marqués de Villafranca, decorated with the Encomienda de Isabel la Católica, the Silver Cross of the Red Cross and an MBA, is a chemical engineer whose business is agriculture. He is married, with six children and a grandchild. Today his *maestrantes* are more concerned with riding as a sport, with good works and with bullfighting. For the Real Maestranza used to administer Seville's bull-ring, the Plaza de la Maestranza, as well as the taurine museum. Known simply as the Maestranza, it is Spain's largest bull-ring and had taken more than a century to build by the time it was finished in 1881. Camilo José Cela called it 'perhaps the most beautiful and evocative of all the rings in Spain'. It is oval, rather than round, and was built to seat 14,000. In 1914 it was remodelled and enlarged. Today, however, the bull-ring is run by a private company.

The Real Maestranza is an anachronism, but one which still survives in a class-conscious society like Seville's. Its rules are watertight, even if it has lost its eponymous bull-ring. Félix Moreno's wife, for instance, came from a family which belonged to the Real Maestranza, but she had to leave it when she married a man who was not a member. Yet, Félix Moreno points out, one of his sons is soon to marry the sister of the future Duchess of Alba, and the Marqués de Motilla is another son's father-in-law, so is not everything relative? He cites another member of the *alta burguesía* who comes into the top rank of Seville society, but who is also not a *maestrante*. This is the urbane José Luis de Pablo Romero, *Hermano Mayor* of the Hermandad de la Macarena, the earthly representative, as it were, of Seville's most famous virgin, and one of the richest men in the city.

The middle classes in Spain are a relatively new phenomenon and owe their existence to the dictatorship. This was particularly the case in Andalusia, where society was clearly delimited into 'the haves' and 'the rest'. From the middle of the twentieth century grew a group of professionals, many of them tied to the State as tenured civil servants in an enormous bureaucracy. Their proportions in Seville have increased in the last ten years with the arrival of many new politicians and bureaucrats to administer the regional government and its multiple offspring. Most of them work in newly converted 'designer' offices, all white paint, white marble, and postmodern lighting and furniture. A model of this is the chamber of commerce on the north side of the Plaza de Contratación. The building opens on to a central patio which has been glassed over and covered with the usual blind. But this one has been painted with allegorical scenes. The top floor, meanwhile, appears artfully to have been only partially restored.

The banisters diminish into nothing, the plaster gives way to brick and back to plaster again as if a section has been cut through the building. Some of the supporting beams are exposed, others are hidden. Of necessity the lift has to be squeezed into a narrow corner; houses with patios were not made for lifts.

The waste of space in these buildings with large patios seems extravagant to one used to the cramped offices of northern Europe, especially in such an overcrowded city. But again and again, this is the surprise of Seville. Like the secret garden of Frances Hodgson Burnett's fancy, there is the essential space and calm behind some of Seville's walls, if you can only find the key to unlock it. While tourism has opened up most of the cities of the world, Seville still keeps much hidden away.

Before we go too much further we should pause to consider the military and the Church, two organisations which dominated Spain for centuries, especially the latter, but which are today in decline. If the military is less of a threat and less of a force than it was, it is still physically much in evidence in Seville, for there are barracks all over the place. Part of the reason for that is that there is still military service. However, the *'mili'* lasts less than a year now and various categories of community service can be chosen instead. Outside the barracks, young soldiers are to be seen on guard, sitting on chairs, their feet up on a low wall, reading the paper or joking with their colleagues. When I primly compared them unfavourably to the rigid guards of the UK, a senior officer roared with laughter: 'We've never taken that kind of thing as seriously as you have. There are many more important things in a soldier's life.'

The socialists came into government in 1982 with a military top-heavy with generals and senior officers. They are gradually being eased out and they congregate instead in the city's clubs, recalling past glories. The dangerous beast has had its teeth and claws drawn, but is not quite dormant yet. Younger officers are turning into professional European soldiers, busily learning English and French; their complaint is that they did not play a large enough part in the Gulf War. Popular opinion was strongly against the war, and bad feelings were exacerbated by the continued presence of the American bases – the base at Rota is just an hour and a half away from Seville, on the coast – introduced by Franco.

As to the Church, it too has a strong physical presence in the city. There are always black-garbed clerics to be found buying sweeties or trainers in El Corte Inglés. The San Pablo religious bookshop in calle Sierpes usually has a mother with baby outside, begging for alms from the steady flow of priests and nuns. In practice, the Church is reeling under the pressures of today's materialistic society. Less than a third of Spaniards attend mass regularly. Since 1988 Spaniards have been able to choose whether to donate a tithe (actually, 0.52 per cent) of their taxes to the Church, or whether they would rather have it directed to social projects. Last year thirty-eight per cent chose to make a donation to the Church – a small decrease on the previous year. The Church is nevertheless present at all the rites of passage; there's no question but that it still sanctions births, marriages and deaths. Javier García, a young civil servant newly graduated in law from the university, is busy enjoying life in the city with his first pay cheques, like any other young man of his age. But when he gets married, 'of course' he'll do it in church. (In his spare time Javier García has started APREF, Asociación [de] Profesionales en Formación, the Association of Professionals in Training. With some cash from the Ayuntamiento to set up an office and print their business cards, a group of young law graduates offer their services free to anyone in reduced circumstances who needs to go to law. This way, the APREF members, especially the ones who are unemployed, keep in practice, while the fee of the experienced lawyer who presents the case in court is greatly reduced, because all the lawyer should have to do is to check over APREF's work.)

On Sundays in May the streets froth with pint-sized brides and sailor boys off to church to celebrate their first communion. The gift shops join in with sickly displays of white leather-effect Bibles and photograph albums, crucifixes and other holy knick-knacks. The main religious shops in the city do healthy business at all times of the year, often as crowded as any of the *ultramarinos* – grocers' stores. People queue up for a carved and painted Virgin, or a portrait of a favoured Christ from one of the local churches. Miniature models of parts of the body can be bought as votive offerings.

The reduced attendance at mass is obvious in the city; this can partly be explained by the fact that more *sevillanos* have cars and second homes and leave the city at weekends; but also women, the majority of worshippers in the churches, have much busier lives, which leave scant room for the Church except on special occasions. Mother María de Pablo Romero, sister of the *Hermano Mayor* of the Hermandad of the Macarena, and the well-connected, well-educated, well-travelled head of the school run by the Madres Irlandesas in calle Bami to the south of the city, acknowledges the changes. Apart from the attractions of the material world, 'people are more afraid to commit themselves. You see it in marriage, and the fear of perpetual vows. We see it in the decreasing numbers of girls who wish to become nuns.'

I first met the Madres Irlandesas in 1972, when the college in calle Bami had just been built. At that time, they had the reputation of educating the aristocracy, or, at least, their daughters, in their two schools in Castilleja de la Cuesta and in calle Bami. Twenty years on, democracy has brought new pressures to bear on the church schools. Those that wish to receive a state subsidy have to conform with ministry regulations. This is a contentious issue: supporters of state education believe that this subsidy, especially to the Church, siphons off money from state schools; while the private schools protest loud and often at the requirements of the government. One of these is greater social integration. The Madres Irlandesas always took local children from poor families, but there is now a much greater mixture of social classes. Students are accepted on the basis of how close they are to school. This also means that they can benefit from going home for lunch, traditionally the main family meal of the day in Spain. The Madres Irlandesas now have 1,400 girls at calle Bami (taught by nine nuns and thirty-five lay members of staff), and 1,200 boys and girls in Castilleja de la Cuesta. Co-education is an innovation, but one that is extremely popular. Mother María likes it, using an argument in its favour that I had not heard before. When brothers and sisters go to the same school, she says, it greatly increases her chances of effective pastoral work with the whole family. 'If there are a thousand children in a co-educational school, then there are about 500 families. So you get to know the families much better and can help them all.'

The government made religious education voluntary in schools in 1991. Mother María regrets this greatly, and says that ninety per cent of her parents want a religious education for their children. The school naturally provides preparation classes for communion, as well as masses and confession. Mothers and fathers, as well as past students, come in to help with the catechism for confirmation classes: 'It's very lively; and it's important that we can all learn together from one another.' The founder of the order believed that girls should be taught just as the Jesuits taught boys, and that women could do great things: 'What a prophet she was!'

Today, Mother María carries on those teachings, also believing that students should feel as welcome at school as they do in their own homes. Only a short time ago society demanded that her girl students became professional home-makers. Now they can be educated for more independent lives; they can choose whether to be engineers or artists. After their time at the school, she believes that her students should have acquired four qualities to guide them through life: a sense of freedom; a sense of justice; sincerity; and a sense of joy. Mother María, despite the severity of her blue suit and uniform shoes, demonstrably has all four. Generations of women have suffered from a convent education, though sometimes to the enrichment of literature. Is Mother María de Pablo Romero an exception as a headteacher, or a sign of the way forward?

Very few students go on to take their vows. The material world is too attractive. But those who choose the religious life are much more likely to join an enclosed order. 'They are frightened of belonging to a teaching order, where they have to be good teachers as well as good nuns. We feel a long-term satisfaction in this when our old students come back to see us. We are *contemplativos en acción*, contemplation and work are one for us. But many more girls prefer the life of prayer. In the USA the *conventos de clausura* [enclosed orders] are full up.'

Santa Paula, just off the calle del Sol, is one such *convento de clausura*, though the sisters would hesitate to say they are overflowing with applicants. Still, with forty-three nuns, the signs are healthy. Santa Paula is a very up-market convent which has had many daughters of top families in its order. Today there are fewer vocations among Spanish girls, so fifteen of the sister come from the Indies – the Caribbean – and Africa. The word *clausura* is a misnomer for the lives they lead. It is true that when you visit them they sit formally behind a large iron grille in the *locutorio*, like prisoners, and there are definite limits beyond which you do not pass. Yet they will come out from behind the bars to show you the treasures of the convent and their chapel, and step out and gossip in their leafy courtyard when you pass the window where they are sewing. A wise, spry sister says that they never want for visitors: 'And it's a delight when all our families come. They bring all the little ones and the patio is full of children running around playing football, just as if they were at home.'

The word '*clausura*' implies silence and prayer, and to an outsider a cruel imprisonment; in visiting hours, while the nuns retain the selfless calm which comes from years of contemplation, they reveal themselves as a collection of merry souls.

Closer to the centre of the city is the enclosed convent of Santa Inés, founded by the fabled Doña María Coronel who escaped the lustful King Pedro el Cruel. The nuns prefer the version in which she disfigured herself with boiling oil. Her embalmed body is displayed once a year on 2 December. Today the convent is less vigorous than it used to be. There are eleven nuns left and they are all getting older – one of them is ninety. The convent is known for its biscuits and cakes, especially the *bollitos de Santa Inés*, but there are fewer nuns to work in the kitchens.

The *Hermano Mayor*, or president, of the brotherhood of Jesús del Gran Poder (the Pontificia y Real Hermandad y Cofradía de Nazarenos de Nuestro Padre Jesús del Gran Poder y María Santísima del Mayor Dolor y Traspaso), has a diplomatic answer to the Church's current difficulties. Antonio Ríos Ramos is a small, intense man, built like a champion jockey, a bachelor devoted to his honorary role. He prefers to emphasise the humbling aspects of his job as the representative of the brotherhood of the most famous *paso* of Christ in Holy Week. The Church's temporal power, he says, is clearly in decline, the archbishop is no longer the powerful man his predecessors were. At this, he looks across at the impressive painting of the austere and influential Cardinal Archbishop Spínola, who less than a century ago was one of his predecessors as *Hermano Mayor* of the Gran Poder. Antonio Ríos Ramos believes that instead the Church's spiritual power is increasing. Now that the compulsion has gone from people's lives, he says, people live a more authentic Christianity.

No mention of the Church of Seville can avoid Papa Clemente. For Seville has not only a Roman Catholic archbishop, but it is also 'blessed' with the antics of an alternative pope, a cross between Archbishop Lefèvre and Hadrian VII. Clemente Domínguez decided to set up a religious order and had himself ordained a bishop by the Bishop of Vietnam. He then ordained a number of bishops himself. When Pope Paul VI died, Domínguez's bishops elected him Pope Gregory XVII. His church is in Palmar de Troya, a village south of Seville. Popular gossip credits him with all sorts of lurid sexual permissiveness with both sexes.

*　　*　　*

Despite its fall from temporal power, the Church, in the persons of the papal nuncio in Spain and the Archbishop of Seville, Monseñor Carlos Amigo Vallejo, was naturally present at the most glittering event of the social calendar for many a year, in June 1991. This was the occasion of the king's name day (the *onomástica* is treated in Catholic countries as birthdays are elsewhere), and was an excuse for Juan Carlos to check on the progress of the Expo buildings and tour Andalusia. For the first time since his accession, he had chosen to spend his saint's day outside Madrid and he chose the newly restored gardens of the Alcázar for the usual glitzy party. Juan Carlos is only the last of Spain's monarchs to leave his mark on the palace, though perhaps the most thoughtful: airconditioning has now been installed in the royal apartments. Seville was swooning, and not just with the heat; those with invitations because they had been invited; the rest of the city because it was one-up on the rest of the country. (It has to be said, though, that there were plenty of *sevillanos* who expressed not the slightest interest, except for irritation at the traffic jams. The *alcalde*, for instance, put the usual full-page advertisement in the press, calling on *sevillanos* to come out on the streets to welcome the king. He was greeted by a fair crowd, but there was only a thin straggle of onlookers waiting to applaud his departure as the cavalcade of Mercedes swept by.)

The whole family was there: the king and queen, the Infantas Cristina and Elena, and the heir to the throne, the Príncipe de Asturias, Spain's only royal prince. (When Franco nominated Juan Carlos heir to the throne, he gave him the new title of Prince of Spain, to indicate that he, Franco, was creating the monarchy, and there was no question of succession from the previous generation and its titles.) The 2,000-plus guests included the prime minister and his wife (who, like the foreign secretary's wife, was wearing a dress she had worn before, the press noted); the heads of the autonomous governments; the mayor and council of Seville; members of the Andalusian parliament; various members of the royal family including the Duques de Calabria and the former pretender Don Carlos de Borbón; the Duques de Alba, Medinaceli, Osuna, Feria and Gor; the Marqueses de La Granja, Valencina and Motilla; a bevy of ambassadors; the heads of the Southern Military and Second Air regions; judges, businessmen, the Expo bosses, any intellectuals, artists and big names who happened to live in the region and any other members of the smart Aero and Pineda clubs and the Círculo de Labradores. Inevitably the *Teniente de Hermano Mayor* of the Real Maestranza de Sevilla, Luis Manuel Halcón de la Lastra, was there, as was the *Hermano Mayor* of the Hermandad of the Macarena, José Luis de Pablo Romero. A wide variety of singers were represented, from Plácido Domingo to the popular singers Rocio Jurado and Silvia Pantoja, the flamenco singers 'La Niña de la Puebla', Manolo Mairena (stepbrother of the great singer Antonio Mairena), 'Caracolillo' and 'El Mani', in addition to the dancer Cristina Hoyos. The former bullfighter Manuel Benitez, better known as 'El Cordobés', and the current heroes of the ring, Miguel Báez, 'Litri' and 'Curro' Romero, were joined by the *ganaderos* or ranchers Eduardo Miura and Salvador Sánchez Guerro, and the presidents of the local football teams.

The newly finished gardens of the Alcázar were a mass of dark suits and brilliant satins, though one local duchess bemoaned the fact that so few women had ordered full-length ball-gowns; the knee – and thigh – were firmly back in fashion. 'It never used to be like this. It's always been obligatory to wear a long dress on the king's name day. But since he's celebrating it in Seville this year, and no one here wears long dresses, they've had to change the protocol.'

The eponymous shop, Vittorio Lucchino, Sevill's leading fashion designers at the Plaza de San Francisco end of calle Sierpes represents the Andalusian version of the new wave in Spanish fashion. But while Madrid and Barcelona are open to innovation, Seville is much more conformist. Bright colours, tailored suits and plenty of gold or glitter is the regulation, while every other man wears a navy jacket, pale blue shirt and light trousers. Thus the two designers are alternately fêted and disdained. They had just eight commissions for the party, revealed the *sevillano* Lucchino – more formally known as José Luis Medina del Corral – but selling their designs is uphill work, even among the aristocracy: 'The nobility here is very special, very English. The duchesses go shopping in slippers and chintzy frocks smelling of cologne. Their solution for parties is to make do and mend with a bit of antique lace. Then they put on their family's jewels and you realise they are great ladies.'

Juana de Aizpuru has also discovered the difficulties of selling something new to the *sevillanos*. She is a one-woman monument in her labours to promote contemporary Spanish art. Despite the trials of the cultural desert of the Franco years, she recalls that things were even harder in the art world in the years immediately after he died.

> We didn't have a thing, we had no laws, no parliament, we had a king, and that was all. Everything had to be started off new and everyone was involved in politics. The dictatorship wasn't as bad for us as those first years of democracy – they were terrible, nobody sold anything, nobody came to the gallery, we were abandoned.

Spain had been isolated for so long from the rest of the world that no one thought of taking its art seriously; it was not until 1986 that the international dealers began to contemplate buying contemporary Spanish art. Then the market boomed, but the *sevillanos* still have to gain the taste for contemporary art that their fellows of Madrid and Barcelona acquired so long ago. Juana de Aizpuru opened a gallery to sell the best of modern art in Seville twenty years ago, and says despairingly, 'People here still don't understand what building a collection means.' Seville, she says, should aspire to being like New

York, Paris, or Madrid. So far none of the paintings she has sold has stayed in the city, not even in the Museo de Arte Contemporáneo, a wonderful museum created out of the old cathedral tax house, a light airy space beside the Archivo de las Indias. The Juana de Aizpuru Gallery in calle Zaragoza and the Pepe Cobo Gallery on the Plaza de Cristo de Burgos are bravely trying to educate the *sevillanos*, but Juana de Aizpuru's staff are as depressed as she is: '*Sevillanos* aren't ready for art. They have their classical city and their fixed dates in the calendar – *feria*, Semana Santa – and things change very slowly. But there are some northerners who have moved to the city who are showing an interest, and some of the aristocracy are too.'

Young *sevillanos* are critical of the artistic life of their city, despite the recent changes: 'Culture? What culture?' declared a friend, who felt that the only culture was the – admittedly impressive – popular displays of Semana Santa, the *romería del Rocío* and the *feria*. 'There is virtually no theatre to speak of, the cinema is all American imports and none of the great writers today is from Seville – or, indeed, from Spain.' The Junta de Andalucía and the Ayuntamiento have been working to dispel this reasonably justified criticism. After the Civil War, most writers and artists of note went into exile, and thirty years of dictatorship did little to foster a new generation of artists. In those years when people were forbidden to sing in public (*'prohibido el cante'* was the sign in every bar) and the censor was at work, artistic enterprise was crushed. So today, as the authorities are discovering, creative artists do not spring into life overnight.

One of the larger projects in the city is the CAT, the Centro Andaluz de Teatro, based in an old Jesuit palace complete with catacombs in the calle San Luis in the centre of the Barrio de la Macarena. This is another of those instantly identifiable new enterprises: white paint, glass, scant furniture, greenery and computers. In this brave new world, there is not a single book on the librarian's desk. Instead, she sits in the corner of her huge room doing all her work on a computer. The CAT is a private company funded with public money with a dual function, to train actors and technicians, and to work as a production centre, doing co-productions and performing its own works. It reminds me of nothing so much as a *convento de clausura* of the twenty-first century: the merry voices, the distant hum of music (rock, not plainsong), the white-painted cloisters and the enthusiastic commitment for the task in hand. Everything is sparkling new: rooms for rehearsals, for make-up, for costumes, for practice at the barre; and the theatre itself. If its output is of variable quality, it also scores golds. Its presence is welcome. In a city where the theatre is so obviously on the streets, formal theatre has not flourished since the Golden Age.

The city does not lack for festivals, even if its theatrical performances are still scanty. The Expo organisation, while providing more venues for performances, also funded a number of festivals. In dance, Seville is certainly making an international mark, with the annual festival, held in June and July in the Roman amphitheatre at Itálica. The dance agent Doni Scrimgeour is typical of an increasing number of foreigners, especially in the art world, who have been attracted to Seville; since he could carry out his business with a phone and a fax, he did not need to be in London, Paris or New York. Why not settle instead in Seville, with a much more congenial quality of life?

Pepe Sánchez, as befits the image of his job, favours jeans. He is in charge of encouraging musical activity for the Ayuntamiento, and is another of these laid-back civil servants, working in a large, empty white-painted room in a converted old building, round the corner from El Corte Inglés. In a city like Seville his remit includes everything from flamenco to rock and church music, as well as arranging the annual music festival, 'Cita en Sevilla', held in April, May and June. He also attends to classical music, including promoting concerts by Taller Ziryab, a group of musicians who are reviving the music of medieval Spain, with a scholarly purpose. The Andalusian government has just distributed to all its schools a book on the Seville school of music in the 'Age of Discovery', written by Taller Ziryab, together with tapes of music played by them.

The Orquesta Sinfónica de Sevilla has a broader role in performing classical music in the city, but not without criticism for the large numbers of foreign players who make up the orchestra. But it takes time to create local players of high quality. However, the prospects for classical music have been raised with the opening in 1991 of the Maestranza Opera House. This brought high society out for its initial programmes, though they seemed more concerned with their jewellery than with the music.

As for flamenco, the symbol of Seville has also become the symbol of Spain, its national music. But why is it that Spain has no really good rock or pop stars? Why, given Seville's musical heritage, this shadowing of the Anglo-Saxon world? In the Franco years, says Pepe Sánchez, using the English language was a form of rebellion against the regime. They were heavily influenced by the American military bases; the best rock in the 1960s came from there. In the 1960s he played in a group; inevitably they copied Cream and Pink Floyd and became friendly with the groups when they came to Spain. The problem for the local groups remains promotion and distribution: the Anglo-Saxon world dominates them and blocks the prospects of any Spanish groups. Flamenco, however, is one of his main preoccupations. Like Indian music under Ravi Shankar, flamenco is becoming more Anglo-Saxon, more commercialised. It is no longer a regional delicacy with an unpredictable flavour.

Magdalena Hernández knows nothing of the efforts to promote flamenco or the arts in the city. Sitting at home, she is quite content to watch it all on the television. She has just discovered to her delight that Carlos Saura's film *El Amor Brujo* is about to come on. Culture hunters in any other country would queue up to see this in an art movie house, but for Magadalena it simply reflects part of her everyday life as a *sevillana*. She rushes to the window and screeches to her neighbour above to join her. They sit down to a box of honeyed *pestiños* (*anís-*

flavoured pastries) bought from a *convento de clausura*; they
tuck the red velvet cloth over their knees and settle in for a
night of high emotion.

6. The city on the streets

A Seville morning: the water drips from the freshly watered red geraniums down on to the pavements. At least, that's the romantic picture. The reality means hopping from side to side of the narrow streets avoiding the drips – where there are geraniums, that is. The *barrio* of Triana was once famous for being frilly with flowers, but they are much rarer today. Far above, the sky is its perpetual blue. At only 8 a.m. it is a lure and a threat: it means uninterrupted sun, but also burning heat.

There is a delicious relish in the mornings. Sleep has erased the painful memories of yesterday's sufferings, and today's heat is still a few hours off. The climate has transformed a beautiful city into a great one, influencing the *sevillanos'* lives as it has their architecture, their agriculture, their cuisine and above all their *manera de ser*, the way they are. For a visitor this last can be the hardest: finding out what is happening and why, and discovering how to be an unobtrusive part of it. Sometimes it seems that everyone else is having the fun. The classic example is the *paseo*, when the world goes out for a walk in the evening cool. Where are all these crowds going arm-in-arm? The answer, of course, is nowhere. But let's begin in the morning, with the dripping balconies and breakfast.

All *sevillanos* look tired in the morning. Because of the heat, they like to enjoy the cool of the evening and go to bed late. A siesta in the afternoon gives them the stamina for the long evening, but there is never enough of the night left for sleep. In summer most *sevillanos* work a *jornada intensiva* or 'intensive day', from eight to three, thus saving them from having to return to work after lunch, when the sun is at its hottest. Even so, travelling back home for lunch is unpleasant. (In the old days, there was a patchwork of different timetables, with offices and public buildings opening and closing at different hours, which made everything from seeing a man about a dog to visiting the Museo de Bellas Artes hugely inefficient. Museums and monuments still work to the old timetables, and to visit more than one or two in a morning requires careful forward planning. At least in offices the intensive day is widespread, with the great advantage that you can be pretty sure when is a good time to telephone.)

The day starts quietly in the city, apart from the angry traffic and bells pealing irregularly, and rarely on the hour, for mass. It takes the city time to wake. Little old ladies are to be found dropping into mass. The buses bringing workers in from the satellite towns and villages are squashed full and they stand in noisy, noxious (Seville's petrol is not lead-free yet) queues of cars, lorries and motorbikes. Given that the commuters set out early, breakfast at home may have been no more than a cup of coffee. All the additional sustenance required through the day can be provided by the bar which will inevitably be beside or below the place of work.

All *sevillanos* wear shirts and blouses with knife-sharp creases in all the right places, the freshness and the quality of the ironing proclaiming a devoted wife or mother as loudly as if the individual was carrying a banner. Or it always used to. Spain is no longer the traditional Catholic country of large families and overburdened housewives; the average number of children to a family is 2.1, and in parts of northern Spain it is half that. The number of gay couples is meanwhile on the increase.

The first shops to open are the bakers, providing fresh bread and often also dairy products for the morning, joining the postman with his capacious satchel. But for anything else, often including a newspaper from a kiosk, you have to wait until ten. Streets that were alive the night before at 9.30 p.m. will be silent twelve hours later. Even calle Sierpes, the symbol of Seville's passion for shopping, becomes just another short cut to get to work. Bejeaned students with cardboard folders under their arms join businessmen with their slim black brief-cases. Women come out to sweep their front step or peer over the balcony. The Barrio de Santa Cruz seems eerily empty. Coach parties of tourists have not arrived to disturb the peace of the hangover morning and to hear once more the story of Susona or look at the plaque to Blanco White in calle Jamerdana. The gift shops are consequently closed and the contrast with the rest of the day is marked.

The builders work to an earlier timetable. Already the lorry reversing into the building site in calle San José to deliver bricks is causing a traffic jam. Passers-by stop to give their advice and soon a crowd develops. The scene is repeated all over the city. Seville's children are walking to school, some-times accompanied by parents, sometimes in laughing groups. The ones from the private schools are instantly identifiable in their overlong kilts and cardigans.

With the workers tucked away in their offices we enter the period of earnest shopping for food, the hours when the tra-ditional housewives come out to buy the food for lunch and the old people can do their shopping in relative peace. Seville's old ladies are a doughty lot. Having survived the climate, the Civil War and the tourists, they are not going to let anything stop them now. The killer instinct comes out on the buses. Not for them a stern frown if someone takes the last seat and they wanted it. They will locate another old lady on the bus and start a voluble discussion on the trials of life, designed to embarrass the sitter into relinquishing the seat in question. If anyone pushes you on a bus, it is bound to be a short, solid old lady. The younger generation are taller, thanks to an improved diet, and slimmer, thanks to the twentieth-century obsession, and less cantankerous. Old gentlemen make the most of their passing years. Once they reach sixty they fling off their suits and change into loose pale blue or grey shirts-cum-jackets, with several rows of decorative pin tucks down either side of the front buttons. This liberating garment is classless informal wear and encourages its wearer to sit comfortably whenever possible. Old men never argue on buses. Perhaps the difference in temperament can be ascribed to their clothes. Their wives, wearing tighter outfits, feel the need to explode at regular intervals from the pressure the fabric puts on them.

While their wives are busy shopping, the men may drop in to one of the clubs within the city, whose glass fronts enable the gentlemen to sit peacefully looking out on the world. In the nineteenth century men would sit by the window, or on chairs in the street outside, ogling any woman who passed. Nowadays the roles are reversed. Today's independent women are just as likely to stare in at the men hiding from the stresses of the outside world.

The Nuevo (new) Casino (no connection with gambling) is more hidden away. Its members broke away from the original Casino years ago, and they now meet on the ground floor of a featureless modern block in Los Remedios, close to the river. Nowhere could be more unlikely. The club's glass windows are opaque – the more up-market you are, the less you need to be seen. The Nuevo Casino is a long, dark, narrow room furnished with dark furniture. A number of the deeply upholstered leather chairs are copies of the chairs in the gentlemen's clubs of London. They look as if the sitter is sitting back-to-front, cowboy fashion; the seat is reversed and the sitter leans his hands on the 'back' of the chair. The oldest members ease themselves into these chairs with alarming difficulty. Will they ever ease themselves out again?

The Nuevo Casino has eighty-three members, ranked by their seniority – the oldest is in his late eighties. At twelve o'clock there are two people in the room. By 1 p.m. there are fifteen enjoying a drink and a *tapa*. The waiter has the air of an army batman, as befits a club which numbers retired military officers among its membership. There is much discussion of old times over the bottles of chilled *fino*; one member produces from his wallet for me a photograph of Franco with his children. In this club they can escape from the metropolis: 'We are among friends. This way we don't have to rub up against the world if we want a drink and a chat.'

Paco Hortal, a mere stripling compared with the club's senior members, is still working – for González Byass, whose Tío Pepe lubricates so much of Seville life and business, and is much in evidence in the Nuevo Casino. Paco cannot drop into the club as often as the regulars. But he welcomes the chance to see the same faces when he can. Seville has grown so fast and has so many visitors each year that the old 'village' of his youth has all but disappeared: 'There were all those bars you could drop into and have a drink between one and three. Twenty-five years ago you'd walk into one of them and you'd know forty-five of the fifty people in the room. Now you'd be lucky if you knew two.'

Less 'privileged' *sevillanos* set up their own networks of favourite bars, where they go with friends or colleagues. Some of the bars will be used because they are close to work and are just the thing for a reviving coffee and a bun or sandwich at 10.30. Others are the 'locals', the favoured bars close to where they live. And finally there are the well-known bars, which are good for music (such as La Carbonería in calle Levies, a large, relaxed space with a cool patio for performances), for fish (such as La Alicantina in Plaza del Salvador), or for the view (such as the Triana pavement bars beside the river), where the itinerant shoe-shiners are often to be found with their knee-high perspective on life.

Wherever they are, *sevillanos* always have a choice. The tourist guides are very keen on picking out the best. Having marked the monuments out of three, what can they do but start on the bars? Yet it is one thing to 'do' Golden Age Seville and its monuments in a day. It is quite another then to spend an indigestible evening hunting for what one guide has decided to choose as Seville's five, ten, fifteen best bars, which may be spread out all over the city, on both sides of the river. Strolling from one bar to another is a very pleasant way of spending a pre-lunch hour or two, or the entire evening, and you will be sure to discover some excellent ones. Orienteering through the streets of Seville in search of some miraculous *tapa*, and feeling incompetent if you fail to find it or irritated because *rabo de toro* was 'off' that night, is ridiculous.

The *tapa* hour starts at midday and lasts until about 2.30 or three, when lunch takes over. Shoppers will drop in for a beer or a coffee, teenagers for a coke, businessmen for a *fino* or a brandy. In such an exclusive city there is a welcome democracy in the *tapas* bar, where the world rubs shoulders. Everything shuts for the afternoon, except El Corte Inglés, the department store. With its air-conditioning and non-stop opening hours, it is a good place to go during the siesta or on a Saturday evening, when most other shops are closed. That's if you want to buy what it has to sell. There is usually something for everyone, including a corner of tourist kitsch: three mugs that stack together into a picture of the Giralda, a brass-effect Giralda that lights up and little metal Giraldas of all sizes, plus plastic bulls, flamenco-dressed dolls, castanets, leather water-bottles, tiny *gitanas* and *caballeros* with miniature bulls and castanets, and of course flamenco dresses.

If you must buy a Spanish souvenir, much more alluring are men's braces in the red and yellow of the Spanish flag or the green and white Andalusian colours. I first noticed these on the chest of Graham Hines of the Sherry Institute in London. Nothing brightens up a gloomy English day more instantly than such mind-expanding, eye-brightening elastic.

El Corte Inglés does not have to close during the siesta, because shopping is a *sevillano* obsession. *Sevillanos* were shopping before the New Yorkers even thought about it. Part of the pleasure is in accumulating packets, however small, and most shops still wrap their parcels in paper, by hand – there are no paper bags here. Drop into a little corner shop on calle Mateos Gago for a roll of sticky tape and the owner will wrap it in a small corner of brown paper. The chemist down the road is more elevated. He uses white paper overprinted with his name in one colour. The toy shop at the Plaza de San Francisco end of calle Hernando Colón adds a gold sticker decorated with a teddy bear to its packages. The patisseries add ribbons to their paper parcels. Even postcards are sold with envelopes. The chain stores and supermarkets have converted to flimsy plastic bags, which they distribute liberally. Yet so much of Seville has remained committed to paper so long that it may still be using it when other cities come full circle and abandon plastic, because of the pollution it creates. (There are environmental arguments against the excessive use of wrappings of any sort, but it will be hard to wean the *sevillanos* off packaging altogether.)

The central shopping area runs betwen the Plazas del Salvador, Nueva and Duque de la Victoria, with calle O'Donnell running off to the west. Seville's Fifth Avenue and Oxford Street is calle Sierpes, 'Serpent Street', winding north–south across the centre. Sierpes has its own Pied Piper legend. The story goes that in the sixteenth century the city's children were disappearing at night, never to return. A slave offered to find them in exchange for his liberty. This version has a happy ending: the slave discovered that the culprit was a serpent that lurked in the street, and he killed it.

The name of the street is a surprise: *sevillanos* have a superstitious fear of snakes and reptiles generally, which contrasts ill with the bustling good humour of calle Sierpes. Every literary visitor has extolled its virtues, but it is hard to be quite so excited about it in the late twentieth century. The city has mushroomed and the number of its shopping streets with it. Yet at the turn of the century it was the street of the *casinos*, the gentlemen's clubs, and of bars, a social street, for passing the time of day with anyone who came. Today a few traces of the past remain, such as El Cronómetro, the clock shop, but many of the bars which were so important in Seville's former political and literary life have closed.

Several of the smart clubs were in Sierpes. Perhaps the smartest is the Círculo de Labradores, or 'farmers' circle'. This misrepresents its status as a club which unites high society. It has extensive sports facilities just over the Triana Bridge in

Los Remedios, with a splendid view over the river, best enjoyed from the enormous dining room. Here is where (parts of) Seville can shut themselves away from the hustle and reassure themselves that the city is still their own. They will entertain you graciously here, with a genuine warmth, but you will never forget you are a guest.

Strolling up and down calles Sierpes, Cuna and Tetuán is an easy way of working off the *tapas*. Here you can find more wedding dresses than there are brides in the city and more shoe shops than there are feet to be shod. Some parts of the streets are shaded from the sun by canvas canopies. In the many fabric shops you will find women browsing for material for their flamenco dresses for the *feria* amongst lengths of spotted and floral fabrics and lace trimmings of every colour and variety, and searching for the fragile tall combs that support their lace mantillas in Holy Week and on special occasions.

Interlarded with these shops are wonderful *ultramarinos*, 'overseas' or grocers' shops, which would rank as museum pieces in other cities. Dried beans, hams, *chorizos*, cheeses, sherries, tinned fish are bursting from the shelves of the gloomy shops. The twentieth-century passion for cling-film has not arrived here. In this world of waxed paper packets, they have escaped the terrors of contamination.

Tucked away there are several tiny shops glowing with the most baroque earrings imaginable. No wonder they call them *pendientes*. They hang from the ear-lobe in tier after tier, each one larger than the last. There are jewellers everywhere, to feed the jackdaw taste for gold that infects all *sevillanos*. A gypsy will pride himself on his gold teeth; a *señora* on her ornate necklace and rings.

The dress shops are full of pink linen suits with gold buttons and strapless evening dresses with frilly hems. Nearby will be the inevitable film shop to service the snap-happy tourists. One of the most remarkable of these is a chemist which also sells artificial limbs and trusses. (There used to be far more of these shops, but the Civil War veterans with missing limbs are dying off and the improved standards of living and of health care also mean there are fewer customers with disabilities.) The pharmacy is the essential shop in the city: *sevillanos*, like many *andaluces*, are neurotic about coughs and colds, and the city centre is extensively supplied with chemists who specialise in dispensing patent medicines and concern – and *preservativos*, condoms – with a severe white-suited, pseudo-scientific wrapper. By contrast, the bookshops of the city have a more bohemian air, heavy with intellectuals and silent reading.

Inevitably there are shops selling ceramics all over the city. Since early times Seville has been a centre for potters on account of its fine clay. What has come down to this century is the decorated pottery that follows the Islamic patterns of up to 1,200 years ago. The difficulty is that ceramics have become such an obvious souvenir that some of the charm of buying them has been lost. Perhaps that's why the sterile showrooms of the Barrio de Santa Cruz are not as full of shoppers as they used to be. Across the bridge in Triana, some ceramics shops are more cheerful, working on the perilous pile-em-high basis. A distinctive *sevillano* style is the pottery formerly made at La Cartuja, the charterhouse where the Expo site now is. An Englishman, Charles Pickman, took over the monastery after the Church estates were expropriated by the state in 1835, and set up a modern, industrialised ceramics factory. At the same time he also laid waste much of the historic site. Pickman china is still made, on the road to Mérida, outside the city. Its shapes are much more English and it has a faintly Victorian air, its cream-coloured ware overprinted with a distinctive pattern in the centre in a single colour.

After its siesta, which may be spent asleep, watching the television news and a soap opera, or simply eating a long, but not necessarily large, and leisurely lunch, the city shifts into gear. At 4.30 or 5 p.m. the shops open again, and shopping and window-shopping recommence. Now there are more couples on the street. Both will have finished work if they are on an intensive day. They can hunt for bed linen or furniture for their dream home – or, indeed, for shoes. The *confiterías* come into their own, providing a sugary boost for the late afternoon of cakes or ice-creams. The latter are more popular with the tourists, for the Spaniards eat less ice-cream than their European and North American fellows. But while the ice-cream made in cones is generally good, the packaged ice-lollies and ice-creams are dreadful. Perhaps the Spanish are just being sensibly discriminating.

The evening brings the ritual of the *paseo*. Refreshed from their siestas, changed out of their working clothes, *sevillanos* can stroll up and down in the cool air, stretching their legs, watching the world go by. The natives of the Iberian peninsula have not always been so enthusiastic, as the Roman historian F. J. Wiseman noted:

> When the members of a local tribe visited a Roman camp for the first time and saw Roman officers parading up and down merely for the sake of exercise, they supposed them to be crazy and tried to induce them to return to their tents, thinking they should either remain quietly seated or else be fighting.

Whether in Roman Spain or today, the *paseo* is something you never do alone. The whole point is to go arm-in-arm with an acquaintance, friend or relation. Young lovers, parents worn down by their over-excited little ones, retired couples, mothers and grown-up daughters all take part. There is no obligation to do it every day, but the fresh air of the evening is very enticing. In Seville there are many places to stroll: in the centre it is pleasant to walk along the river past the Torre del Oro, or through the Parque María Luisa, or over the San Telmo or Triana bridges and back. One of the most alluring pleasures is to sit at the river's edge during the *feria* and watch the world in its finery walking over the San Telmo bridge to the fair. While on your *paseo* you may come across a wedding, since the early evening is a popular hour. The bride will be dressed in the traditional white, as she was for her first communion, and her girlfriends will all be in what were once known as cocktail dresses.

Gradually it becomes cool enough to overcome languour. The city's prostitutes begin to stir. Plays and concerts usually start at 9 p.m., and dinner is not until ten at the earliest. The Spaniards are renowned for their late hours, but none more so than the *sevillanos*. I was sitting in a restaurant with some friends one evening at 10.45 and they were apologising to me for the fact there was only one other table occupied. They felt uneasy, because every *sevillano* abhors a vacuum. 'We must have come too early,' they said, 'it will fill up eventually.' *Confiterías* and grocers' shops keep the same late hours and may still be open at eleven. But life does not stop when the shops close. Bars will be open and *sevillanos* will be easing the night away until 1.30 or 2 a.m. and often later in the night clubs. In the summer there seems little point in going to bed, when the breeze of the night is pleasant and the *dama de noche* bush sheds its powerful scent.

Shopping in Seville is not just an activity carried out behind doors. The streets are busy with vendors of all kinds. Some of the most obvious, by their sheer quantity, are the blind and partially sighted people who sell tickets for the lottery run by the ONCE, the national organisation for the blind. With strips of label-sized tickets clipped to their lapels or blouses, and with their white canes, they work their patches of the city, mostly on the pavements but sometimes in bars. Wherever there is a gathering of people – a football match, a bullfight – they will be found. Spain is a land of lotteries; the declaration of 'El Gordo', 'the big one', the top prize in the national lottery, is headline news. Kiosks that have sold a winning ticket will advertise the fact, even though one might think that lightning never strikes twice. Yet *sevillanos*, despite the energy of the sales people and their fascination with the declaration of the winning numbers, buy few tickets and consequently seldom win.

In Franco's day there were many beggars (mostly Civil War veterans) on the streets, often with limbs missing. Today, they have almost disappeared, and have been supplanted by the street sellers, who can usually be found at work outside the cathedral. They gather at the doors which open on to the Plaza de la Virgen de los Reyes, just like the medieval merchants: lottery sellers, gypsies with red carnations, vendors of strips of postcards and touristic trifles. The gypsies are also busy during *feria*, entering private *casetas*, marquees, with their bundles of flowers and daring any man with a woman beside him not to buy her a red carnation. They are well aware that they are a cliché of Seville and they play up to it. Then there are the little old ladies who sit stifling in tiny kiosks, selling penny chews to children. Their stock is scanty and unappealing, and usually kept in tatty cardboard boxes. These ladies are not to be confused with the owners of the newspaper kiosks, who stock more magazines and papers than they usually have room to display, and greatly disapprove of browsing.

Nor are they to be confused with the impressive caravan trailers that come to sell all manner of confections, particularly during *feria*. The towering trailers set up their pitches at the Prado de San Sebastián and around the outskirts of the *feria* site, and drop down on one side to reveal their contents. Soon domesticity is established: the women who sell the sweets (nary a man to be seen) have the washing hung out to dry on a line between the caravan and the trailer each day. Business is non-stop: by day, a continuous trickle of passers-by who may succumb to a little packet of honeyed almonds or pistachio nuts, but by night there is a solid stream. The temptation is to browse, but each stall has the same stock. Teenage Mutant Ninja Turtles and *turrón*, brittle nougat, are the stand-bys – but more of that in Chapter 7.

The *turrón* lorries come only at festival time, but all year round there are markets on the streets. The city's classic flea market is much more attractive in the prospect than the actuality. Every Sunday, the Alameda de Hércules overflows with junk, sinks, fridges, 'rare' Chinese vases mysteriously available from a number of stalls, cassettes, fabrics, DIY equipment, a few books, clothes, shoes, secondhand copies of *Playboy*, fans and cheap toys. There are also floppy discs and software, and a collection of the sort of hippy jewellery and Moroccan oddments that went out of fashion in Britain years ago. A salesman is busy demonstrating a citrus juicer at a small table – on one side he has a pile of oranges and lemons, on the other a steadily filling jug of juice. The question is not how effective is the juicer, but what on earth will he do with the juice in this dry, dusty, drainless place when the jug is full? The answer is, the crowds were too pressing, and I shall never know. A gypsy woman is squatting nearby beside a basket of succulent cherries; another is selling garlic. On one of the aisles there is a stall that makes almond brittle, spreading the caramel out on the metal sheet to set hard. This is the local colour that the guidebooks love. Don't expect to purchase a bargain print of old Spain, though, but it may be just the place for a nice white lavatory pan. Altogether it is a very male affair; there are remarkably few women. Perhaps they are cooking lunch? Or have they gone to mass? At the opposite end of the Alameda from the Roman columns there is a particularly distinctive Men Only section, crammed with car parts and plumbing equipment.

The historic *jueves* or Thursday market, in the calle Feria, is similar, if less seedy, and also sells antiques. (Seville has some particularly good antique shops, but nothing is cheap.) On Sunday mornings, in the Plaza de la Alfalfa, there is a pet and bird market, if you like that kind of thing. There are often puppies for sale outside the central El Corte Inglés, while in the square in front of the department store there is a daily hippy market of still more jewellery and crafts. In the little Plaza del Cabildo, through the alleyway opposite the cathedral on the Avenida de la Constitución, there is a market for coins and stamps on Sunday mornings. The semi-circular plaza also contains the tempting little shop which stocks pastries, biscuits, jams and sweets made by the nuns from enclosed convents all over the city. This is the place to go to inspect the range of their produce.

On Sundays going to mass in the cathedral is one of the better ways to enjoy the building. It is also one of the things you can do there without paying, and so saves a good deal of aggravation in this house of God. During mass, one's eye is distracted from the gilded enormity of the reredos by activity nearer the ground. On either side of the high altar are two doorways into the reredos, and from these peek at various intervals a pair of acolytes, just like the married couple in the toy houses that predict the weather. One is in jeans and trainers, though near the end of the service he reappears in his church robes. The other has already changed, but neither seems to have his mind on the holy matters at hand. A fat prelate strolls by, fanning himself. The congregation – a mixture of nationalities and faiths, some standing to pray, others kneeling, some just sitting according to their custom and their faith (or lack of it) – look around, trying to spot the most devout. They are also more captivated by the occupants of the choir stalls in purple and lace than the sermon, which seems not to captivate the other four celebrants lined up behind the altar either. This is production-line faith; in an hour's time another bunch of worshippers will be lining up here for the sacrament, and in half an hour there will be a group of punters crowded into the chapel of San Fernando. And suddenly the service is at an end. The collection has been passed round. The gates into the choir are closed to keep out the curious, the lights are switched out and God is off for another half hour.

Time, instead, to cross the city to the San Fernando cemetery beyond the Macarena Gate. In the thirteenth century Christians were buried inside the city in their parishes; only the Jews and the Moors were buried outside. But the city has grown and *sevillanos* now have to travel some distance to pay their respects to their loved ones. At the cemetery you will find a fair slice of Seville on a Sunday. The florists' stalls at the entrance sell them a selection of flowers and sprays. Red carnations, inevitably, but also cheerful sprays and bouquets

SAN LORENZO

EMPRESA DE POMPAS FÚNEBRES
DE
JOAQUIN FERNANDEZ Y LOPEZ
PALMAS, 85.-TELÉFONO, 191

Gran surtido en aparatos de gran lujo.
Cajas del reino y extranjeras.
Paños bordados en oro, gran novedad.
Mausoleos y lápidas para Cementerios; y todo lo concerniente á una defunción.

SERVICIO PERMANENTE

Esta casa se encarga de los embalsamamientos y y traslaciones de cadáveres de una provincia á otra y al extranjero,

En la repetida casa hay tarifas para todas clases de entierros. La persona que desee conocerlas se le facilitarán en las oficinas de dicha Empresa.

such as one might use at a wedding. To an English eye the sight of these sprays being carried along the avenues by visitors looks incongruous. Have I come to the wrong place? Is this the short cut to a party? Or is it a political rally? Certainly the numbers of people walking up the avenues imply that someone's having fun. As if in preparation for a party, there are women all over the cemetery collecting water in green buckets from standpipes. These have thoughtfully been supplied by the cemetery in order that the womanhood of Seville, in its role as mother and maidservant, should carry out its traditional duty of washing and cleaning. The gravestones are scrubbed, the carnations refreshed and the family reputation, whether in the street or in the cemetery, remains sparkling.

Further back by the entrance are the big names. The Pickman family tomb, they of the pottery, are here, and several bullfighters. Most prominent is the monument to Joselito 'el Gallo', after whom one of the streets in the *feria* is named. Joselito's coffin is shown being carried on the shoulders of bearers, one of whom is the bullfighter Ignacio Sánchez Mejías, a good friend of the poet Federico García Lorca. In the group of grieving gypsies portrayed following the coffin is another well-known figure. This is Manolo Caracol, a flamenco singer who became internationally famous after the Civil War; here he is shown as the young boy he was in 1920 when Joselito died.

Even today, there are a handful of fresh carnations strewn across Joselito's tomb. The red flowers, so symbolic of the city, cast against the black of the tomb are a reminder that neither fame nor domesticity can prevent the triumph of death. At the heart of the *alegría*, of the joy and happiness of the *sevillano*, there is always tragedy.

7. *Tortilla, tapas, tomates, turrón*

We would do well to remember Ziryab, a musician at the court of Abd al-Rahman II in ninth-century Córdoba. But it's not for his music or his skills in hairdressing or perfumery that we owe him our gratitude. It is for his preoccupation with what we eat and the way we eat it. Thanks to Ziryab we eat in the sequence we do today, with sweet following savoury and meat before sweetmeats. And thanks to his compatriots Spain enjoys the foods that become the cornerstones of cooking in Seville and in Spain, and are important ingredients – now that any foodstuff can be imported anywhere – the world over. The Islamic conquest brought with it a language and a culture, but it also brought its most enduring legacy, food. The invaders joined the cooks of Seville with the cooks of Damascus in a chain that swept across the Mediterranean, linked by common spices and staples. The effect of the Muslim occupation of Spain may still be argued over, but the influence of their foods is indisputable.

*   *   *

Seville's historic buildings are daily reminders of its history of invasion and colonisation. Just as much are its foodstuffs: olives, olive oil, salt, rice, fish, almonds, vegetables, fruit. Fundamental are the olive and olive oil. The olive tree flourishes throughout Andalusia, but tradition has it that the tastiest and best olives are those grown within sight of the Giralda, the *manzanillas de Sevilla*.

The Romans exported vast quantities of Seville's olives and oil across the empire in *amphorae* made by the potters of Triana. Latest research shows that they made a sensible choice: if you care about your heart, then it is the mono-unsaturated fat of the olive you should make a point of consuming. The Muslims used olive oil in preference to other fats, as did the Jews, whose dietary laws prevented them from combining animal fats with meat. Inevitably, then, when the Christians conquered southern Spain, they reacted against the olive oil of the infidel, substituting it where possible with lard. They were more successful in this in the northern, strongly Castilian parts of Spain, where lard and butter are still widely used. Seville and Andalusia, however, hung on to their Muslim and Jewish heritage. A priest writing at the time of the Catholic Monarchs, at the turn of the fifteenth century, commented of the Andalusians:

> They have never lost the Jewish custom of eating dishes of onions and garlic fried and refried in oil, which they put in the pan instead of lard . . . meat cooked in oil is what makes the breath stink . . . and they smell just like the Jews because of the food they eat and because they have not been baptised.

The Phoenicians introduced the practice of salting and preserving foods. Even today anchovies are carefully arranged in vats for salting, and cod is dried and salted and sold in large, unappealing, hairy hunks as *bacalao*. The salt flats the Phoenicians knew along the coast towards Cádiz are still in operation and produce rough, creamy-coloured crystals with a crunch.

The almond symbolises Islam's influence on Spain. The tree with its pretty blossom shades and enchants the garden, while its milky white fruit enhances both sweet and savoury dishes. In *ajo blanco*, a cool white soup is made of ground almonds and (raw) garlic and decorated with white grapes; it is a dish typical of Málaga and eastern Andalusia. The almond thickens and enriches soups and stews. As a sweet, its uses are legion. Top of the list must come *turrón*, in its two varieties. *Turrón* is often translated, though misleadingly, as nougat. Although the ingredients are similar, the Spanish *turrón* bears little resemblance to the French or Italian nougats.

The hard variety, which I much prefer, known as *turrón de Alicante*, is made of whole almonds, egg white and sugar, and then wrapped in rice paper. It is only for those with the strongest teeth. The contrast of the sticky crunch of the sugar with the chewy crunch of the milky nuts, combined with the slight terror of it all – will it be this time I break a tooth/lose a filling? – adds a frisson. An additional uncertainty comes from breaking it up to eat. *Turrón* comes in 100 gram or 150 gram chunks, not in daintily prepackaged portions, and you need strong wrists to break them. When it breaks, what will it be, too large or too small?

Turrón de Jíjona, by contrast, is soft and easily cut into squares. It is essentially an almond version of halva and much more like the sweetmeat the Arabs would have eaten. A bonus in these days of additives, artificial colours and stabilisers is that *turrón* is entirely E-free; this is a commercial product that tastes as good as anything home-made just because it contains nothing that you could not find in the domestic kitchen. As we shall see later with the *tortas de aceite* of Castilleja de la Cuesta and the *dulces* of the *conventos de clausura*, Seville produces a basket of delicacies that taste delicious just because they still make them 'like mother used to'.

Turrón is made to be eaten at Christmas, though it is sold at festivals all year round. Look at the sell-by date. Though *turrón de Alicante* is worth eating at any time, it will go soft eventually. The almond confectioners have spawned all sorts of inventive marzipans: marzipans cut into shapes and glazed, marzipans sparkling with glacé fruits, chocolate and coconut marzipan . . . The blocks ripple out across the stalls, though none of them is quite as tasty as *turrón de Alicante*. Another delicacy are *alfajores*, rather rough-and-ready-looking rice wafers sandwiching a paste of honey and ground almonds. Or for a sweet snack, nibble some whole almonds in a honeyed coating.

The Arabs introduced sugar-cane to Andalusia, unleashing a repertoire of syrup-drenched pastries which decorate the shelves of *confiterías* to this day. Nearly 1,300 years later Magdalena Hernández, despite her heart problems, secretly indulges in *pestiños*, little pastries made with oil, flour and white wine and flavoured with aniseed, deep fried in lemon-flavoured oil and soaked in a honey syrup. Like all pastries they are wrapped up in cellophane, paper and ribbons by the *confitería*, but beware the syrup, which always leaks on the way home, over the pavement, the bus and one's legs.

The Arabs also greatly extended Seville's agriculture and irrigation and introduced rice, second now to bread as the city's staple. Today, the Mediterranean province of Valencia may have the greatest reputation for its rice and rice dishes, most notably *paella*. But there are many who think that Seville's rice is far superior, and the cooks of Seville just as expert in their rice dishes. In the five centuries of Muslim occupation of the city, Seville absorbed the conquerors' flavours and tastes. *Comino*, cumin, a very distinctive, slightly sweet spice redolent of the East, was introduced, as was *anís*, aniseed, the basic flavour of many biscuits. *Canela*, cinnamon, and *azafrán*, saffron, also resound through the centuries, as do *hierbabuena*, mint, *nuez moscada*, nutmeg, and *cilantro*, coriander. The market stalls of the spice vendors of the day were as colourful and as pungent as any in Morocco or Istanbul. The figs, bananas, dates, peaches, citrus fruits, so many of the contemporary riches of the Guadalquivir basin, owe their origins to the Arab occupation. Seville's figs were especially highly prized (there are two words for fig in Spanish: the more common is *higo*; *breva* is the early variety). The vegetable gardens of Arab Spain were famous for their abundance: aubergines, artichokes, celery, onions, carrots, leeks, spinach, chard, radishes, asparagus and several varieties of beans. From the Arabs comes the practice of combining savoury with sweet, adding raisins and pine kernels to stews and spinach, or cooking lamb with honey. Vinegar, too, appears in sweet dishes, to add a bite of the sour.

The influences on Seville's cuisine did not stop with the Arabs. The city's position as both *puerto* and *puerta* brought it a basket of products from the Americas which conquered the world: potatoes, tomatoes, sweet and hot peppers, turkeys, chocolate. The potato created the classic *tortilla* – potatoes cooked in oil, then drained and mixed with beaten egg. The omelette is then fried on both sides until it forms an unctuous gateau, golden on the outside, warm and oozing slightly in the centre. *Tortillas* are for those with no fear of salmonella, for there is nothing worse than one set hard. Some prefer to vary the contents, adding *jamón serrano*, cured ham, *chorizo*, pork sausage, or peppers to the potatoes. Whatever the recipe, the *tortilla* has rightly become a national staple, a simple, delicious food for farm labourer and king alike.

The tomato is so fundamental to the *sevillano* diet that it is hard to believe that it too is a relative newcomer. Now it forms the basis of that other local delicacy, *gazpacho*. Under the mass tourism of the *costas, gazpacho* became as debased as *sangría*, the sparkling drink based on lemons and red wine. But it remains a perfect soup based on local ingredients.

Just as the heat affected the architecture, so it demanded a cold soup which needed no cooking in a hot kitchen, but could be simply pounded in a mortar in the shade. It illustrates once more how the climate has helped to create the unique features of Seville. The proportions depend on the cook's taste, but the basic ingredients are tomatoes, cucumber, green peppers, garlic, sweet red pepers, sherry vinegar, olive oil, pepper and salt. Some prefer to add white breadcrumbs, to thicken it; some grind almonds in; some like a soup which is still reasonably thick; others prefer a fine soup thinned with water, over which they can sprinkle more of the same ingredients, finely chopped, as well as chopped hardboiled egg. Everyone adds ice-cubes.

This is the pleasure of so much of *sevillano* cooking – there are no hard and fast rules. It avoids the tiresome regulations of international cuisine. Recipes which have been handed down through the generations inevitably vary from person to person and town to town. Following a set recipe for *tortilla* or *gazpacho* would go against the grain for the independent *andaluz*. That's why you will look in vain for a shelf of cookery books in a *sevillano* kitchen. Families used their own recipes, and only recently have cookery books and foodie personalities started to multiply.

The peppers from the New World are equally well-integrated: stuffed; roasted, skinned and dressed in oil and vinegar; chopped and sliced into salads and stews; adding sparkle to rice dishes. The small hot peppers, however, are less common in the kitchens of Seville – they make their mark in Basque cuisine. The American turkey is less common on the menu, though it is eaten increasingly at Christmas, but given Seville's proximity to the coast, many families still prefer to celebrate by cooking a whole fish. Chocolate, of course, is everywhere, but the *sevillanos*, like the Spaniards in general, do not nibble a bar of chocolate if they are hungry, as the British and the North Americans do. They have a much wider variety of street food, savoury and sweet, to choose from, though habits are changing, in food above all else, as Europe becomes more homogenised. Seville does not have the sweet shops familiar to American and British children stocking fifty-seven varieties of chocolate bars; the city's infants are still in the 1950s era of jellies, boiled sweets, liquorice bootlaces and bubble-gum. Chocolate, especially milk chocolate, is bought in the supermarket in family-sized bars to be shared out at home after lunch or at tea, or eaten in a sandwich after school. Thus the Spaniards eat less than four kilos each of chocolate a year, compared to the French who eat more than five kilos, and the British who eat eight.

There are still dishes that remind us how chocolate was once used – as an unsweetened flavouring that enhanced meat stews. Today's recipes use small amounts of chocolate, of the best plain variety that can be found, to provide a subtle richness. Typical is *perdiz*, partridge, in a sauce flavoured with chocolate. There is also a classic Catalán dish which successfully commits all the apparent heresies – lobster with chicken and chocolate. (The Catalán taste for meat and fish together has been widely taken up in the USA as 'surf 'n' turf'; but the idea of putting chocolate with fish or meat has never quite caught on outside Latin America.)

Chocolate was also originally used as a beverage and the *sevillanos* managed to keep the recipe for making it a secret from the rest of Europe for a century. They have never lost the taste for it, though they have made it a good deal sweeter over the years. The drink is made with water, though increasingly milk is added, and thickened with cornflour to give it the consistency of a wintry soup. It is alarmingly sweet, though sometimes alleviated by a sprinkling of cinnamon. There are still a couple of old-fashioned *chocolaterías* which sell nothing but drinking chocolate and in some old bars you will find the chocolate in copper vats which keep the unguent smooth and warm throughout the day. Chocolate can be enjoyed, depending on the powers of your digestion, at all times of day. It is a breakfast drink, whether it be first thing or late-morning breakfast, or a morning-after-the-night-before breakfast enjoyed with a bundle of freshly made *churros*.

Churros were another gift to the Spanish stomach from the Arabs. Long tubes of dough are extruded in circles sixty centimetres in diameter into great vats of boiling oil. As they crisp up to a golden brown, they are ladled out and cut into sticks perhaps fifteen centimetres long. The Muslims dipped their *churros* in boiling honey; today they are rolled in sugar, which makes them easier to eat. *Churros* have been compared to doughnuts, because their ingredients and method of cooking are the same, but they are crisper and less bready. They certainly have the same effect on the digestion and should only be eaten when you are really hungry. One of the best times, therefore, is at the end of a long night at the *feria*, when one is in need of something both soothing and reviving. The bars selling *churros* and *chocolate* will be at full stretch. In the city centre, some bars make their own *churros*; not every bar makes chocolate. Look for the sign that says *'Hay churros'* or *'Hay chocolate con churros'*. Alternatively you can buy a bundle in a paper wrapper from a little *churrería* in the street or market place if you can find one, and take it along to the nearest bar to dunk in your coffee or chocolate. One becomes quite expert at hunting the *churrería*: look for the plume rising from the heat of the vat, or for concentrations of people eating them. (The *churrería* converts itself into a chip shop in the afternoon, piling high its counter with cellophane packets of fresh potato crisps, tasting the way potato crisps should taste – of potato, oil and salt. Be sure, though, that you are given a fresh packet. There is no air-tight seal and they lose their crispness quickly. You are likely to be palmed off with a stale packet if business is slow.)

Long before the Islamic conquest, *sevillanos* were exploiting the abundant fish and seafood of the region. The Roman invaders exported vast quantities of garum, a fish paste, to liven up their diet in the outposts of the empire. Today, the city's tastes range widely across cod, both fresh and dried, hake, monkfish, bream and sardines, to tuna and swordfish, as well as prawns, mussels, langoustines, crayfish, squid, octopus, crabs and lobsters. The passion for fish comes together in the classic *pescado frito* (fried fish), which even the *sevillano* will admit is most closely identified with Cádiz. It is merely a dish of fried fish from the sea, but this is fish as it should be eaten. A selection of fishes large and small – small hake *(pescadillas)*, small soles *(acedías)*, red mullet *(salmonetes)*, whiting *(píjotas)*, anchovies *(boquerones)* – are dipped in seasoned coarse flour and quickly deep fried in olive oil or a mixture of oils. The coating is thin and lightly crunchy, the fish a brilliant white, cooked to perfection. A plate of mixed fried fish with wedges of lemon and a salad of sliced lettuce, tomato and onion, dressed in salt, olive oil and sherry vinegar, mopped up with a crusty roll of fresh bread, make a simple, nourishing, healthy dish. It is as far from the excesses of international cuisine as one could desire. For that reason it was despised by the venturesome foodies of central and northern Spain, who saw the *andaluz* diet as meagre and under-developed. Today the trend for restaurant eating has swung back towards simple ingredients well cooked and the *pescado frito*, along with the *gazpacho* and the meat and bean stews, are coming into their own again.

A variation on *pescado frito* is a portion of whitebait *(chanquetes)* or of whole baby squid *(chipirones)* fried together into a crunchy bundle, or of rings of squid *(calamares)* in a fresh batter. The nearest relation to the British fried fish are the fingers of *bacalao*, dried salt cod, reconstituted and fried in a crunchy batter. They are known as *Soldaditos* (little soldiers) *de Pavía* after the yellow-jacketed soldiers of General Pavía who crushed the Andalusian rebellion in 1873. All of these dishes require only a few local ingredients; what they do need is a cook who cares. There is nothing nastier than overcooked squid, *pescado frito* from fish that is not fresh, tasteless *tortilla* or vinegary *gazpacho*.

I should add that while there are delights to be enjoyed when eating out in Seville, there is a strong chance that you may be disappointed. It is possible to eat one bad meal after another in the city, especially if you stay around the centre, near the cathedral. The restaurateurs and waiters can perhaps be forgiven for their treatment of tourists, given their bad experiences. Though tourists are changing, the attitudes of many waiters and restaurateurs in the old centre are not – tourists are a captive audience for the mediocre *tapa* and the uninteresting set menu; they (used to) know no better; even if they do complain they are not staying long enough to come back; and many of them (used to) want safe, unadventurous foods. However, if you keep to the places where you see *sevillanos* eating, and if you order the local dishes rather than international foods, you should make some discoveries of your own. Keep an eye on the prices. If you wander off from the mediocrities of many a restaurant set menu – *gazpacho, pollo y patatas fritas* (chicken and chips), *flan* (caramel custard) – you may get stung.

At the Bar Cáceres, Antonio does not have time to dwell on the historic influences on the food he serves. He works a fourteen-hour day more or less single-handed, and when he's not cooking or serving, he's ordering the next day's supplies and tidying the counter and the chiller cabinet. He has been working for thirty years in the calle San José, close to the church of Santa María la Blanca (a synagogue until 1391, until the pogrom of the Jews; it was converted in 1659 into the exuberant baroque church it is today). He's been at his present bar for some thirteen years; before that he was just down the road. There is room for ten stools along the bar. The place is designed for customers who want to stop for more than a moment, so he provides enough stools for almost everyone, as well as a couple of tables and chairs squeezed in beside the fruit machine. Further into the city centre, the bars are busier and stools take up valuable drinking space. So rather like the children's party game where a group of children fight for a decreasing number of stools, the closer you get to the city centre the harder you have to fight for a perch. Of course, the point about having a drink and a *tapa* is that you should be able to stand to eat. Sitting down does not come in to it. But for a weary visitor not wanting to pay the extra for a seat at a table outside, perching at the bar is a good compromise.

Breakfast at the Bar Cáceres is therefore a civilised, sit-down affair – even though it lasts ten minutes at the most. Most people have a *bollo*, a soft roll, or a *tostada*, either the whole or a half of a large, fresh crusty roll, the inside toasted on the hot plate. This is the first of several such rolls that the average *sevillano* will eat in a day. The counter is laid out with trays of jams and spread for customers to choose their own toppings. Some take the northern European route and have jam, or butter and jam, on the bread, and there are even little jars of sweet Seville orange marmalade, a relatively rare sight in the city where the bitter fruit trees line the streets. Others have cheese spread or sprinkle on olive oil. Still others have pâté, or *sobrasada*, the Mallorcan version of pâté, a spread of *chorizo*, lard and paprika. Orange juice in the city's bars is usually fresh. Antonio's waste-not-want-not method involves peeling several oranges and juicing the whole lot. What rises to the top is an unexpected creamy froth of pulp and stray bits of pith. Give it time to settle and you can drink the juice through the topping.

His first customers for a coffee and a roll are often the builders from up the road; next come the office workers. There are also a few tourists from the hotel over the way who have discovered that breakfast in any bar is better than that in (almost) any hotel. The atmosphere will certainly be livelier; even first thing in the morning everybody is talking and the noise level rises as the day goes on. A couple of builders will be arguing over the result of last night's football match, Antonio will be joking with one of the young women at the bar and a couple of dark suits and briefcases will be in discussion, leaning on the chiller cabinet by the front door. Antonio is tall for his generation of *sevillanos*, a skinny fellow who knows his customers and is ready to share a joke with any of them. He does not aspire to run the best bar in Seville. But the Bar Cáceres is like so many of its kind across the city, a one-man business where you can drop in for a friendly chat, a drink and a bite to eat at any time of day.

The wall behind the bar is a riot, full of diversion for the few who cannot bring themselves to talk in the mornings. Inevitably there are the rows of sherry bottles. The brandies on the shelves recall people and events of Spain's great past: Cardenal Cisneros, Gran Capitán, Gran Duque de Alba, Felipe II, Cardenal Mendoza, Alfonso el Sabio, Lepanto (the sea battle in which Cervantes fought, where the Spanish fleet helped defeat the Turks). Over one's *tostada* or *tapa* one can contemplate the eternal *sevillano* theme of the ephemeral nature of life, that in the midst of life is death . . .

There are also the compulsory half-empty bottles of obscure

and evil-looking liqueurs. Can anyone really drink these? Yes, Antonio assures me, they're very popular, especially as after-dinner drinks. There are soft drinks of every variety, including flavoured milks, with a further selection in the fridge below the counter. The back wall bustles with tins of white asparagus (though they have plenty of excellent fresh asparagus of their own, *sevillanos* have an inexplicable liking for the tinned, thumb-thick variety), mackerel and tuna, and bottles of mayonnaise (Antonio is not allowed to use real mayonnaise any longer because of the health risks). There's the latest winning number from the lottery run by the ONCE, the organisation for the blind; a few bars of chocolate and some packets of crisps; and of course the espresso coffee machine, which works as hard as Antonio, pouring out steam for coffees and hot milk, and hot water for infusions of camomile, mint or tea. Tucked into every corner there are keys, cigarette lighters, boxes of cigarettes, matches, photographs, bits of paper, bills, reminders and souvenirs. The television is at the far end of the bar high up on the wall, with the lavatory (the light switch for the loo is behind the bar, so customers have to ask Antonio to turn it on and off) and the telephone beside it. Antonio has to make all his phone calls to his suppliers from this payphone in the centre of a busy bar.

During the morning, people working in businesses nearby have been dropping in for a quick coffee or a bun, but business has been relatively slow. By twelve o'clock the demand for drinks and *tapas* is building up. Much enthusiastic guff has been written about *tapas*, especially in Britain since *tapas* bars began to be opened as themed refits for pubs and wine bars. A few years back it suddenly became very smart to eat *tapas* – it was all part of a Princess Diana syndrome of eating small meals, and often being charged high prices for them. This fad for eating *tapas* out of their normal habitat was not altogether understandable: *tapas* are miserable shadows of themselves outside Spain. They take on the guise of the ornate hors d'oeuvres and canapés of the 1950s, impaled with pimento-stuffed olives and topped with sliced hard-boiled eggs. All they need are miniature Spanish flags on cocktail sticks to recall the full horrors of the cheese and wine party. It has to be said that *tapas* are not always all that they are cracked up to be on their home territory. But for those with an appetite for it, there is no better place than Seville to practise the gentle art of *tapear*. The climate and the cuisine, and the charm of the city, all conspire to make Seville one of the *tapas* centres of Spain.

To start with a little etymology, *tapa* literally means 'lid'. In the past, bartenders would serve a glass of sherry and cover it with a slice of cured ham or cheese, making a lid. The general assumption is that, by transference, any little dishes, cold or hot, from a few olives to a small portion of *riñones al Jerez*, kidneys in sherry, have come to be called *tapas*. A double-sized *tapa*, roughly equivalent to half a full portion, is a *ración*. A *ración* and a *tapa* or two will make a good substitute for lunch, and are usually cheaper than a restaurant meal. Bars will serve *tapas* before lunch, roughly between 12 and 3.30, and again in the early evening until closing time.

As I stressed in Chapter 6, orienteering through Seville searching out bars recommended in guidebooks is no way to enjoy yourself. Part of the pleasure lies in dropping into a local bar, not walking across the city in the hope of locating a guidebook favourite, ignoring four promising bars on the way. Few *sevillanos* will get into a car and drive across the city and then hunt fruitlessly for a parking space in the hope of a beer and a bite, though they may walk five minutes further to a particular bar rather than merely go to the one round the corner. So when looking for a *tapa* rely on your own common sense. Does the bar look reasonably clean? Are there any other *sevillanos* using it? If they are beginning to put the *tapas* out, are they fresh? Is anyone else eating them? If you have enjoyed breakfast or coffee at the bar, then it may be worth going back at lunchtime for a *tapa*. Don't worry too much about the rubbish on the floor. Be pleased that all bars are hygienic enough to provide you with tissues to wipe your mouth and fingers with for no extra charge. The floors will be swept, and, indeed, in some of the bars in Arenal, west of the cathedral, and in other old parts of the city you may find they still use sawdust on the floor to assist the process.

Once discovered, the pleasure of finding good bars far out-weighs the bad experiences you will be sure to have had. I shall not quickly forget two *tapas* I ordered in one of the highly recommended picturesque bars in calle Mateos Gago, near the cathedral. My first was a stuffed green pepper. Its meat filling was an unpleasant solid pink lump, and the whole was covered with a pale grey sauce, sickly and tasteless. It also failed the usual *tapa* test of fast food: it was impossible to eat with the tiny three-pronged forks that are normally all you need for *tapas*. Desperate for something better, I turned to the *tortilla*. The omelette was pale and dry, and tasted alarm-ingly of reconstituted egg. To crown it all, it had been bathed in the same sickly grey sauce that drowned the stuffed pepper. Yet a *tapa* of *calamares fritos*, six or eight deep-fried rings of squid, in the Bar Miami just over the river in the Triana district – or any good bar with seafood – made the most appe-tising taster, as did a terracotta dish sizzling with *gambas al ajillo*, prawns fried in garlic and olive oil, eaten near the city centre.

The ideal accompaniment for such *tapas* is *vino de Jerez*, sherry. Sherry is made from the grapes grown on the white *albariza* soils enclosed by the triangle of towns Jerez-Puerto de Santa María-Sanlúcar de Barrameda, and is produced by a method of moving the ageing wine from cask to cask known as the *solera* system. The label 'sherry' obscures the treasure house of wines that are produced by the *solera*. Although Seville is outside the golden triangle of sherry towns, there is nowhere better for tasting the variety of wines, and enjoying them with *tapas* as you do so. The taste today is for dry wines, for the *finos*, but especially for the *manzanillas* (not to be confused either with *manzanilla*, camomile tea, or *manzan-illas*, small, fine olives) which are made in the seaside town of Sanlúcar de Barrameda. They have a special taste, said to come from the salt breezes wafting in to the bodegas. Every *feria* in the south will have its own semi-official *finos* or *man-zanillas*. The Seville *feria* is so large that no one brand prevails, though González Byass' *fino* Tío Pepe and Hidalgo's *manzanilla* La Gitana predominate.

The sweet wines of Jerez have become somewhat debased over the years, as people have come to assume that they are the tipples beloved of old ladies and pubs, which serve them in unspeakable glasses. In fact the old sweet wines, with a suitably hefty price tag, reveal the glories of their ripe maturity and should be drunk lingeringly and with relish. The *finos*, on the other hand, are lighter wines, just right for oiling the wheels of business, as well as the *feria*, as we shall see in the next chapter. (The sherry families are as almost as widely known in Seville society as their wines. A number of them married into English or Scottish families, many were educated at English schools, most of the older generation dress more convincingly in tweeds than any English gentlemen. When four of the patriarch and rancher Alvaro Domecq's grandchildren died in a car accident near Jerez in spring 1991, the local tragedy was treated as a national disaster, a symbolic message of the risks of driving on Spain's roads, and was given a silent salute by the crowds at the Maestranza bullring.) Seville also produces a local white wine of the sherry variety in the Aljarafe, but it tastes curiously greasy by contrast with a good *fino*. The sherry-type wine of the condado de Huelva, on the other hand, is a better attempt at flattery, if not imitation, as are the *montilla* wines from near Córdoba.

The *tapa* slows the absorption of alcohol into the bloodstream and eases the impact of these fortified wines. It is a civilised way of sampling the fruits of the kitchen without having to eat a full meal. After a few stops on the *via crucis*, the Stations of the Cross, or the Spanish version of a pub crawl, you soon discover what is worth trying. Most bars have a solid, sculpted mound of *ensaladilla rusa*, Russian salad, which is an insult to that nation, or what remains of it. The mixed vegetables, usually tinned or frozen, are coated with bottled mayonnaise and piled high. Potatoes and tuna both come *al aliño*, in an oil and vinegar dressing, often with finely chopped green pepper and tomato. There will nearly always be *tortilla*, which should be a reliable stand-by. *Paella* or another rice dish is often served as a *tapa* or a *ración*. There's another *tapa* which the *sevillano* adores: snails. *'Hay caracoles'*, 'snails here', goes up on hand-written notices in bars all round town in season.

As you become familiar with the litany of *tapas*, you will jump when you are offered something a little different, say a hot dish like *albóndigas en salsa* (meatballs in tomato sauce) or *rabo de toro*. As *riñones al jerez*, kidneys in sherry, is to the city of Jerez, so *rabo de toro* is to Seville. It is usually translated as 'oxtail', but in this city the more literal translation of 'bull's tail' is correct. Not for nothing is there a bull-ring down by the river-side. At the gentlemen's club, the Nuevo Casino in Los Reme-dios, *rabo de toro* is on the menu. It's a rich and glutinous stew, which they ginger up with cayenne pepper. To mop up the juices there is the traditional little round of 'French' bread; 'dry' dishes are always served with a handful of *picos*, or minute breadsticks, which are not as sweet as the Italian variety.

The Casino offers the three traditional *tapas*. The first is of course a little dish of olives. While the small fine olive, the *manzanilla de Sevilla*, with plenty of flesh and a small stone, is the most admired, there are lots of other varieties. There are many more ways of preparing olives than simply curing them in brine. Lourdes March and Alicia Ríos, in their com-pendious reference book on the olive, list the following poss-ible flavourings in decreasing order: garlic, thyme, Seville orange, lemon, green pepper, paprika, oregano, bay leaves, fennel, cumin, chilli pepper, cloves, coriander and pepper. Vast tubs of flavoured olives, especially the *gordales*, the extra large olives, can be seen in the markets, and many cooks have their own recipes for olives at home. At the Nuevo Casino, however, they prefer them plain.

The second traditional *tapa* is *manchego* cheese, cut into wedges, its salt taste an excellent appetiser for a glass of sherry. The third is *jamón serrano*, the local delicacy from Jabugo in Huelva province, ham cured in the mountain air, which has a salt edge but a creamy richness which is restrained by the wafer-thinness of the slices served. Every bar has its own ham on a carving board, and some will have more hanging up from the ceiling, each with it own little paper cup to catch any drips of fat or moisture that may accumulate.

There are bars in the city that do not serve *tapas*, or only *jamón*; their purpose is sherry, and the sherry casks and bottles line the walls like a *bodega*. The atmosphere in these bars is usually wonderful, recalling a more leisured, if less affluent past, One such is Casa Morales, in calle García de Vinuesa. Another which is heavy on atmosphere, but serves a full range of *tapas*, is El Rinconcillo in calle Gerona. Founded in the seventeenth century, it is reputed to be Seville's oldest. Set well away from the tourist centre it manages to remain much more authentic than some of the old bars in the Barrio de Santa Cruz.

The flamenco singer Peregil runs an atmospheric small bar of the same name not far from the spiritless bus station in the Plaza de la Encarnación. His name is a play on *'perejil'* which means 'parsley'; it was the nickname of his great-grandfather, whose surname was Perez Gil. Despite being asked to perform for the king, and having constant commissions to sing *sevillanas* at weddings, parties and at Christmas, Peregil still keeps his bar going. A tall, charming, tanned fellow, with a distinctive lisp, he comes from the village of Manzanilla and the bar has a very rustic air. There are 200 families from the same village in the city who all keep in close contact. The *manzanilla* sherry (no relation) is kept in a green enamel teapot in the fridge. While washing the glasses at the bar, he sings. His mouth opens wider, and wider still, until it seems that his lungs are practically exposed. Over the noise of the traffic the voice soars out. Amongst the usual detritus of the bar counter and the back shelf there are cassettes of him singing, for sale. But he is the proof that flamenco only really works live and in a bar. Apart from the teapot, the fridge is pretty empty; the customers come for Peregil, not his *tapas*.

Expensive, international bars are not always the best places for an authentic *tapa*. Take, for instance, the bar attached to Egaña-Oriza, the smart Basque restaurant which is renowned for its food. It is a pleasant bar, heavy with the gossip of businessmen and lecturers from the university over the road. It can conjure up an excellent breakfast and many traditional *tapas*, yet one of its standbys is baby croissants stuffed with savoury fillings. In a city with such an inventive repertoire of *tapas*, who needs a stuffed croissant? Better to try somewhere like the Bar Europa on the corner of calles Alcaicería and Siete Revueltas, which has been refitted in a turn-of-the-century style. It may not be authentically old, but its *tapas* are authentic reproductions.

The repertoire of the Bar Cáceres changes little. Antonio came with his own recipes and thinks up others from time to time. His menu is written up on the wall, but it tells only half the story. Always ask the waiter what is on for the day, even though the catechism of the reply will be given at such a pace that it will be practically impossible to follow. Imperceptibly the bar shifts gear into lunch. Some drinkers will change from sherry to *tinto*, red wine, or *tinto con casera*, red wine diluted with a slightly sweetened fizzy drink. Many will stick to beer, which has just become Spain's most popular alcoholic drink. Antonio always provides one solid main course, a stew based on beans, *menudo* (tripe stewed in a tomato sauce), a rice dish, or a thick soup.

A popular compromise between a *tapa* and lunch is *Huevos a la flamenca*, a typical dish which has variations round Andalusia. To a tomato and onion sauce are added cooked peas, chopped ham, green beans and *chorizo* sausage. The vegetable sauce is put in the bottom of a terracotta dish, topped with an egg, and cooked on top of the stove until the white is just set. The yolk will be wonderfully runny, just right for dipping plenty of fresh bread into. Seville has some of the best white bread in the world and it is made for dipping into egg yolks and mopping up soup.

Antonio will also conjure up a salad out of his tins and mayonnaise bottles, a practice which always surprises me in this city of bountiful produce. Part of the reason is supply and demand, which are important for a small bar; at least this way he doesn't have food going bad in the back room. Antonio's son has come in to help now lessons are over for the morning. He'll soon be leaving school. Will he come to join his father? No way, this is no job for anyone, Antonio replies smartly. 'I started when I was very little, just helping out, and then when

I was fourteen I left school. But the hours are terrible; some-times during *feria* I don't close until 4 a.m. When can a man get to see his family?'

Finally, the bar cools down for the afternoon. Antonio's only visitors until the late afternoon are tourists, especially pairs of Australian or American girls, dropping in for a glass of water or to buy a *bocadillo*. The sandwich in Seville is as unpretentious and as nourishing as could be. No butter or cholesterol-rich spread sullies the inside of one of the ubiqui-tous crusty rolls. The filling provides fat enough: *jamón ser-rano, manchego* cheese or, the jumbo version, a whole fresh *tortilla* cut in two. Do not be deceived into thinking that by virtue of being a simple sandwich, it will necessarily be cheap. *Manchego* and *jamón serrano* are both expensive foods, even in small quantities.

Business warms up again in the early evening. A mixture of coffees, brandies, teas and cakes are consumed as a reviver after the siesta, and an increasing quantity of *tapas* as people come out to stroll in the gardens at the edge of the barrio de Santa Cruz, and enjoy a glass of *fino* or *manzanilla*. The focus of the city has shifted elsewhere, and around 9 p.m. Antonio can shut up shop. Over the river in Triana life is only just beginning. At the west end of the Puente San Telmo there are three bars with an excellent view of the city. The best view of the Torre del Oro is from the Río Grande, or the Kiosco de las Flores on the south side of the bridge. Sitting out on the pavement by the embankment at midnight in one of the great cities in the world, eating an enormous platter of *pescado frito*, one understands at last that this is not an activity dreamed up by the tourist office, but part of city life for many *sevillanos*. It's as noisy and wide awake as a market place at 10 a.m., with traffic roaring over the bridge and everyone talking at the tops of their voices. The fact that it is the middle of the night disturbs no one at all. Only now is it cool enough to enjoy oneself.

*   *   *

Seville

Only a matter of years ago, the bustle of Seville's bars contrasted with the atmosphere of its expensive restaurants, which were very straight-laced. Those who could afford to eat out, the old guard of the Franco years and the upper classes, were conservative in their tastes. The menu inevitably included the classic *pato a la sevillana*, duck with olives. The fish restaurant La Dorada, which has branches in several cities, rightly won acclaim for the excellence of its fish and the way it was cooked. Its party piece was undoubtedly *urta a la sal*, bream cooked inside a coat of sea salt to keep it wonderfully moist, and served with boiled potatoes and a selection of sauces. The only drawback of this particular delicacy is that there is an excessive amount of boiled potato and baked white fish to eat. But La Dorada stayed close to its local ingredients and recipes and fared better than many other smart restaurants, which went for increasingly international dishes cooked with little distinction.

Today, it is a different story. One of the major impetuses has been the appearance of a new group of consumers, the *nueva jet*, the civil servants and Expo people who have money to spend and a taste for good cuisine. Seville's smart restaurants are now filled with equally smart middle-aged men and a smattering of women. When I mentioned to one such new-wave civil servant the criticism of a traditionalist that Seville's restaurants were full of younger men in trendy suits, he replied, 'Well, at least we all have the chance to go out and eat. In the old days, the conservatives wanted to conserve it all for themselves.'

The newer restaurants popular with the politicians and Expo people are modern white reflections of the equally modern white offices in which the diners work. One such, Bailén 34, named after its position in the street of that name, provides a menu that draws on the prime ingredients of the region and the classic recipes, while adding some variations of its own. Its cool, crumbly goats' cheese from the sierra is served not with the traditional *membrillo*, quince paste, but with three different fruit conserves. One of the things that marks it out is that the restaurant is run and the food is cooked by women. Traditionally women have only cooked in the home. But the kitchen in Bailén 34 is run by four women, none of whom has had any professional training. They cook for love and from experience, and the kitchen has a domestic warmth quite lacking in the military rigour aped by male chefs.

Another untrained cook who has risen to the top of Seville's restaurants is Esperanza Flores, the chef at Parabere, a restaurant which opened just over a year ago at calle Narciso Campillo 4, an inauspicious little side street, but usefully sited just a block away from the offices of the Junta de Andalucía. The decor is discreetly post-modern, and the clientele try to live up to it. Again, the menu rescues classic ingredients, such as *trigueros*, the wild asparagus, and recalls historic influences, serving meat with raisin sauces, echoing the Arab combination of sweet and sour.

Parabere has an extensive list of salads, popular with self-conscious businessmen watching their weight, but generally uncommon in this city where the average salad consists of lettuce and tomato. Eating out in Seville the one thing I miss is vegetables, and I discussed this one afternoon with Esperanza Flores in a taxi on the way to the *feria*. The taxi driver soon joined in, saying he liked nothing more than a plate of greens that had been cooked, and then fried with raisins and pine nuts *(piñones)*. It's a classic dish, but to one accustomed to enjoying reasonably plain vegetables with a main dish, I sometimes regret the emphasis on stuffed, stewed and baked vegetables that stand alone as individual courses.

We had finished lunch that day at 4.30, but it would have been just as possible to finish at 5.30. Lunch is the main meal of the day. Because of the *jornada intensiva*, lunch may not begin until half past three or even four. Thus the *tapa* at midday is not just a pleasant diversion. A little dish of *calamares* or *boquerones en vinagre*, anchovies in vinegar – or even the ubiquitous *ensaladilla rusa* – is essential in order to keep going until lunchtime. The whole family can sit down and eat this meal together, though children are more inclined to bolt their food and rush off to play. This is the meal that will be served with a little ceremony, even though the television will usually be on throughout. Rafael Delgado, an engineer, does not get back home until well after three. By this time one of the children will have bought more fresh bread from the *panadería*, and the table will have been laid with napkins and a lace tablecloth, bought in Ayamonte, the nearest Portuguese border town, where lace tablecloths and duvet covers flap from every other shop front to attract the trippers.

The meal begins with soup, in summer most likely a *gazpacho*, with their favourite garnishes. A thin soup, such as *sopa de cuarto de hora*, simply made from strong home-made chicken stock, with a little minced ham and some thread noodles or leftover cooked rice added near the end, makes an equally light starter. Sometimes Rafael's wife Rosa prepares a cold vegetable to start with, such as roast, skinned green peppers in oil and vinegar dressing. The main dish is hot, or at least warm, even in summer. If Rosa has been too busy to cook in the morning, it may be *pescado frito*, bought from the *freiduría* round the corner. The *freiduría* is as far from the British chip shop as could be, selling a range of crisp fresh fish, to be eaten at home, or taken to a nearby bar and enjoyed with a glass or two of cold beer. There is not a potato chip in sight, though the shop may also sell roast chickens. On other days, if Rosa has been to the market, she will fry the fish herself.

Another quick dish which is popular with the children is thin veal fillets, *filetes*, egged, breadcrumbed and fried, served with home-made potato chips. If she has had more time to cook, there may be a rice dish, perhaps *arroz a la marinera*, a version of *paella* cooked with a selection of white fish and seafood. Rosa always makes a quick, simple salad of lettuce, tomato and onion, and pours over the separate items of the dressing, the oil, vinegar and salt, one at a time, and then stirs them together in the bowl. 'I don't like buying tinned things like tomato sauce, when I can do it myself,' she says. 'And I don't like things like frozen *empanadas* [small pasties, originally a Galician speciality] which just have to be heated up, because you don't know what's in them.'

In winter the meal is altogether more solid. It may begin with a thick soup of brown lentils with chunks of *chorizo*. Or the meal may be a combined soup-cum-stew. Every region has its own variations, but the principle is the same: the liquid is served as a soup first, and the solid pieces are eaten with a knife and fork next. The Andalusian *puchero* is, like many such dishes, named after the pot it is cooked in. The basis of the *puchero* that Antonio Lara's wife Susi makes is chick peas *(garbanzos)* and rice. Chick peas and lentils are the most common pulses in Seville; in northern Spain haricot beans prevail. Susi soaks the chick peas overnight, and then cooks them with half a chicken, a ham bone, a wedge of pork belly and an onion, for three to four hours. The family eat the chick peas, rice and vegetables first as a meaty soup, mopping up the liquid with plenty of fresh white bread, and then eat the pieces of chicken, ham and bacon to follow.

The *pringá* is another local variation on the *puchero*, except that Susi adds *morcilla*, black pudding, and *chorizo* sausages, thickly sliced. A third variation in her kitchen is the *cocido*, best known as Madrid's staple dish, but eaten everywhere; this has the same basic ingredients as the *puchero*, but without the rice or the ham bone. Later Susi adds green beans, pumpkin, carrots and potatoes, green pepper, a whole head of garlic, *morcilla* and *chorizo*. The *puchero* is the most limited dish of the three in its list of ingredients. In this it reflects the impoverished history of the Andalusian agricultural labourer. But in this day of the monosodium glutamate-enriched stock cube made with hydrogenated vegetable fats, it tastes deliciously of simple ingredients, plainly cooked.

Most days there is no special pudding in the Delgado household, simply a piece of whatever fruit is in season. Fortunately, in Seville this is usually no problem, because of the bounties of the Guadalquivir valley. Like the bread and the chocolate bars, the fruits grow in family-sized pieces, even the grapes and the apples, though the apples are nothing special (the fruits selected for export are more delicately sized to suit smaller families). The one fruit that palls is the bumper, family-sized *sandía*, the water-melon, whose monotonous taste far outweighs the attractions of its brightly coloured flesh.

At weekends or on special occasions, the family may enjoy a gateau or tray of little cakes from the *confitería*. These are frequently a great let-down. The cakes in the *confiterías* look appealing enough, but are usually made out of cheap, dry biscuit and sponge mixtures. The icing may be exuberant, but the fillings are pathetic. However, when the *sevillanos* abandon their pretensions of aping the French *patissiers* and follow their own classic recipes, they are far more successful. The classic repertoire of *postres*, desserts, is small. Inevitably *flan*, caramel custard, comes top of the list, followed closely by *tocino de cielo*. *Tocino* is lard; and *tocino de cielo*, 'lard of the skies', or 'heavenly lard'. Essentially *flan* without the milk, *tocino de cielo* is an enormously rich confection of egg yolks and sugar (the recipes begin, 'Take twelve egg yolks . . .'). It is cut into mercifully small squares and an unctuous portion goes down well with a strong black coffee and a good brandy. A more domestic dish, and one that is beginning to appear on the menus of restaurants rediscovering Andalusian cuisine, is *natillas*. This is nothing more than home-made custard, but it sounds much more appealing in Spanish. The custard is usually mildly flavoured with lemon and topped with grated nutmeg or roughly chopped walnut pieces. *Cuajada*, junket, is another domestic dessert whose star is rising in the smarter restaurants.

Sometimes, though less often, the Delgados have a little cheese for dessert. Spanish cheeses are usually made of sheep's or goats' milk. The land is not as arid as one might think: the Roman historian Strabo cites the legendary Geryon, whose herds gave milk so rich that they produced no whey. The most famous cheese today is *manchego* from the central plains of La Mancha, which varies greatly in its strength depending on its age. There is a great repertoire of cheeses in Spain, from mild goats' cheeses to strong blue cheeses, which deserve to be much more widely known. If you are offered cheese as a *tapa* in Seville, however, it is very likely to be *manchego*, Don Quixote's favourite. When the Delgados have it as a dessert, they eat it not with bread or biscuits, but with wedges of *membrillo*, the thick quince paste. The contrast of the salt creamy cheese and the sweet, mildly fruity *membrillo* seems to me to have been made in heaven.

If the Delgados have friends or family to lunch at the weekends, then the meal runs on easily until perhaps 6 p.m. There is no reason to move, and the coffee and brandies just keep flowing . . . The children will be demanding their *merienda*, tea – of cakes and biscuits – by about this time. No one's thoughts turn to supper until eleven or even midnight. When the night is cool, it is finally time to think about food again. Supper is a simpler meal. The Delgados enjoy having eggs at this hour: *huevos a la flamenca*, or eggs lightly fried in olive oil, with fresh bread dipped in the yolks. Supper is a good time for finishing up lunchtime leftovers: cold *pescado frito* or tortilla, or warmed-up *sopa de cuarto de hora*.

Seville has not forgotten its fesival foods. In a world of increasing homogenisation, where the seasons have disappeared from the fruit and vegetable racks of the supermarkets, *sevillanos* still enjoy special foods at certain times of the year. One of the typical meals during Holy Week is *garbanzos con bacalao*, classic lenten fare which nourishes the mind and the body for the rigours of following or taking part in one of the processions. Magdalena Hernández pre-soaks the dried salt cod and the chick peas, and cooks the chick peas in some of the water in which the cod was soaked. These two unspectacular ingredients produce a warming stew; it is another of those simple dishes of Seville which do not require long hours standing over the cooker. On the other hand they do need someone to plan and shop ahead; they presuppose the existence of a good woman with sufficent time on her hands. Another lenten dish with chick peas is *espinacas con garbanzos*, in which the spinach contrasts in texture and colour with the pulses.

There are also sweet cakes associated with Holy Week. First, there are the *pestiños* beloved of Magdalena Hernández, the *anís*-flavoured pastries bathed in honey. I have a sentimental preference for *torrijas*, but clearly the essence of all of these is to eat them in liberal quantities before you make your choice. *Torrijas* are slices of bread, soaked in lemon-flavoured milk and then dipped in egg and fried. Once fried they are soaked in a white-wine syrup and left until they are completely oozing with gorgeous stickiness. The best *torrijas* are made with thick country bread. Sadly, many of today's *torrijas* are made for ease with Bimbo and are a poor shadow of the real thing.

Torrijas, like *pestiños*, can be enjoyed at any time. However, they come into their own during Holy Week, in the early hours of the morning before dawn. One's blood sugar level is at its lowest, and one or two of these sugary cakes will give the body the necessary blast to carry you through until dawn. I vividly remember being taken to a flat above calle Feria on the very early morning of Good Friday. We had come to watch from the balcony as the Macarena, one of the most popular representations of the Virgin in Seville, passed down the street, where she always received a passionate welcome. Having spent the whole of the previous evening chasing Virgins, we were all physically weary. But our hosts had put out a tray of syrupy cakes and pastries with whisky and gin, and we were soon revived.

At Christmas, as I have said, many families in Seville prefer to eat fish rather than turkey, though the increasing popularity of turkey at Christmas is another sign of the creeping homogenisation. This is the season of *turrón* in all its varieties, and marzipan sweets. On New Year's Eve, everyone, whatever their age, tries to eat twelve grapes, one for each chime of the clock. It makes a big difference how big the grapes are, and whether they have pips or not. On 6 January, the *Reyes Magos*, the Three Wise Men, come and children leave *turrón* out for them to eat. On this day it is traditional to eat the *Roscón de Reyes*, a sweetened yeast bread shaped into a ring, decorated with candied fruits and sugar. Lent comes in with *buñuelos de Cuaresma*, light, sugary fritters. The *buñuelos de viento* sold for All Saints' Day are similar. Also sold on All Saints' Day are *huesos de santo*, almond-based sweets filled with candied egg yolk, just like marrow-filled 'saints' bones'.

For the *feria*, all kinds of street food is on sale. The towering caravans selling *turrón* predominate: at the top every boxed brand is piled up, hiding the sales people behind. Below there are trays of crystallised fruits and *alfajores*, and in front of them, running along the edge of the stall, trays of nibbles packed into cellophane tubes selling at *veinte duros*, a hundred *pesetas*, a time: pistachio nuts, whole peanuts, shelled peanuts, hazelnuts, whole and shelled sunflower seeds, roasted almonds, *almendras garrapiñadas* (almonds candied with honey and sugar), pine kernels, tiger nuts, roasted chick peas, Smarties and jellies, as well as a few bags of crisps, though not in the sort of volume that would compete with the crisp fryers. Alongside each there is a tray, constantly refreshed with running water, of coconut slices. The vast edifice of sugared delights, a monument to Islamic Spain, is decorated with plastic gewgaws: miniature guitars, pink and green, drums in the Andalusian white and green, pink and orange telephones, red and yellow water-bottles, monstrous black machine guns, golden pistols and old-fashioned children's diabolos in peaceful baby blue. Every stall is exactly the same and there's no sign of fierce competition. They fill every available space in the Prado de San Sebastián, which becomes a car park and bus stop for the *feria*, and they line calle Presidente Carrero Blanco along to the *feria* itself. The *turrón* vendors do not hawk their wares, unlike the people who have come in their lorries to sell china, cutlery, linen and the usual fairground stock, who quickly set up a relationship with the passers-by. When the *feria* is over they will be off to the next one the following week somewhere else in Andalusia, offering the same comfortingly familiar temptations wherever they go.

In villages and smaller towns the towering caravans may be replaced by individuals pushing carts. Their stock is much the same, there is just less of it. The advantages of these carts for the vendors is that they are mobile and can be pushed amongst the crowds awaiting the carnival or Holy Week procession.

Chocolate and *churros* are *imprescindible*, essential, at the end of each evening, but before that there has been a whole day of eating. The *casetas* or little marquees which run side to side and back to back along the avenues of the *feria* have only rudimentary temporary kitchens. However, since *sevillanos* basically cook on top of the stove, the facilities are not vastly different from those of any kitchen in the city. A few *casetas* provide a full meal with the tables laid; more commonly waiters will bring a plate of *paella* to be eaten, often with difficulty, in the cramped conditions of a popular *caseta* (and any *caseta* that provides a good lunch is sure to be popular). The *paellas*, the *cocidos* and the *rabos de toro* will be brought in to the *feria* site from local restaurants. Throughout the day and night the kitchens will be providing *tapas* to soften the effects of the copious quantities of drink. One or two of the larger *casetas* are more public affairs and will run to *pinchitos morunos*, 'Moorish kebabs', usually of pork, prepared in a dry marinade of paprika, cumin and thyme, and served on a wooden skewer. Very occasionally a *caseta* may provide a tray of little cakes from a *confitería* to nibble in the early evening, but the essence of the fair is sherry tempered with meat and cheese.

Seville is not just traditional in the foods it eats, but also in the way it prepares them. Even where the demands of commerce intrude, there are still those who stand out against industrialisation. By the quality of their produce, and their resistance to change, these are the kinds of goods that will keep their identity in the single European market, if their small size does not cause them to drown. One such is the family business of Andrés Gaviño, the mainstay of *sevillano* and Spanish breakfasts, which makes biscuits and cakes in the village of Castilleja de la Cuesta. The village is in the hills of the Aljarafe outside Seville, on the way to Santiponce and Itálica, and was the home not only of the Conde-Duque de Olivares, adviser to Philip IV, but also of Rita Hayworth. The Madre Irlandesas have a school here, in the white, airy palace in which Cortés, the discoverer of Mexico, died, embittered and forgotten.

Castilleja de la Cuesta has always been known for its *dulces*, its sweet biscuits and cakes, although their commercial manufacture is relatively recent. Gaviño call their brand 'La Primitiva', on account of its being the first to make the biscuits commercially in the village, though it started as recently as 1952. They are quick to explain the brand name, because they don't want it to be thought that they are in any way 'primitive', in the sense of being uncivilised. However, given their method of working and the equipment they use, they deserve to be described as primitive in the very best sense of the word.

The factory started up in the back of a private house, where there was already a bread oven, in the small and charming main square of the village. Carmela, *'la del Horno'* (the baker, or 'she in charge of the oven'), decided on the recipes, and is in charge of what more jargonistic enterprises would call 'quality control'. She is proud of her biscuits, and rightly so. The recipes she selected were traditional local ones, to which she has added a few variations. None of the biscuits has any additives, preservatives or colorants, and like so many of Seville's foods they are simple recipes simply made with care and attention. There is the minimum of machinery, which looks well-loved, if not of the latest design. The dough and the egg whites are beaten in giant basins by ancient paddles, and the biscuits are shaped by hand, baked in an old bread oven and stacked to cool on wooden racks. The company has already invested in some newer ovens, but the men who slide the trays in and out of the ancient oven are better than any machine at judging the right moment to withdraw the fragile biscuits before they burn.

The cornerstone of the bakery – and the Spanish breakfast – is the *torta de aceite*, which is popular throughout Spain with a cup of coffee in the morning. This translates literally, but unappetisingly, as 'oil tart'. The *torta* is a deliciously thin and crisp pastry biscuit about twelve centimetres in diameter, made with refined olive oil so that it does not taste strongly, and flavoured with *anís*. The finished biscuit is rolled in sugar. The superior variety, my own favourite, is sprinkled with chopped almonds as well as sugar after baking. In both cases, some of the sugar melts on the hot biscuit and forms small patches of caramel. The biscuits are weighed and cut by machine, but each *torta* is patted into a circle by hand.

The manager, Ana María Soriano, who looks far too young to be running the enterprise, is immensely proud of 'her girls', many of whom have been with the factory since it started. Sitting in front of a pile of flour, each girl pats the dough into almost perfect rounds, even enough to fit neatly into a prefabricated plastic pack at the end. Once baked and cooled, the *tortas* are sorted and packed. Then comes the *tortas'* 'unique selling proposition'. Each one is wrapped by hand in a square of transparent, quasi-greaseproof paper, overprinted with the company's logo in blue. The pleasure for the eater is to break the biscuit before unwrapping it, to eat the bigger pieces, and then finally lick the sugary, nutty crumbs out. This only works because the paper wrapper is so large. A custom-made, machine-wrapped packet would be too small to keep the crumbs. The Gaviños have semi-mechanised other parts of their production, but the *tortas de aceite* remain sacrosanct as an *artesanal*, craft product. What happens to the imperfect ones? Most are given to the nuns to dispose of, but Ana María Soriano likes to eat a few. Like the real enthusiast she is, she prefers the broken ones.

An equally traditional biscuit is the *polvorón*, or shortbread, which, rather unappetisingly, is made with lard, not butter. But when you watch the enthusiastic baker Sebastián heaving a great fat block of the purest white lard into the mixer and hear him eulogise about the quality of their lard as it melts into the flour and sugar, your reservations melt away too. The biscuits certainly melt in the mouth, just like in all the best advertisements. The *polvorones* are, sadly, machine-wrapped in cellophane; it means that you have to be a bit more inventive about getting the last crumbs out without spilling them all over you. *Polvorones* now come in several flavours: chocolate, coconut and almond, but the best is the original recipe.

The *tortas* are baked daily. A particular delicacy of the region that the Gaviños also produce, though not so often, are *cortadillos de cidra*. These little squares, hand-wrapped in the same distinctive greaseproof paper, are tiny sandwiches of a *polvorón* mix, encasing a layer of *cabello de ángel*. 'Angel's hair' is an excessively sweet preserve made out of candied strings of pumpkin flesh, which is a popular filling in these parts for pies and biscuits. The *cortadillos* work so well because of the contrast between the melting biscuit and very sweet strands of the filling. Also in the repertoire of biscuits is the *bizcochada*, a boat-shaped biscuit piled high with meringue and sprinkled with sugar before baking.

As for the cakes, the Gaviños also make the sweet buns called *magdalenas*, which are so popular for breakfast and tea, and a plain sponge cake, or *bizcocho*. This, again, is made with a refined olive oil, rather than animal fat, and is a longer-lasting variation on the traditional Victoria sponge. Nothing could be further from the commercial jam and ersatz-cream-filled cakes of the UK baker. In Seville they still work to simple recipes and the customer adds the jam at home.

Between the factory rooms and the house on the square is a domestic patio, with tubs of flowers and some chairs for sitting out. At the front of the building is the factory shop. Across the marble-topped counter the Gaviños sell their *tortas, polvorones, bizcochadas, magdalenas* and *bizcochos* to all comers. A portrait of Jesus Christ wisely blesses the fortunate citizens of Castilleja who have such delicacies on their doorsteps.

In the city centre, the nuns of a number of the *conventos de clausura*, enclosed orders, are noted cooks, creating an array of sugary delights along with their daily prayers. The convents date from the time of the Reconquista. The nuns who came from Christian Castilla to set up the first foundations brought their recipes with them. These were changed and developed over time, and inevitably took on a number of the flavours and styles of the Arab cuisine of the city, predominantly the use of almonds, cinnamon, aniseed, sesame seeds, olive oil and plenty of sugar and honey. In due course the nuns took their recipes with them when they went out to the New World to set up sister houses amongst the heathen. A cookery book found in the archives of a convent in Puebla in Mexico has an extensive range of recipes which give clues to the nuns' Spanish heritage. It has been suggested that the reason why Galicia's most famous desserts, the *tartas de Santiago* and *Mondoñedo*, are made of almonds when Galicia has no almond trees is the same: nuns travelled from Seville to sister houses in Galicia and took their predilection for almonds with them.

The most famous of their delicacies, without doubt, are the *yemas de San Leandro*. *Yemas* are egg yolks, and in this distinctive sweetmeat, egg yolks are cooked in a sugar syrup until a soft paste is formed. The *yemas* are shaped into little cones and dipped into a sugar syrup which dries into a crust over the richly yielding egg underneath. Each *yema* is then wrapped in a screw of distinctive grey greaseproof paper, over-printed with the stamp of the convent, and packed in wooden boxes. This hardwearing packaging makes them popular to send through the post to homesick *sevillanos*, much as clotted cream used to be sent in tins from Cornwall. *Yemas* could only be made in a city which has no fear of salmonella poisoning – or of an excessive consumption of sugar and cholesterol. A typical recipe for *yemas* from the turn of the century starts: 'To make three pounds of *yemas*, take eighteen egg yolks, two egg whites and two and a half pounds of white sugar . . .'

The nuns of Santa Paula started cooking in earnest in the 1950s, when the pope gave convents permission to earn money to support themselves. Some convents took up embroidery, others laundry, book-binding or making wafers for mass. At Santa Paula they began with *membrillo*, the quince paste that is eaten in slices, either alone as a dessert or with cheese. They started in a small way, but today they make 2,000 kilos a year, buying their quinces from a supplier in the Sierra de Huelva. The convent had an old recipe for *membrillo* which one of the sisters would have brought with her when she joined the convent. They also acquired more up-to-date advice from a relative of one of the nuns, who exports *membrillo*.

Gradually they branched out into jams; their flavours today include apricot, lemon, grapefruit, cherry, strawberry, fig, apple and pear. They also make tomato jam. While the saying is that *'entre los pucheros anda el Señor'*, 'Christ walks among the cooking-pots', I think that he must have omitted to pass by this particular jam skillet. While the sisters are to be commended for making jam out of almost anything, tomatoes are a big mistake. Using another local ingredient, they do make a Seville orange marmalade, in which the fruit is very finely chopped, and it is set in a relatively high proportion of sweet jelly. The sisters also capture the essence of the city in their jasmine and orange blossom jellies. They sell purées: of chestnuts, grown in Galicia; and of sweet potatoes, reflecting the presence of nuns from the Indies in the community.

Like San Leandro, Santa Paula also makes a delicacy from egg yolks, *tocino de cielo*, the 'heavenly lard'. 'There's no problem with eating the eggs,' says Mother Asunción. 'People know they can rely on the quality of the eggs we buy. If anything, people are much more concerned about eating so much sugar.' The inevitable question is, what do the nuns do with all the leftover egg whites? In the old days, the sherry industry used egg whites to clarify the wine, much as you would a consommé. There was thus a mutually beneficial link between God and Mammon; the bodegas used the whites and the convents used the yolks. Today, chemistry and hi-tech have taken over from the humble egg whites. The nuns have had to find another outlet for them. Fortunately for Santa Paula, a *confitería* is happy to buy their egg whites to make meringues.

Mother Asunción is quick to rebut any assumption that the sisters are merely cooking. My references to 'the kitchen' are corrected to the *obrador*, or workroom; cooking is simply one of the many tasks they do to the greater glory of God. They work in the kitchen in the morning, between 9.30 and 1 p.m., with sturdy aprons over their habits, but normal timetables are suspended when fruit is in season. When the quinces come in in October, the whole convent joins in the work. Quinces are notoriously difficult to prepare, so the sisters cook them lightly to soften them a little before peeling and coring them.

Just after Christmas come the Seville oranges and in the late spring there is always a rush to prepare the strawberries while they are at their best. The amount of work depends, of course, on the harvest. Sor María Belén, who is plagued with Parkinson's disease but still keeps a sharp eye on the work of the kitchen, says that last year the land was dry and the harvest of quinces poor; this year she fears that it may be just as bad.

The convent of Santa Paula is a lovely building richly endowed with treasures, many as a result of the well-connected women who chose to become nuns here, and the sisters will proudly show you round their museum. There are enough of them for the duties of the convent to be shared out. But Mother Asunción agrees that there are fewer vocations today; her numbers are strong because she has young women from the Indies and from Africa who have come to take their vows.

The sisters of the convent of Santa Inés are in greater difficulties. Their numbers are dwindling as they get older. Everybody has to do everything here; there is no question of taking turns or building up an expertise. The greatest effort comes in the run-up to Christmas, beginning with the festival of the Immaculate Conception on 8 December. They are also very busy over Holy Week and the subsequent weeks to Corpus Christi. ('But we don't make anything special like *torrijas* or *pestiños* for Semana Santa, because other convents do that, and we none of us want to compete.') While they sell their goods throughout the year, the range, as in many convents, is much more limited in the summer. The sisters at Santa Inés have been making biscuits for six centuries, so they say, since the time of their foundress doña María Coronel. They used to give them away as presents; it was only in the 1920s that they started to sell any of them, and it was not until the 1970s that they decided to follow the papal dispensation and manufacture them as a way of supporting themselves. Their recipes came from other convents, and also from a *confitero*, a baker, who gave them his when he retired.

Santa Inés is known for its *bollitos*, or little sweet buns, decorated with sesame seeds, which are delicious warmed up in the oven ('Our cakes are very popular with people who don't like things too sweet. Some people eat them with jam; others with ham'). It also bakes the full range of typical cakes in season ('We make everything by hand, everything is *artesanal*'): *cortadillos de cidra* ('We don't make the *cabello de angel*, we buy it in; it's very expensive'), *tortas de aceite, polvorones* (all three of these are similar to the biscuits of Castilleja de la Cuesta), *tortas almendradas* (almond biscuits), *magdalenas* and *roscos de vino* (a Christmas speciality, made with wine). What, then, is it that makes their cakes so special? 'The ingredients,' says the nun hidden behind the little revolving door in the wall, who sells the cakes. 'We only use the best, and they can't hurt anyone. Our eggs are fresh and come from the countryside. We use pure pork fat and refined olive oil, which we've been buying from the same factory for forty years. That's why people come here to shop, because they can tell the difference.' This last sentence was said with the greatest humility; when God is your marketing device you don't need subterfuges.

In the past the nuns used to be given their ingredients by a grateful populace. Nowadays they have to go out to shop and pay for the raw materials. Yet despite the pressures on their incomes, all the convents give away sandwiches to the needy, of salami or *chorizo* or cheese. 'We prefer to give them food, rather than money, but if a family we know is in real trouble, if they can prove the electricity is about to be cut off, then of course we'll pay the bill.'

The cooking convents are open for the sale of biscuits, cakes and jams usually between 10 and 1 and 4.30 and 6.30. Each is slightly different. At San Leandro and Santa Inés, there is no one in sight, and nothing at the entrance apart from the open door to indicate that sweet temptations lie inside. Across the other side of a silent courtyard is the small rotating door in the wall and a price list beside it. There is also a bell to summon the vendor. Visitors have to know what they want; asking what each thing is does not always help. Nearly everything is made of flour and sugar, so it can be hard to differentiate. You order your kilo, or fraction of a kilo, of what you want and put the money on the shelf. The shelf rotates and

Seville

after a pause back comes the change and your bag of shopping. The convent of Santa Clara has its own shop out on the street, while at the convent of Santa Paula the difficulty lies in deciding which of the several doors in the little plaza is the entrance (it's the one on the left as you face the convent, and it has a tiny iron grille which is open during visiting hours). The visitor walks across a courtyard, where there is plenty of peaceful activity of sisters sewing, and the sister who sells the jams comes out to greet you. Shopping for sweet things from the *conventos de clausura* has to be one of the best ways of getting to know secret Seville. For an initial introduction to the range of the sisters' products, drop into the shop in the Plaza del Cabildo opposite the cathedral, mentioned in Chapter 6.

In a charming orange-painted house with white detailing at number 1, calle Mesón de Moro, in the Barrio de Santa Cruz, work a group of enthusiasts. The air is thick with talk of *manzanillas, hojiblancas* and *gordales*. These are the olive exporters and their constant aim is to conquer the world for the Spanish olive as Fernando and Isabella tried to do with Christianity. The United States leads the world in its consumption of Spanish olives, despite the increasing competition from Californian olives; the UK hardly figures on the statistics. No doubt it is because of the embarrassment with where to put the stone; the stiff-upper-lip British prefer their olives stoned. José Tomás Carmona, the director of Acemesa, the exporters' association, enjoys telling the anecdote of the days when he was just another olive grower and exporter. A visiting Japanese businessman was perplexed about where to put the stones. Sr Carmona explained that there were small china frogs with gaping mouths made for just this purpose. El Corte Inglés stocked them and he would be happy to leave a couple at the Alfonso XIII, where the man was staying, for his entertainment. This he duly did. Just before the businessman returned to Japan,

182

Sr Carmona received a request to ship 600 frogs out to Japan. Shortly after, a cable arrived from Japan. Could Sr Carmona change that to 6,000? 'I never sold that man a single olive,' he laughs, 'but at least there must be lots of people in Japan who know what to do with the stones!'

The British, lacking china frogs, like their olives stuffed with pimento paste, mainly to make their food look pretty rather than taste different. Like the mustard that is left on the side of the plate, the olive growers make their money in the UK from what the British are served but do not eat. Sr Carmona fondly remembers the dry Martini, an excellent vehicle for the stuffed olive, even if if he could never understand how anybody could drink such a powerful cocktail. The dry Martini has more or less passed into history, at least as far as the olive exporters are concerned. But the arrival of salad bars in supermarkets has made a big difference, especially to the paltry exports to the UK; there, olives are served loose, and also garnish ready-made salads. On the other hand, the big supermarket chains have too much power over pricing, and at this Sr Carmona clutches his throat. 'They're really squeezing us,' he emphasises, twisting his hands together in another expressive gesture. In all, the olive industry has some 25,000 people working in activities related to it. 'How can we make employees redundant, when you know them all and their families? You've seen them married, you've been to their children's first communions. What are you supposed to do?' he asks despairingly.

Sell more pizzas, is one solution. For pizzas, with their garnish of black olives, have also been most satisfactory in getting the world to eat Sr Carmona's product. But the green olive, the small perfectly formed *manzanilla, 'el coñac de las aceitunas'*, 'the cognac of the olives', is what puts him into ecstasy. 'My grandfather wouldn't touch an *hojiblanca,*' he says of the variety of olive which looks similar to the *manzanilla*, but has a larger stone which comes away less easily from the relatively lower proportion of flesh. It is also the variety which is extensively shipped to the UK, for the 'undiscriminating' British consumer. As managing director, Sr Carmona's public view has to be much more even-handed: 'Every variety has its enthusiast,' he says.

Picking olives is an immensely labour-intensive task; no machine has been found to better hand-picking. Yet today it's unpopular work, and with the current problem of the government subsidies to unemployed agricultural workers, employers believe the people don't want to work. The olive is picked while still green and in the commercial process is passed through a caustic soda bath to take out the bitterness. After thorough washing it goes through a lactic fermentation to bring out the sugars. Black olives are similarly produced by a chemical process, or by a newer process of oxidation, which the Spanish olive-growers learned from a chemist who was sent over from California. Andalusian technology has had a chance to shine here, producing machinery which can stone up to 2,000 olives a minute: '*Una barbaridad,*' beams Sr Carmona proudly of the enormity of it all.

The growers of many foodstuffs have banded together to create the quality mark for their product, the *Denominación de Origén*. This mark is an assurance that the product comes from within a demarcated region and is up to certain standards. The DOC, as it is called, is equivalent to the French *Appellation Contrôlée* for wines. Surely Seville olives, of all things, deserve a DOC? The answer is, yes, of course, but only if the producers want it. The Seville olive-growers are an independent-minded lot, reflecting their Andalusian spirit. As one observer commented wearily, 'For a DOC you need a very disciplined group of producers and they're not.' In the meantime, they face increasing threats as Spain enters the Single European Market. For years, Spain had a gentlemen's agreement with California that it would not compete with their black olives, if California did not compete with Spain's green ones. This agreement has now been broken. Consumption of olives has increased worldwide and, at present, production and consumption are more or less in equilibrium, but production is on the increase. The *sevillanos* see the greatest threat to them close at home, in Morocco, which has plans to have 300,000 hectares under olive production in twenty years, using the *picolín*, the olive that works equally well for eating and for oil, which will give Morocco flexibility for the future. Sr Carmona is particularly concerned because Morocco's ties with France give it 'easy entry to the EC markets, without it having to pay the extra taxes it should pay'.

Olive trees surround Seville and cast their special silvery shade over the arid landscape. In the city itself the tree that gives shelter and relief from the burning sun is the bitter orange, apparently as resilient amid the fumes as the plane in London. But how much more beautiful, with its shiny leaves, its gentle perfume, its decorative blossom and its colourful fruit is the Seville orange. Though it came to Seville with the Islamic conquest, could have been invented just for such a city of romantic symbolism. But if the olive is more or less holding its own, the Seville orange, as an agricultural product, is in grave decline. According to the EC it does not even exist. Today there are only three main co-operatives, one smaller co-operative and five private companies who are involved in the business, and they all have other burgeoning interests in related fields. The export of fresh oranges to Britain just after Christmas for the ritual making of marmalade is now really no more than a token.

Bitter oranges would have been exported from the fifteenth and sixteenth centuries, but it was not until the nineteenth century that the trade with Scotland was established. Antonio Romero Carmona, a stalwart of the Seville orange business for many years, describes Scotland as *'la cuna de la mermelada'*, or the 'cradle of marmalade', in the loving terms in which one might talk of the 'cradle of civilisation'. There are various stories about how marmalade was invented: was it perhaps Mrs Baxter having to dispose of a batch of unexpected oranges in Dundee, doing what any frugal housewife would do and turning them into jam? Whatever the story, British companies became involved and the exporting was based on a mixture of Spanish and British capital, just as so many of the sherry companies had been. While marmalade was the smart thing on every well-dressed British breakfast table, it was never as popular as, say, strawberry jam. The growers had no great incentive to increase their production, and neither grower nor producer wanted to be involved in the risks of marketing a product for which there was limited demand. The fact that there was never a demand for the product in Spain is underlined by the fact that there is no generic word in Spanish for bitter orange jam, what in English we call marmalade. *Mermelada* and *confitura* both mean jam of any variety – including bitter orange.

Today Seville produces between 12,000 and 25,000 tonnes of bitter oranges a year, depending on the weather, of which it exports up to 20,000 tonnes. The UK takes some ninety per cent of the exports, but only some three million kilos are fresh oranges, a fifty per cent drop on the quantity of fresh oranges exported just ten years earlier. Fresh oranges are always a problem, in that they deteriorate so quickly, but even so the collapse in the fresh bitter orange market has been dramatic. The bulk of the oranges arrive in the UK already part-processed, to be made up into jams and jellies in the UK throughout the year, and it is at this stage that the orange arrives cut up into the miserable slivers we are supposed to like. For a month of the year the processing factories in Seville are worked to capacity, cleaning and preparing the oranges; the rest of the time the machinery lies forlorn, reeking of oranges despite relentless cleaning. The exporters have therefore been much more interested in extracting the essence of the orange, but this is now under threat with the arrival of chemical analogues. It is no wonder that the growers are uprooting their trees and replacing them with a more commercial product such as peaches or nectarines. Demand and supply are in almost exact equilibrium. The producers have therefore had to start harvesting for commercial production the oranges that decorate the city's streets. Not all of them: no one would want to eat the polluted oranges of the Avenida de la Constitución facing the cathedral. But next time you are sitting under an orange tree in a square, eating a *tapa* or enjoying a meal at midnight, take a look at the fruit growing above you. It may be about to find its way into your pot of marmalade.

JOSE
GONZALEZ
SEVILLA
CANOVAS DEL CASTILLO 16

AZULEJOS
NUEVOS MODELOS
CUARTOS DE BAÑO

SUCURSAL EN CORDOBA
GRAN CAPITAN 19

8. One continuous party

'*Hoy es fiesta*' was one of the first phrases I learned in Spanish. I could never understand why I had been taught it. Not until I came to Seville, and discovered that 'today's a festival' is a phrase that can be used in conversation practically every day of the year. There is always something to celebrate, and if, by chance, life should be slack in the city, then one of the nearby towns or villages is sure to be celebrating something.

The first major festival of the year comes at Epiphany, with the Three Kings. Despite the barrage of Hollywood films about Santa Claus, Spain still holds true to the *Reyes Magos*. With enormous patience, children have to wait until their presents come at Epiphany. During this time they can visit the nativity scenes set up throughout the city. On 5 January three well-known *sevillanos* – a politician, perhaps, and a singer, and a bullfighter – dress up as the kings and are led in a long procession through the chilly streets. The children shout with delight as the brightly-coloured kings throw them sweets from their carriages. At home that night children put out on the balcony, a pair of shoes belonging to each member of the household, and in the living room three glasses, some brandy and *turrón* for the kings, together with some water and straw for their camels. Next morning the food and drink have gone and in their place are the family's presents. Each of the shoes, too, will have some little presents inside. On 6 January, everyone eats the *roscón de reyes*, the sweet bread ring decorated with crystallised fruits and sprinkled with sugar, hoping that they will be the lucky one to find the little porcelain charm inside and be *rey de la faba*, or king ('of the bean') for the day.

February brings *carnaval*, the traditional time for the Catholic world to let off steam, before Lent begins. In Spain the steam still comes off with more of a blast, because *carnaval* was banned throughout the Franco years. Under the dictatorship of national-Catholicism, *carnaval* was altogether too expressive, too anarchic and too critical of authority to be allowed. A number of villages and towns in the province celebrate *carnaval* with cavalcades and entertainments, and undoubtedly the best place to go is Cádiz, on the coast two hours away. For several days the already crowded city on its little peninsula is crammed to bursting with people who have come to watch the *carnaval* processions, to join in the eating and drinking and to hear the singing. Choirs from all over the province compete in producing the funniest and rudest songs. Many of them are short, just a matter of a few couplets, ending up with a resounding punch-line, and they parody anybody well-known – singers, the manager of the local football team, and especially politicians. The Prime Minister Felipe González, his former deputy Alfonso Guerra and Alfonso's brother Juan are frequent targets. As *sevillanos*, they are more or less local boys, and therefore easy to bait. There is a treatise to be written about the contrasts between those two historic cities of Seville and Cádiz and their people. There is no doubt that Cádiz is the place to go for a laugh; its citizens, the *gaditanos*, tell the funniest shaggy dog stories I have ever heard. The *sevillanos* are above that kind of thing. Their great sense of fun does not descend to the belly laugh.

If Cádiz is the national focus of attention for its *carnaval*, then Seville undoubtedly is for Semana Santa, Holy Week. Every hotel, *pensión* and floor space is booked up far in advance. Semana Santa has become a grand lure for tourism in the last fifteen years, one of the most striking spectacles in the world, but one of the hardest for the outsider to follow. In brief, fifty-seven brotherhoods or *cofradías* take to the streets between Palm Sunday and Easter Sunday. Each brotherhood has between 500 and 2,000 people processing with two, or sometimes three, *pasos* or floats, one representing one of the stations of the cross, the other a stylised portrayal of the grieving Virgin.

Do not be deceived into thinking that this is simply a remarkable demonstration of faith by a mass of believers. The Church's temporal power in Seville is waning rapidly, and its spiritual influence is being battered by the materialistic culture of our times. But you do not have to be a confirmed Catholic to feel its impact. In the processions there is indeed an expression of religious belief for some, but for many the sentiment comes from taking part in the annual renewal of the history of a city and its people. There is the whole culture of the *bulla*, the crowd, of being part of the large throng in the street or *plaza*, moving with it and sharing its moods. There is drama, which seduces the *sevillano* who is accustomed to the sounds, the bright colours and the passion the *pasos* display. And there is death. The *pasos* are about death, and for a week death walks the streets, in the midst of the bustle of city life. Only one *paso* concerns the life-enhancing message of resurrection, and that is the single *paso* of 'Resurrection Sunday', belonging to a brotherhood which dates back only to 1982.

Many of the brotherhoods have their beginnings in the old trade guilds. The bakers' brotherhood is popularly known as 'Los Panaderos', though more properly as the Pontificia, Real, llustre y Fervorosa Hermandad y Archicofradía de Nazarenos de Nuestro Padre Jesús del Soberano Poder en su Prendimiento ('the seizure of Jesus'), Nuestra Señora de Regla y San Andrés Apóstol. In 1575 the guild of silversmiths founded a brotherhood; when it subsequently moved to the building which is now the Museo de Bellas Artes, it naturally acquired the nickname 'El Museo'. 'Los Negritos' was founded under the patronage of Archbishop Gonzalo de Mena for black and mulatto slaves, to prevent them being maltreated by their owners, and it admitted only black brothers up until 1847. Similarly 'Los Gitanos' was founded by gypsies in 1573 to prevent racist persecution or repression by the authorities.

Most of the floats have a story behind them, if you do but ask. The Christ of 'Cachorro', for instance, which comes from the former gypsy district of Triana, represents Christ at the moment of death. Tradition has it that the sculptor copied a dying gypsy known as 'El Cachorro'.

Today the brotherhoods are still very influential. If you want to get anywhere in Seville, except for politics, I was repeatedly told, then you have to be high up in a brotherhood. One observer put it more succinctly: 'You don't tangle with the *cofrades*.' The Calvario is known as a closed circle for *sevillanos* with plenty of money and power; the Silencio is another such, whose *Hermano Mayor* or head is the well-connected Eduardo Ybarra Hidalgo; the Gran Poder has a reputation for being right wing.

The first brotherhood was founded in 1340, and the first procession in Semana Santa was held sixteen years later. In these early processions the brothers merely carried a cross, but by the fifteenth century they had incorporated floats of the Virgin and of Christ. The greatest sculptures were carved in the sixteenth century, by artists of international rank such as Pedro Roldán, his daughter Luisa Roldán de Mena, Juan de Mesa and Juan Martínez Montañés, but images are still being created today, either for new brotherhoods, or to enlarge existing tableaux of Christ, or to replace damaged figures. (In 1991 the Cristo de la Sed was lifted so suddenly that his fixing broke and he fell from the crucifix against one of the other figures on the *paso*. The Christ had to be laid down on the *paso*, and it processed in silence, 'making a sad entry to its church', as the radio reported.) It is important to remember that none of the floats is a static design. The processions may look unchanged from the sixteenth century, but each year the brotherhoods are adding to and changing the floats, and investing in jewels for the ornate costumes of the figures.

Some of the *pasos* can be very big, with five or six figures of apostles, Romans and soldiers, a horse or an olive tree, in addition to the Christ himself. The Virgin always comes last, at the very end of the procession. She stands alone, wearing an expression of grief, under a canopy or *palio*, embroidered in gold, silver and silk. The *canastilla* on which the statues stand is of carved wood, gilded or covered with sheets of silver, and is perhaps the ultimate expression of Spanish baroque. The *pasos* are lit by candles, most distinctively by *candelabros de cola*, cascades of candles in glass vases that spill unexpectedly down the backs of the *pasos* of the Virgin. Every vacant space on the float is filled with flowers. Though there are variations, the *sevillanos* are as traditional in their floral decorations for Semana Santa as they are in the rest of their lives: red carnations or small purple irises represent the blood Christ shed for us; white carnations and gladioli the purity of the Virgin. Semana Santa is a monument to the labours of the florists of Seville. A *paso* of the *misterio*, of Christ, takes some 3,000 carnations; a Virgin, 1,800. It takes three hours to decorate one of these floats, pinning on each flower individually. Many flowers are used to create a carpet, but they also decorate the float in sprays. Unfortunately in the 1950s they developed a custom of shaping the bouquets into solid globes on stands, like topiary. But while topiary has a certain appeal, nothing could be more unnatural than these lumpen sprays.

The *nazarenos*, who walk in pairs with the *pasos*, wear the hooded, peaked hats once worn by the Inquisition, and subsequently taken up by the Ku Klux Klan. This connection with the KKK gives the observer an unintended frisson. There are all kinds of complicated symbolisms and messages flying about in Semana Santa for those with a will to catch them, but a racist intent to murder blacks and their white collaborators is not one of them. For the visitor with a taste for kitsch the sweet shops of the city sell little dolls dressed as *nazarenos* during Semana Santa.

From whichever Church they start, the *nazarenos* must process to La Campana, the beginning of the *carrera official*, the official route. (La Campana is a central space, neither crossroads nor *plaza*, well known for the *confitería* of the same name, with waitresses in Laura-Ashley-ish aprons. A *campana* is a bell tower, but there is none there now.) One of the best views in La Campana must be from the balconies of the floors above the Macdonalds there. The fast-food ground floor of the building is alien to this city (though it is not the only burger bar), but the upper floors with their wrought-iron balconies look as if nothing has changed.

All the way along, the routes will be lined with people; *plazas* will be entirely filled. Once on the official route *nazarenos* cannot stop for a drink or leave the procession. They must move slowly up calle Sierpes, across the Plaza de San Francisco between the city council's stands for its guests, up the Avenida de la Constitución and through the cathedral. Once out of the cathedral they can relax if they wish, though some brotherhoods prefer to keep in disciplined files until they have returned to their church. The newspapers include guides to the timetables: *ABC* publishes a daily pull-out: *El Correo de Andalucía* has an equally useful supplement with interesting features. The basic information is also contained in a handy paperback sold by the brotherhoods' magazine, *El Cofrade*. There are seven or eight processions a day, starting from midday and finishing after midnight, some of them lasting as much as twelve hours. In addition, there are processions during the night of Maundy Thursday and the early hours of Good Friday, *La Madrugada*. With only the briefest break on Good Friday this makes one almost continuous thread of processions from 3 p.m. on Thursday afternoon with the *salida*, exit, from their churches of the brotherhoods of Los Negritos and Las Cigarreras, to the *entrada*, or entrance, to its church of El Cachorro sometime around 3 a.m. on Saturday morning. Not all of the *nazarenos* are by any means *penitentes*, but walking the route in the stifling mask amid the crowds is as exhausting as it is exhilarating.

The formal ceremonies for Semana Santa begin with the *Pregón*, a speech reflecting on Semana Santa in Seville, and its particular qualities, delivered by a Seville dignitary. This is usually published in book form. When Palm Sunday comes, a number of the larger houses will decorate their balconies with a large palm frond, which will stay up long after Easter is over. This practice is much less common than it used to be, having become, for many, a symbol of the right-wing bourgeoisie. Palm Sunday is a cheerful day, full of anticipation of the extraordinary events of the week to come. After mass, people go visiting the decorated floats that will be out on the streets in the afternoon. It's a very social activity, an extension of the *paseo*, as one strolls to church in one's best clothes, stopping to talk to friends on the way. Monday is quieter and more solemn, but by Wednesday the excitement is building up.

Eusebio Sánchez has been taking part in Semana Santa since he was three. He's twelve now, and very calm about the afternoon's impending procession. He's sitting watching the cartoons on the television, drinking *cola cao*, chocolate milk, and eating *magdalenas*, while his mother and grandmother rush about getting ready. His robe and cape are hanging from the lamp in the sitting room. His *capirote*, the sinister-looking hood with its cardboard cone and two slits for the eyes, sits on a chair; his white nylon gloves beside. His father, Eusebio Senior, pauses from his late lunch of a *bocadillo* and a beer in front of the television to lace the 'silver' buckles to his son's shoes. Everyone has to go shod in silver buckles in this brotherhood; many of the adults in the procession will have had shoes especially made.

Eusebio's little sister Carmen, aged eight, is in her best dress for this special day. It goes down well below her knees, to give plenty of growing room. The dress has an enormous white collar which will require regular smoothing by anxious adults as the evening progresses. She's chewing a *bocadillo* very slowly, while her mother brushes her luxuriant hair and restrains it with a velvet alice band. Thus attired, she has the doll-like air of the Mediterranean infant. (This is the intention. The affectionate '*!Que muñeca!*', 'What a dear little doll'!, is a term of great praise to children.)

At the last minute, to avoid creasing his robe, Eusebio is

dressed. First he dons the gown on top of his jeans and shirt. It is yellow cotton, with red buttons running from neck to hem and up the cuff. Next comes the gilded medallion of the brotherhood on a red silken band, and the gloves. This is the last year that Eusebio will be able to wear this particular robe. It is getting too tight across the shoulders and will need to be exchanged for another. Eusebio picks up his membership card, which tells him where and when to assemble in the church. The organisation of the numbers of the *nazarenos* in and around their small churches bears a great resemblance to school fire-drill. The cape and *capirote*, together with two kilos of boiled sweets to hand out to children in the street, and a bottle of water and a bag of *bocadillos* to keep the pilgrim going, are carried down to the car.

Eusebio's grandmother lives in an eastern *barrio* of Seville. It is worth taking the car into town to save a weary walk back later. But there is nowhere to park: the buses have been terminated early, and the centre of town is cut off. It is a risk in Holy Week; if you leave it too late to get out of town at lunchtime you may find yourself stranded at 3.30 p.m. in the centre with no buses or taxis. Still, having the car a few hundred metres closer is better than nothing when it comes to the end of the evening and going home. Once in the street Eusebio dons his cape, with its crest of the brotherhood on the shoulder, and his *capirote*. He runs ahead to meet his cousins and stepbrothers in the *estanco*, the tobacconist, at the Puerta Osario. His grandfather used to run the well-known *estanco* at this crossroads, and the family, who are all in or following the procession, have chosen to meet here. There's also a *nazarena* among their number, one of the teenage girl cousins, taking advantage of the fact that Seville now allows women to join in. What, one cynic asked, is the point of women dressing in such anonymous costumes? The point about Semana Santa, he said, is for women to be seen in their finery, especially on Maundy Thursday and Good Friday, not to be devout incognito.

From all quarters people are strolling into the city centre. They walk in couples and families, arm in arm. Teenage girls are a particular hazard with their habit of walking three abreast. Baby buggies add to the perils. We spill on to the road as the last cars make their escape. The ones that are left risk damage from weary spectators and from uncontrolled *pasos*. We pass El Bacalao, its shop windows full of unappetising sheets of bristly, grey, dried salt cod. Throughout Lent the shop has been doing excellent business, as families substitute fish for meat in such traditional dishes as *garbanzos con bacalao*.

Eusebio's father takes his son off to find his place in the procession. Eusebio Senior still pays his dues to the brotherhood, but chooses not to join the processions any longer – 'I had a crisis of faith,' he laughs. When his son was little, though, he used to go with him. He returns to tell us that Eusebio is in the fourth group in front of the *paso* of the Christ on the right-hand side. This is essential information, since there is no other means of recognising one's beloved amidst 599 other pilgrims. We learn, too, that Eusebio's stepbrother will be carrying one of the immense silver trumpets in the front row. There's still another hour before Eusebio's procession is scheduled to leave the church, and it will be another quarter of an hour after that before we catch sight of him. We therefore leave him to watch some of the other processions, and meet up again at the end of the Alameda de Hércules opposite El Pájaro Loco, a pet shop selling vitamins, collars, bird seed and frozen meat for pets.

Eusebio is not exactly pleased to see us; he does not wish to have the women in his family rushing up to offer him food and drink. Still, he takes a refill of boiled sweets. Many of the younger *nazarenos* carry such a supply of sweets to dole out to the children lining the route. It is not a matter of waiting politely until the gift is offered; the children run up and down the processions, tugging at the *nazarenos'* robes, demanding sweeties. You have to choose your *nazareno*. Those who are in the procession for spiritual reasons disapprove and are likely to be rude. The children also pester for wax from the *nazarenos'* candles, since the *nazarenos* are fair game on their interminable stops along the route. An assiduous collector can have a holy tennis ball by the end of the evening. Eusebio's sister decides to make a start with a piece of silver paper at the core, but after burning her hands with the wax and getting it down her cardigan she decides against it and demands candy floss instead.

There's a lot of eating going on in the crowd: popcorn, salted nuts, boiled sweets, ice-creams and *bocadillos* in the street, as well as the full array of *tapas* in bars. The mingled smells of food, perfume and flowers would be gorgeous were it not for the invasion of tobacco from the crowds. Much of the food is junk, admittedly, but essential to keep you going as the long evening wears on. Seville's bars do excellent business during the week, and put up their prices for Semana Santa as they do for *feria*. It is vital to make good use of them if you want to keep going. The ideal, of course, is to have a friend, or as is more usual a friend of a friend of a friend, who has open house the day(s) the procession(s) pass by his or her balcony. Then you can sit and eat and drink until the moment the first *paso* arrives and then recline in comfort until the next one.

Eusebio's brotherhood, La Lanzada, is particularly well endowed with small children and the solemn procession is interrupted by fond parents running in and out of the lines with video cameras. The little ones come in a batch, so as not to lower the tone of what follows. It is also easier to organise this way, as weary infants can be taken home as the evening passes. The toddlers carry baskets from which to dole out their sweeties. The babes are carried, or pushed in buggies like little archbishops. All the children are in the uniform, though without *capirote*; some wear clerical gear rather than *nazareno* style. The effect is like that of performing dogs in their circus ruffs; it raises the eyebrows rather than warms the heart.

Eusebio carries a cream candle. As we get nearer to the *paso*, the colour changes. In La Lanzada the dignitaries carry red candles; for La Macarena they are green. Either way, it's a sign that the *paso* is near. Just before the *paso* itself come the four or six *ciriales*, or huge candlesticks. (If you stand in a square and watch a procession leave its church, the *ciriales* are the sign that the long waiting is coming to an end and that the *paso* is imminent.) And then suddenly the *paso* of the crucified Christ is upon us. The space is too narrow for it and we have to squeeze together to let it pass. The forty-eight *costaleros* are taking the corner too gently, and the full weight of the *paso* bears down upon a parked car beside us. We scream out a warning and the *paso* veers sharply round, just missing the car. The crowd stretches out to touch the silver sides of the juggernaut, as the Christ towers above us. Then it is gone down the street to be followed immediately by the band.

Very few *pasos* go out in silence. In general, the standard of music is poor, relying on some fifteen drummers to provide the drama that the rest of the brass band lacks. Part of the problem is that too many bands are needed to accompany all the processions, and not all of them are up to it. Much of the music sounds tired and tawdry, even 'Amargura', 'sorrow', the march which has become practically the official theme tune of Seville's Semana Santa, composed in 1919 by Manuel Font de Anta. The journalist Nicolás Salas has discovered that 'Amargura' was played at the anarchist leader Buenaventura Durruti's funeral in Barcelona in the middle of the Civil War in November 1936. Certainly, he remarks, no one can have realised the implications of the tune they were playing. Los Servitos, on Saturday afternoon, is one of the few processions that can be relied upon for good music. The music, of whatever quality, echoes not just through the streets, but also through the bars, many of which play the popular tunes of Semana Santa.

As the Christ processes round the square, we wait interminably for the Virgin. La Lanzada takes about three-quarters of an hour to go by, and it is one of the medium-sized processions. The square is packed, and there are balloon-sellers around, another sure sign that a *paso* is close. The balloons are of the expensive, silvered helium variety, and the *tortugas ninja* predominate. Look for the turtles, find the Virgin. Now come a group of *penitentes, nazarenos* who have chosen the tougher route. They wear the *capirote*, but without its supporting cone, so that the hood lies flat down their backs. Some are carrying crosses; some are walking in socks; a very few are barefoot. Their crosses look insubstantial and mass-produced. Some *penitentes* have two or three crosses taped together to increase the penance. The days of the obvious gestures, the flagellation and the chained feet, are past. The brotherhoods *de sangre*, of blood, who were renowned for flagellating themselves until the blood came, were outlawed in the eighteenth century. However Canal Sur, the local television station, usually manages to find a few good examples of the ankles of contemporary *penitentes* chained together for their daily bulletins from Seville and all round Andalusia.

The Virgin comes at last, lit by tens of candles. (Somewhere in the procession you can be sure to find a man with a wheelbarrow. He carries spare candles and collects the ones of the *nazarenos* who drop out. They are expensive, so the leftovers can be melted down for next year.) In front of the Virgin comes the man with the miserable – though clearly blessed – task of relighting the candles. Even on a still night the movement of the *paso* will be sure to blow most of the candles out between each stop. So there is one official whose job is to walk backwards in front of the *paso*, forever relighting the candles from a long pole.

The Virgin, carried by her thirty-six *costaleros*, looks reasonably ethereal. But the effect is destroyed by the noise she makes, reminiscent of the betraying thumping and heavy breathing of the ballerina. Each Virgin's canopy is composed of pieces of silver plate which – there's no other word for it – clank with a certain lack of elegance. With her passing, and that of her band, La Lanzada moves on. We leave it to go and have a beer and *tapas* with a friend who lives in the centre and is glued to the football on the television. Eusebio meanwhile has joined the official route to the cathedral. Once out of the cathedral the discipline is inclined to lapse; the performance is over. Discipline is not maintained inside the cathedral. A friend who was a *nazareno* for the first time in 1991 was struck by the way the processions broke up, as *nazarenos* had a smoke and wandered off to the lavatory. There may be several processions in the cathedral at once, so the potential for confusion is great.

We met up with Eusebio after the official route was over and took him to La Alicantina, a classic seafood bar in the Plaza del Salvador, for a well-deserved *tapa*. At 1 a.m. we all needed something to keep us going. Across the city, bars were full of off-duty *nazarenos* and their families. The Plaza del Salvador was as busy as a weekday – busier, if anything – and the waiters were as hardworked as the *costaleros*. We sat under the full moon, illuminated as if on a stage set. We were weary. Even the children were drooping. And then Christ appeared in the *plaza* and the dream was complete.

In other, smaller towns and other years, I have seen Christ walk in the streets. But the *bulla*, the bustle and mass of humanity in Seville, frequently distract the mind and the spirit from the *paso*. I marvel at the strength of the *costaleros*, the endurance of the *hermandades*, the size of the crowds. But only rarely does Semana Santa touch me. That night in the Plaza San Salvador was one. It had been an evening dominated by this-worldy concerns: would Eusebio survive the procession, would his grandmother's feet last out, would his sister stay awake? But then the *paso* of the Christ of La Lanzada ('with the spear-wound') came slowly up across the square in front of us, casting vast shadows on the walls. On the *paso* the Virgin, St John and the three Marys look on as the Roman Longinus pierces the side of the crucified Christ with a spear. The statuary of La Lanzada is not outstanding. But the theatre of Semana Santa worked for me then under the bright moon. I saw the Christ in his suffering for the world. And I felt secretly relieved that I was only drinking mineral water. What if He had found me drinking something stronger?

A fortnight later I sat in the *plaza* one lunchtime on the steps of the church of San Salvador, waiting for a friend. It took me a few seconds to realise it was the same *plaza*. Only the Bar Alicantina next door to the church confirmed that this empty square, with just a few shoppers and a boy playing football, was the same place. Then I felt the shiver that this was the place where I'd seen the Christ. This is the power of

Seville

Holy Week: not the crush and the spectacle, but the subsequent recollection of the presence of Christ and the Virgin
incarnate in the city.

Thursday and Friday are both public holidays. Many *sevillanos* take advantage of the *puente*, the bridge or long weekend, to go away to the country or the beach and avoid the
crowds in the city – only to be confronted by crowds on the
beach if the weather is good. The rest of the city is out on
the streets on Thursday morning, visiting the *pasos* in their
churches. Every morning during Semana Santa it is customary
to visit the *pasos* in their churches – a favourite one, or a few
– that are due to go out that afternoon. Each church gives the
visitors a tiny strip of brightly coloured ribbon to pin in their
lapels; those who have chosen to tour the churches of the city
can end up with a decorative display of little ribbons flutter-
ing in the breeze. Thursday and Friday are especially busy.
Many women dress in black and drape black lace *mantillas*
from the tall ornate combs in their hair. To relieve the
solemnity they also wear red carnations in their hair and on
their dresses. Their partners will be in dark suits and ties,
or navy jackets and dark trousers, their hair slicked back,
their posture proud and erect. One of the papers, *ABC*, a
national with a local edition, changes into awed and
devotional prose during Semana Santa. So it says of the
Thursday *paseo*: 'Because God is here amongst us, the
sevillanos put on their party clothes.'

Jesús Casado, a lecturer in the university's education department, is an *aficionado* of Semana Santa and an ideal companion for the week. He follows Semana Santa as it should be
followed, running from street corner to street corner to catch
the *pasos* and avoid the miles of *nazarenos*. (No one crosses
a procession while it is moving, and even when it is stationary
it can be intimidating to pass between the *nazarenos*, standing
at ease with their long candles. Better to avoid them
altogether.) He examines the newspaper timetable like a stud-

202

ent of racing form, calculating when he can see the best processions in the best places. He starts with a splendid lunch for his friends, to set them up for the long afternoon ahead. It ends with an enormous iced sponge gateau, sixty centimetres in diameter, as baroque as any *paso*, which has been bought for the occasion in the country village of Trigueros.

In the gardens below his flat the *costaleros* from the neighbouring brotherhood of Montesión, the men who carry the floats on their necks, are getting ready, as we fortify ourselves with coffee and cake. Each of them wears a uniform white shirt with the symbol of the brotherhood. Other brotherhoods are less formal; I saw one *costalero* wearing a tee-shirt with 'crew' written on it. The rest of the costume owes little to twentieth-century devices to spread or relieve the pain. They wear simple black trousers and black espadrilles; in some *cofradías* the *costaleros* wear shorts. Around their waists a fellow *costalero* straps a deep black belt as tightly as possible. This supports the back against the immense weight. On their heads they wear a rectangle of stout cloth, with the back flap folded to form a thick pad on the back of the neck. Despite this, their shoulders are rubbed and bleeding from the task. In the old days, the *costaleros* were usually dockers. In 1973 some students from the university were the first amateurs to do the task when they carried their own *paso*. Now the *costaleros* are nearly all amateurs who pay fees to the brotherhood, though some are assisted by professionals who hire themselves out during the week. There is no textbook to teach the *costalero*. He learns by experience, standing next to an old hand, perhaps practising first in one of the less important Semana Santa processions in a nearby town.

The bearers take turns in their tasks, but each *paso* needs at any one time between thirty and sixty *costaleros*, depending on its size, simply to carry it, hidden underneath the draped *canastilla*. In Málaga, the *paso* is carried on long rods like stretchers and the carriers are plain to see. In Seville in Semana Santa the *paso* arrives in a moment of real artifice, apparently untouched by human hand. The *paso* is controlled by the *capataz*. He beats the knocker on the front of the *paso* three times, and the *paso* is up and off. He decides when to stop, for frequent breaks are essential, and he guides the *paso* through the narrow streets with their perilously overhanging balconies, shouting out instructions to the invisible bearers. I remember being caught in a crowd in calle Cuna, as the *paso* of the Panaderos, of Jesus in the Mount of Olives, came bearing down upon me, and feeling a moment of absolute terror. There was no escape in front of the *paso* as it marched on, and behind me was a wall of people five deep who had fought for their standing room and did not want to yield a millimetre. The seconds passed and eventually I was frightened enough to fight my way out past the disgruntled crowd. Calle Cuna is not especially narrow. The problem there is the crush of people. Calle Alcaicería, on the other hand, is called a suicide spot, because of the risks of being caught in a crowd with a *paso* coming. Young people enjoy the risks in the same way as those that go bull-running in Pamplona.

Much of the fascination of the processions comes from an appreciation of the skill of the *capataz* and his *costaleros*. To leave and enter their churches, the *costaleros* usually have to go down on their knees to move the *pasos*. This will be greeted with roars of appreciation and applause from the watching crowds. When a *paso* of the Virgin passes another church, it will make a half-turn and curtsey, to the delight of the onlookers. In calle Aguilas, the Virgin of the Negritos curtseys to the nuns in the convent. The nuns are clustered behind a small grille and the candlelight of the *paso* highlights the delight on the sisters' faces. Sometimes you will find members of the public walking backwards in a group, facing the Virgin. Walking with them, part of the procession, creates a feeling of intense excitement. You have to trust with the strangers around you that you will all move together and not trip over as you stare at the *paso*. Above you towers the Virgin, lit by tiers of candles. On either side, the onlookers press themselves to the walls to make way for you. The next day the street will be empty, with few signs that there was ever such a crush of people or such a *pièce de théâtre*. But something about the street, a balcony or the pattern of a lamp, will remind you of the power of that experience, and that is a sense that remains, however faintly, all year.

At the end of the street, in the Plaza de Pilatos, the procession stops again in front of the Casa de Pilatos. The Duke and Duchess of Medinaceli are standing alone on the balcony of the house and various members of the household are watching from the windows. (Royal-watchers and gossips in the crowd scan the windows excitedly, certain that this year they can see one of the *Infantas*, the king's daughters, watching from a window.)

Grasping each other firmly by the hand for fear of getting lost in the engulfing crowds, we run after Jesús Casado from street corner to street corner, to catch the passing of the Cristo de la Exaltación or the Virgen del Valle. Enthusiasts like Jesús Casado and his friends stay up all Thursday night in order to watch the greatest processions, of La Madrugada (dawn), pronounced '*Madrugà*' by the *andaluces*. This is the one night of the year, exceeding even New Year's Eve, when *sevillanos* do not go to bed if they can help it. There are three great rivals: the Virgen de la Esperanza Macarena (the 'Virgin of Hope' from the Macarena district), probably carved by Martínez Montañés, with 2,300 *nazarenos*; the Virgen de la Esperanza de Triana, which dates from the nineteenth century and has some 1,600 *nazarenos*; and the Jesús del Gran Poder ('Jesus of the Great Power'), by Juan de Mesa, with 2,000 *nazarenos*.

The competition between the Virgins' supporters is particularly strong. The Esperanza de Triana comes from the Triana district on the other side of the river; like the Macarena district, it was traditionally working class. Triana had a greater proportion of gypsies and sailors among its residents and is the acknowledged Seville home of flamenco. Both districts are equally vociferous in praise of their Virgins of Hope. Much of the argument centres on which has the more beautiful and sensitive expression. The general consensus is that La Macarena is *más guapa*, prettier; La Triana is *más mujer*, she is more of a woman, she has lived the pains and ecstasies of the women of Seville.

Though both Virgins have associate brotherhoods abroad, Macarena has the international status and has come to be the most representative of Seville's Virgins. She was granted the gold medal of the city, like any outstanding dignitary, and wears it on a red and gold ribbon round her neck. This is lost beneath the enormous extravagance of her dress and cloak and the jewels that decorate every empty space; all the Virgins are ornate, but La Macarena, with her devout following, is more laden than most. The media catch the fever when the heroines of La Madrugada come. 'Here comes La Macarena,' cries the radio commentator, clearly not a member of the Richard Dimbleby school of outside broadcasting, from his post at La Campana. 'It's as if she has come down from the angels to Seville. *¡Que señora, que mujer, que madré!¡ La virgen de las virgenes! ¡Que bonita, que bonita!*' ('What a lady, what a woman, what a mother! The Virgin of all Virgins! How pretty she is, how pretty she is!')

When the Macarena arrives at one end of the street, the atmosphere instantly changes. You cannot see her yet, but you can hear the sound of the crowd. The photographers' lights flash as if at a film star, and the bursts of applause and cries of *'¡Guapa!'* echo down the street. The Macarena is led by an extraordinary guard of a hundred centurions, *los armaos*, a contraction of 'the armed ones', the only Virgin to have her own bodyguard. These are solid *sevillano* citizens in the full Roman army gear, complete with breast-plates, helmets and nodding plumes, who walk two by two along the route. When she arrives at La Campana, at the entrance to the official route, she is showered with rose petals. The best place to view the Macarena is protected from the crowd, upstairs, on a balcony. The most striking place to watch La Triana is without doubt the Triana Bridge, as she crosses to the cathedral at 3 a.m., or returns home some six hours later. She appears to be sailing over the waters of the river in which she is reflected. Both Virgins suffer from the hype accompanying them and carry a huge burden of sentiment and superstition. Can the small doll on the *paso* be worth the agony of waiting? For the crowd it certainly is, and even for the unaccustomed visitor.

For the visitor, the question is how best to enjoy Semana Santa. Undoubtedly, the answer is with someone who knows the city's streets and short cuts, and runs from one *paso* to the next. At the other extreme you can hire one of the small rush-bottomed or folding seats set out along the official route. The most expensive sites are La Campana and calle Sierpes, and the most expensive days are Palm Sunday, Maundy Thursday and La Madrugada.

The disadvantage of this is, first, the sheer tedium. Some of the great processions are interminably long. Second, as Jesús Casado found as a *nazareno*, the crowd on the *carrera official* is like a football crowd – the atmosphere is wrong. When you have stood uncomfortably in a *plaza* or a narrow street for half an hour waiting for the *paso*, you will give it a much more affectionate welcome than if you have been sitting down, eating and drinking your way through the evening. (The piles of litter along the *carrera official* after the processions are over are enormous, as is the quantity of thick wax spilled all across the road. But the moment the last Virgin has gone, the chairs are stacked away for the next day and the street cleaners in their orange suits are out, at whatever time of night, sweeping and hosing down the streets.) The answer perhaps is to spend the first day on the *carrera official*, to learn something about the structure of a procession, but to avoid it thereafter.

One solution is often to find a bar from which to watch the procession, though you have to arrive well in advance and fight for space. Certainly, nothing could be more pleasant if you can find a place than sitting out on the pavement in the Kiosco de las Flores by the river, watching the Virgen de la Estrella either as she crosses into Seville at 6 p.m. on Palm Sunday, or as she returns along calle Betis at midnight. One of the best places to see the processions is in their own *barrios*, where the feeling of the crowd will be that much stronger. The return of the Gitanos to its church of San Román, at midday on Good Friday, the very end of the Madrugada, is dramatic indeed. The procession comes slowly up calle del Sol, through the working-class district. The crowd has been gathering for a couple of hours in the plaza, and the sun is beating down. Tempers rise as people defend their tiny patch of hard-won space, especially if they have a wall or a car to lean on. Crowds are normally extremely good-natured during Semana Santa, but on this one occasion I felt the need to move to an exit. Very soon, a fight broke out. The loser was led off with a bloody nose. But when the Virgin appeared in the plaza all that was forgotten. On one of the crowded balconies a woman sang a *saeta* to the *paso*.

The *saeta* is one of the fundamental features of Semana Santa, though often better in recollection than in action. It has its beginnings in the psalms, though it seems to hark back to the melodies of the *muezzin*. It is a short song, of perhaps five lines, of petition, or praise, of the Virgin or the Christ, or a reflection on the sufferings of both, or a brief illustration of the Passion. From the crowd a voice rises:

> *Viéndote a Ti padecer*
> *morao se puso el lirio*
> *sangre brotó del clavel*
> *y la rosa en su delirio*
> *le llamó Gran Poder.*

('Watching You suffer, the iris turned purple, from the carnation poured forth blood, and the rose in its delirium called You Christ of the Great Power.')

In the mid-nineteenth century the *saeta* began to be sung in the street, but it was not until the early twentieth century that it became really popular. The great flamenco singers of the day – Antonio Mairena, Pastora Pavón, Manuel Torres, 'La Niña de la Alfalfa' – developed the *saetas*, applying the distinctive sound and phrasing of flamenco. Sometimes the *saetas* are impromptu, more often they are prepared. The best singers will have their patch, and the *capataz* in charge of the *paso* will know to stop directly beneath it. Says Pepe Peregil, one of the leading exponents, 'It's the hardest form of flamenco. There's no microphone, no accompanying voices, no guitar.' He prefers it when the crowd hear him out in silence, as befits the seriousness of the song, but more often they break into applause.

The third great procession of La Madrugada is Jesús del Gran Poder. Though there is a *paso* of the Virgin in this procession, the attention of all the onlookers is devoted to the Christ figure. The head of the brotherhood, the *Hermano Mayor*, is the small and wiry Antonio Ríos Ramos, whose spare office in the brotherhood's building adjoining the church is dominated by a portrait of the former *Hermano Mayor*, the Cardinal Archbishop Spínola. Antonio Ríos Ramos joined the brotherhood in 1976, and almost immediately entered its hierarchy. He has now served seven years as *Hermano Mayor*, a post for which there are elections every four years. All the posts are open to election, and it was proudly pointed out to me more than once that democracy existed in Seville from early times, in the brotherhoods, even if at the level of local and national politics it was still lacking. There are 8,000 members of the Gran Poder, 7,000 of them men. Women cannot hold office, but they play an active part in the social life of the brotherhood. Despite the apparent decline in church-going, especially among the young, the majority of the *hermanos* of the Gran Poder are aged between twenty-five and thirty. Something over a thousand members are outside the city, many of these in Central and Southern America, where they have similar processions in Holy Week. The iconography of the Gran Poder travelled with the Franciscans to Ecuador; there are forty-two images of the Gran Poder in the country.

The *Hermano Mayor* admits that the worship of the Gran Poder seems a little austere after the ecstasies aroused by La Macarena and La Triana. It is, Antonio Ríos Ramos says, very popular with bullfighters, because it expresses the physical sufferings they have experienced. The sharp spines in the crown of thorns and the blood on Christ's face represent the same agonies, while his mouth reveals a mixture of the bitterness and sweetness that he feels. During La Madrugada the expressiveness of the Gran Poder is enhanced by the way the *costaleros* walk. A *capataz* taught them the way to sway while walking *(rachear)*, and this makes Christ's gown swing, giving the distinct impression that he is walking through the streets carrying the cross to Calvary.

Semana Santa starts for Antonio Ríos Ramos on the Saturday before Palm Sunday. The Gran Poder is brought down from his usual position in the church, so that people can queue to kiss his hands (the *besamanos*). The sculptures have articulated arms for this purpose. The *Hermano Mayor* takes his turn at washing the hands of the Gran Poder, which become dirty from so many visitors kissing them. He regards the task as a great privilege and 'it brings a lump to the throat to see so many worshippers come.' On Tuesday night the Gran Poder is put in position on his *paso*, and on Wednesday the float is decorated with the red carnations of his Passion. Then on Thursday, everyone comes in their finery to visit the *paso* before its journey to the cathedral. 'It's wonderful to see people's faces. All types of people come, and He has a dialogue with each one of them.'

The brotherhood is busy throughout the year: in the church there are 360 weddings a year, and 'continuous' masses, requiring some seven priests. On Sundays the brotherhood has its own mass, and on Fridays they hold a *miserere*, which gives them time for spiritual reflection. After the *miserere* the members come to the clubroom, which a brother has recently endowed with an excellent tiled bar, where the women will do the drinks, and 'everyone washes up afterwards'.

Antonio Ríos Ramos stresses the importance of friendship in the brotherhood, although his preoccupations lie with its charitable works. In the old days many of the brotherhoods had their own hospitals – they were the National Health and the Social Security. The Hermandad de la Gran Poder has probably the largest charitable fund of any of the brotherhoods, with an income of some £300,000 a year. A committee meets every Thursday to dispense alms, and not just to the impoverished working classes who may need money for medicines or simply to survive. The brotherhood knows many members of the middle class whom it helps confidentially. The twenty-five members of the committee go out to visit the individuals in need to assess the cases, as does the *Hermano Mayor* himself. In other ways, too, the brotherhood supports the local economy: 'A lot of people live off us.' When a new robe was created for the *paso*, for instance, it took thirty-four people twenty-two months and cost the brotherhood £145,000.

Camilo José Cela records the remarkable life of a former chaplain of the Gran Poder, Juan Ramírez de Arellano y Bustamente, who died in 1678 aged 120 from a fall. The good chaplain said mass daily until his death. He was not ordained until he was ninety-nine. Before taking orders, he sailed to the Indies a number of times, learnt seven Indian languages, wrote a book of sonnets to the Virgin, married five times, and had forty-two legitimate children and nine bastards. At his ordination dinner there were more than eighty grandchildren.

The bachelor Antonio Ríos Ramos devotes his spare time to the Gran Poder and its followers. His opposite number at the Macarena, José Luis de Pablo Romero, points out that he has a wife and family, and that he cannot afford to spend the same amount of time. The Macarena is therefore run much like a very efficient business, a BMW in a world of saloon cars. One of the richest men in Seville, José Luis de Pablo Romero knows how to delegate, whether it's the administration or the charitable works. Though the literature of the *hermandades* speaks of being born into one's brotherhood, he proves that this need not always be so. He has risen quickly to the top, despite the fact that he used to belong to the Hermandad of the Gran Poder and changed over. He is in charge of 10,000 *hermanos*, 3,000 of whom are not *sevillanos*, but are spread across Spain and the rest of the world, especially Latin America. He too has illustrious predecessors as *Hermano Mayor*, including the eminent *ganadero* or rancher Eduardo Miura.

As the representative of the Macarena, the *Hermano Mayor* has a distinguished position in society. Whenever something important happens in the city, the recipients of the gold medal are invited, and the *Hermano Mayor* goes along as the representative of La Macarena. Whether it is to meet the king or the prime minister, or to visit the Maestranza bull-ring or the Ateneo, the literary society, José-Luis de Pablo Romero will be there. In fact, as a distinguished member of Seville society, he would be invited in his own right to many of these events.

Relations between the Macarena and the Gran Poder are warm, but they were not always so. At the beginning of the century the two brotherhoods became involved in an unseemly dispute over which should process along the official route first. Finally Archbishop Spínola stepped in and instructed them to sort it out. Today the Macarena follows the Gran Poder. Each year, though, before the procession starts, the Macarena's centurions march to the Church of the Gran Poder accompanied by a band, to do obeisance to the Gran Poder. In return, some *nazarenos* from the Gran Poder, leading members of the brotherhood, go to the Macarena's basilica to reaffirm their agreement. (A piece of one-upmanship: the Macarena's is the only basilica in the city.) The different ways the brotherhoods fulfil their agreement is instructive of the original middle/upper class–working class divide: the Gran Poder's representatives are a solemn deputation of *nazarenos* dressed in black; the Macarena sends her band of merry men.

The Macarena, like the Gran Poder, is very popular with bullfighters. She is identified with the great *torero* Joselito el Gallo, as the Esperanza de Triana is with Juan Belmonte. When Joselito el Gallo was gored to death, the Macarena was dressed in black – to the disapproval of the archbishop. (This is a common practice; when the popular *Hermano Mayor* of La O and former secretary of the General Council of Brotherhoods died last year, the Virgin processed in mourning.) As the most popular representation of the Virgin in Seville, the Macarena is seen everywhere: in taxis, by the check-out desks at El Corte Inglés, on key rings and ash trays. Not even the communist party could ignore her influence. The poet Rafael Alberti dedicated a poem to her at the party congress held in Dos Hermanas during Semana Santa in the early 1980s:

Déjame esta madrugada
llevar tu mente en mi pena,
Virgen de la Macarena,
llamándote camarada,
que no hay bien que se resista
hoy en la tierra
al Partido Comunista.

('This dawn, let me carry the memory of you in my grief, Virgin of the Macarena, calling you comrade, for there's nothing today, on earth or in heaven that can hold out against the communist party.')

Alberti was writing in the first flush of post-Franco enthusiasm. In the succeeding years, however, the Macarena has outflanked even the lures of communism.

The *Hermano Mayor* feels himself part of a club, in which he meets *macarenos*, and therefore friends, everywhere at every level of society, even on holiday in Turkey. He can relate remarkable things that have happened to *macarenos*, though he is cautious not to call them miracles. So what is the continuing attraction of this remarkable sculpture? 'It's because she's the Virgin of Hope, and that's the one thing everyone seeks.' He adds in his best marketing jargon, and with a smile, 'Here at the Macarena, we're in the business of selling hope.'

After the exertions of La Madrugada, the city begins to wind down. The processions are by no means over, but everyone is exhausted and sadly aware that the end is close. In the Church's calendar, Good Friday is the most solemn day of the year, but while the atmosphere in Seville is calmer, no one could call it solemn. On Saturday the most noteworthy procession is the Santo Entierro, the Holy Burial. The brotherhood's *Hermano*

Mayor is always the sovereign. It contains representatives from all the *hermandades* of the city, who each appear dressed in their own colours. It also contains representatives of the city council, the Church authorities and, less appealingly, the military. Under Franco the military were everywhere and it has always seemed inappropriate to have them in civil and religious processions.

This is the only allegorical *paso*, representing the triumph of Christianity over death, showing a skeleton, the cross and a coiled serpent. In 1940 Franco came to preside over Semana Santa, as the monarch had been used to do, and the *costaleros* made the bold and irreverent gesture of getting the awesome *paso* to curtsey to his wife. Semana Santa ends with the last *paso* of all, the relatively new one of the Resurrection, which sets out at dawn for the cathedral, displaying its single *paso* of the mystery, though it hopes to have a *paso* of the Virgin of the Dawn ready for 1992. It returns to the church of Santa Marina around 1.30 p.m., by which time *sevillanos'* thoughts have long gone elsewhere: some to the first of the season of bullfights that opens in the Maestranza bull-ring that afternoon, and many, depending on the timing of Easter, to the *feria*, which starts within a week or two, almost before Seville has had time to draw breath.

Feria! The very word spells excitement. *Feria* means parties, friends, flamenco dresses, seductions, entertainment, dancing, bright lights and bunting, *caballeros* on horseback – and crowds – practically from noon to night and night to noon for a whole week. The world of *la bulla*, the culture of the crowd at which *sevillanos* excel, unable to form a queue but knowing just how to behave in a crowd, transfers itself from the streets of the city to a large patch of scrubby ground to the west of the city, on the edge of Los Remedios. Estimates vary, but one source has it that 100,000 cases of sherry are consumed in the *feria*. It seems feasible, with the newspapers claiming that on the busiest nights a quarter of a million people have crowded on to the site. The Red Cross say that at least people are less drunk than they used to be. They put this down to the fact that people are drinking *manzanilla* rather than *fino*, as well as the fact that most *casetas* have a bottle of vitamin B on the counter.

The statistics abound: in just the first three days of the 1991 *feria* 95,000 people were ferried to or from the fair; 166 were taken in hand by the Red Cross, including seventy-five who were the worse for drink; 14,242 cars parked in the official car parks, 212 were towed away; thirty-eight children and two adults were lost; eight people were arrested; three *casetas* caught fire, but were saved by the local firemen, who have their own *caseta*, with beds in it, on site. (The risk of fire is great. In 1964, half the *feria* caught fire.) In addition, 105 tonnes of rubbish were collected, and on the busiest period, Friday night and Saturday morning, they collected 225 tonnes of rubbish, equivalent to the rubbish produced by a city of more than a quarter of a million citizens.

Every town has its *feria*, often to celebrate a saint's day. This is a particularly Andalusian phenomenon, since it requires parading on the streets under (reasonably) clear skies. In recent years the *feria* has been interrupted by bursts of torrential rain. The rain turns the sand to mud, fine clothes are ruined and the bunting droops. But the moment the sun shines the fun starts up again. The recipe is simple and unchanging: a site in the town permanently dedicated to the *feria*; a funfair at one end, often with a separate section of pint-sized big wheels and dodgems for children; rows of stalls at the entrance selling *turrón*, nuts and sweets of all varieties and mountains of plastic gew-gaws; temporary bars selling *tapas* and *chocolate y churros* in the morning; a huge, brightly lit archway at the entrance, which dominates the *feria* at night and which is specially designed each year using local themes (Paco Hortal buys his wife a gold brooch in the shape of the Seville *feria* arch every year); and one or more rows of *casetas*.

The *caseta* or 'little house' is fundamental to the *feria*. It entirely alters the character of the fair, making it either democratic or exclusive. It is better described as a small marquee, because of its canvas structure. In Seville, the *casetas* are erected in terraces along wide streets named after great bull-fighters, most notably Juan Belmonte and Joselito el Gallo, and each of the *casetas* is numbered like the houses in a street. So when a *sevillano* invites you to his *caseta*, he says, 'Come to Gitanillo de Triana 88', or whatever the address may be. The majority are the size of a small front room, but on the corners and in the middle of the row there are much larger *casetas*, which will be perhaps three or four times the size of a small one. The *caseta* is covered with striped canvas and has a simple iron fence to waist height running across the entrance. Here, at certain *casetas*, stands a bouncer, to keep out *hoi polloi*. Behind there are curtains draped back at either side. At the back of the room, behind the curtain, there is a rudimentary kitchen and bar, and an equally rudimentary lavatory.

Each of the *casetas* is decorated, though some more lavishly than others. A wooden floor will be laid, adequate for dancing. The typical ingredients include candelabras hanging from the ceiling, a large gilt mirror or two, some romantic portraits of Seville and swathes of lace. There are five or six small tables with four or five rush-bottomed painted chairs at each. The effect is like a cross between a brothel and a boy-scout camp. The large *casetas* are set up with trestle tables, provide sit-down meals for large numbers and will usually have a stage set for dancing.

Who owns the *casetas*? Some – very rich – individuals; an increasing number of companies; groups of friends; trade unions, brotherhoods, political parties, clubs. The waiting list is long and always a source of contention. More importantly, who may enter a *caseta*? Only those who are invited, except for a handful of public *casetas*. This is where Seville's fair differs from so many in the south. It looks as if everyone is having a party, with the drink and food flowing. But you can only join in if you are recognised or have an invitation.

In other villages, the position is reversed. Every *caseta* will be public, except for a few that will be for friends or members only. You simply walk in and buy a drink, or a half-bottle of *fino* and some plastic glasses. The *feria*, like Semana Santa, has become another great tourist attraction in recent years. Yet, even more than Semana Santa, it is a spectacle in which the outsider can take no part. You can wander up the avenues and take photographs of the girls in their flamenco dresses and the riders on horseback and soak up all the local colour. But you can do nothing to get underneath the skin of the phenomenon, or the city, without some invitations. This is typical Seville; apparently open-handed, but actually exclusive.

The *feria* begins on Monday evening at midnight, with the mayor turning on the lights, followed by sit-down dinners in the *casetas*. The *feria* has the air of being one of the great traditions of the city. But it is actually one of the newest, since it was started in 1847, by – shameful rumour has it – a Basque. Still, in the interviewing century and a half, enough sentiment has accrued to the *feria* to give it the reputation of a medieval fiesta. Originally it was a horse fair; horses to be bought and sold thronged the city. Today it is more of a market of politicians and pretty women, but its vigour and spirit are unchanged.

Until 1973 the *feria* site, *el Real*, 'the Royal', was in the city centre, at the Prado de San Sebastián, lugubriously enough on the site of an old cemetery. Many *sevillanos* regret the move. The *feria*, they say, was much smaller, much cosier, much closer to the centre. It is to be moved again, and old-timers fear the atmosphere will be entirely lost if it grows any bigger. Today's party-goers catch the special buses or stroll past the Plaza de España, over the Puente del Generalísimo, past the new Tabacalera – a real carbuncle – and the minor gin-palaces of party-goers who have ostentatiously sailed up the Guadalquivir for the *feria*, and then along to the site.

As you draw closer the crowds are swelling: young couples, she in a new flamenco dress, he in his uniform casuals; middle-aged couples with middle-aged spread; yuppies and aristocrats aping each other, the women in parrot-bright power-dressing suits, the men with their jackets elegantly hanging from their shoulders like capes; and tourists looking extremely scruffy by contrast with all this freshly pressed elegance. The cars are all funnelling down into a typical Los Remedios bottleneck, tooting and screaming at each other.

Miraculously, the horse-drawn coaches laden with their picturesque cargoes of laughing, dark-eyed girls in flamenco dresses and their dark-eyed partners survive in the traffic. It may look wonderful travelling in one of these romantic coaches, but the dust, the fumes and the traffic detract from the journey's delights.

The horse-drawn carriages are a distinctive feature of the *feria* and one of the few remaining links with the horse fair of times past. For eleven and a half months of the year, the carriages are tethered outside the cathedral and the Plaza de España. Only a tourist would be seen dead in one. But during the *feria* they come into their own, ferrying *sevillanos* in their finery to the fair. Carriages come from all round Seville, bowling into the city in the morning with the lorries and buses. The horses are trimmed with pompoms and tinkling bells, and the coachmen are dressed either in the traditional high-waisted trousers and short jackets with a cummerbund, or the more florid designs of Goya's day. Not all the carriages are the smartly painted, elegant models of the Regency romance; among them are a good few farmyard carts led by working horses, bearing the agricultural worker and his family in their Sunday best.

In the late 1980s Spain was swept by an equine fever, and as a result there were no horses at the fair. In 1991 the horses returned to captivate everyone. There were carriages drawn by as many as nine horses, as well as horseback riders in elegant outfits. The most striking were the girls who dressed as *caballeros*, far outshining even the girls who rode side-saddle clasping their partners' waists, their flamenco dresses spread out around them. Only the city council was concerned about the crush of horses. The *feria* was so full of carriages that for long periods in the afternoons the traffic stopped moving entirely. After fifteen minutes sitting with a friend in her family's carriage in one such jam, we got down and walked instead. The driver was instructed to return to the *caseta* when he could.

For one week, the streets of the *feria* are bright with colour. Every avenue is decked with strings of red and white or green and white paper balloons. The hangings of the *casetas* are also red and white or green and white, while their architraves are ornately painted in bright colours with stylised leaves and typical Andalusian symbols such as the Giralda and the guitar. Lights are strung across the streets from the lamp-posts, and the tree trunks and lamp-posts are painted white and decorated with spirals of greenery. And among it all are the women in their flamenco dresses. The *traje de gitana* has become more popular in recent years and is widely worn by all ages and sizes. Though the coming of *feria* heralds strict dieting, it is not actually obligatory, as was freqeuntly pointed out to me, to have a waistline at all. It is such a flattering garment that almost anyone with decent posture looks good in it. I draw the line at little children though, babies and toddlers. There is a fashion amongst working-class families to put their's into one of these flounced and frilly dresses. The child typically has gold earrings and no hair, and the floral alice band only enhances the baldness which it is intended to hide. This *muñeca*, or little doll, is then wedged into its buggy, with its dummy jammed in its mouth and bracelets round its pudgy wrists, the ugliest *gitana* you ever saw.

Every child, once grown, is transformed. A floor-length dress of two, three or four flounces, with short, flounced sleeves, a shawl with many hanging strands draped across the shoulders, a deep scoop at the front and tied at the back, disguises many a knobbly knee and thick ankle and emphasises even the smallest bosom. The bright earrings and bracelets and the comb in the hair distract the eye from any remaining flaws.

Like the *pasos* of Semana Santa, the flamenco dress is not a static object. In the 1960s skirts were short, to emulate the mini. Today, skirts are back to the floor, the flounces more exaggerated, the spots larger, the ribbon threaded through the lace thicker. In all, one of these dresses takes between seven and twenty metres of fabric, depending on the style chosen, and can cost anything up to £300 or £400. Some of the dresses are made of vibrant floral fabric which would look better on a sofa.

Esperanza Flores, the chef at Parabere, is much in demand as a maker of flamenco costumes. She disapproves of the trends in today's dresses, especially the florid sleeves, and met me during the *feria* in a perfectly understated dress that was forty-five years old, with tiny spots, gentle flounces and a fine lace edging.

If they are not wearing flamenco dresses, the women of Seville will be in their very best clothes. Every woman will be in an expensive new outfit, most of the young in tight-fitting linen suits, all with plenty of gold buttons and gold jewellery. The key to the peacock display comes in the verb *estrenar*, for which there is no direct translation in English. In the cinema it means 'to première', but it has a special meaning for clothes, namely 'to show off for the first time'. Every woman is *estrenando* at the fair, showing off her new wardrobe, and no visitor can hope to compete. *Sevillanos* of every social class spend large amounts of money on clothes; each stroll down calle Sierpes, for every evening *paseo* is a rehearsal for the *feria*.

If the *feria* is a feast for the eye, it assails the ear. The sound mounts up gently: whispered gossip; trotting horses, with bells jangling; mopeds weaving in and out of the traffic; gypsies selling single red carnations; the men selling split canes that can be cracked rhythmically; groups of girls walking by playing their castanets; shouts of laughter; and the cries and claps and stamping of feet coming from the *casetas* where people are dancing. The city meanwhile appears deserted. The bars and restaurants, if not closed, have scant custom. Yet I know *sevillanos* who stay at home and do not go every year. The crush of people is so great, especially on Friday night, and the old intimacy of the fair so rarely encountered, that they prefer to ignore it.

Amalia Fernández is not one of these. By 3.30 at her *caseta* everyone is busy having lunch. She runs the *caseta* with a group of friends, having been on the city council's waiting list for several years before a vacant *caseta* came up. The friends hire a fixer to organise the furniture, supply the waiters and bring in the food and drink for an overall fee. The artifice of being entertained in a private home, even if it is on the edge of the city in a glorified field, is delicately maintained. Today the lunch is *paella*, another day it will be *fabada*, a bean stew orginally from the northern province of Asturias. Amalia is very tall, slim and blonde, unusual for a Spanish woman, and she looks very striking in her outfit. The hem of her dress and her perfectly matching purple suede shoes are being ruined by the sand that has been churned up by the rain, but she is unconcerned. Children's flamenco dresses are washable, she admits, but hers will be a pig to clean. *Sevillanas* are the incarnation of the childhood admonition that you have to suffer for the sake of beauty.

Amalia works as a nurse, and therefore cannot spend as much time at the *feria* as she would like. But her friends are welcome to drop in at any time and the little *caseta* is crammed with people for seven days. All this hospitality is provided entirely free and no one would dream of discussing the cost. Amalia knows the owners of perhaps ten to twelve other *casetas* which she can visit, but she does not expect her other friends to repay the hospitality. The point is to be able to provide some fun.

Other *casetas* are less busy. My hosts at one such were the elderly parents of some friends, who invited only their children, their grandchildren and a few other close relations and friends. They had always had a *caseta* from the times when Seville was a smaller city, and they still wanted to keep up the tradition, without the expense of opening the *caseta* up to the whole world. Their (grown-up) children were able to go off to meet their friends in other *casetas*, to gossip, to show off their little children and then return to relax. There are other *casetas* that have a determined public relations function, run by newspapers or companies. The press photographers will hover to snap the film stars and directors, singers, bullfighters, ranchers and other worthies, not forgetting the Duchess of Alba or the false 'Pope' Gregory XVIII, who arrives with his 'cardinals' and 'bishops'.

The middle of the day and the early afternoon are the best times to see the classic carriages and horseback riders. In the early evening the carriages will be escorting the *feriantes* to the Maestranza bull-ring, for there are bullfights every day from the end of Semana Santa until the end of *feria*. Going to the Maestranza is still an important social event, just as it is elsewhere in Spain. In Madrid, for instance, the season of bullfights which are part of the celebrations for its patron saint Isidoro lasts almost a month and there's a well-founded joke that senior executives make sure they are not seen at work during bullfight hours, or people will realise that they are not as important as they like to make out.

Most people go home for a snooze or a shower at some point during the evening, for they will be up drinking and dancing until the early hours. The session finishes with the obligatory *chocolate y churros* in one of the temporary bars on the edge of the *feria*. As the week builds up to its finale, the *feria* loses its local, domestic, private air. By Friday night it is crowded out with people from all over the province and beyond. And on Sunday it is over with a great burst of fireworks. Only the British would think of holding their firework festival in November. More sensibly, Seville chooses April, when it is warm enough to sit out at midnight in one's summer clothes – at least when it is not raining. Monday is, inevitably, a public holiday. Recognising that no one would go into work, an understanding mayor made it *lunes de resaca*, 'hangover Monday'. It is the only depressing public holiday in the calendar, when the city goes silent as the weary sleep the week off. On Monday evening the train to Cádiz is full of exhausted young men with six o'clock shadow, their smart suits hanging from the luggage racks as they snore in the seats.

The *sevillanos* have no respite from fiestas. At the end of May comes the *cruces de mayo*, a celebration originally intended for children. Groups of neighbours used to set up crosses in the middle of their shared courtyards in the old rooming-houses known as *corrales de vecinos*. Children would also take small statues of the Virgin out on the streets, with a *capataz* and *costaleros*, just like the Semana Santa processions. But as the *corrales* have been pulled down, and the nature of people's lives has changed, the *cruces de mayo* has almost become extinct. Not quite. Today, the tradition has been revived, with parties and dancing in some of the small *plazas* of the city, such as the Plaza de Santa Cruz, and in the Triana district. Nothing in the *cruces de mayo*, however, could match the drama and intensity of the *romería del Rocío*.

Until the early twentieth century, the pilgrimage *(romería)* to the sanctuary of the Virgin at Almonte, in the coastal salt marshes *(marismas)* of the Guadalquivir, was a local affair. Tradition had it that a hunter from the village of Villamanrique found an image of the Virgin in a tree, which may have dated back to the times of Alfonso el Sabio and the conquering of Muslim Seville by the Christians. The neighbouring villages of Villamanrique and Almonte disputed ownership of the Virgin, and Almonte was victorious. The village named her the Virgen del Rocío ('the Virgin of the Dew'), and for several centuries groups of local villages used to go and pay homage to her. In 1919 she was crowned canonically, and from that time on her fame and her reputation for miracles grew. The building of a road from the beach resort of Matalascañas undoubtedly boosted attendance, as did the boom in car ownership. Today brotherhoods from all over Andalusia, and the rest of Spain, as well as tourists, television crews and journalists from across the world, make the journey, in a mixture of a pilgrimage and presidential rally. Seville sends two brotherhoods, one from the city itself and one from the Triana district.

The *rocieros*, the pilgrims, set out in time to arrive on the Saturday before Whit Sunday, the Seville brotherhoods leaving home on the Thursday. In the past, people travelled on foot, or in Wild West-style cattle wagons with hooped roofs. Today, the car cuts the walker's journey from a few days to a matter of hours, and the tractor often supplants the horse. But the road is bright with decorated wagons, women in flamenco dresses and men in their traditional striped trousers and short jackets. For those who choose to make the journey on foot, walking with the traditional long stick, it remains a powerful experience. In the Franco years, the *romería* was one of the few occasions when the *andaluces* could escape the rules and oppressive morality of daily life, eating and drinking, singing and dancing, seducing and being seduced to their hearts' content. Even the religious fervour was released from the usual pressures. Where most *nazarenos* would walk in Semana Santa as a fulfilment of a penance, the Virgen del Rocío could be celebrated without any tiresome, guilt-inducing sense of duty. For a week, the *rocieros* were cut off from the world and its disapproving gaze. Strong friendships were formed, as in any group that shares its meals and endures the discomforts of such a journey. Many *rocieros* felt that this was the one time in the year that they really lived.

Once at Almonte, the brotherhoods have to process past the *Hermano Mayor* of the village and pay their respects to the Virgin. The number of brotherhoods is growing so fast – twenty-nine were created in the 1980s, bringing the total to eighty-seven, with more waiting to be approved – that the procession now has to be organised over two days. This ceremony, as everything else that follows, stresses the ownership of the Virgin by the people of Almonte. Originally their quarrel was with Villamanrique; today they are holding off the world. In this the *romería* differs from many pilgrimages, and from the processions of Semana Santa itself. The people of the village, the *almonteños*, are fervent in their ownership of their Virgin. This becomes plain in the early hours of Monday, after the solemn mass of Pentecost on the Sunday. At a certain point, never specified, the young men of Almonte gather in a crush around the shrine and leap over the railings that protect the Virgin. The *paso* is then taken out with *almonteños* shoving and fighting each other for the privilege and turning on any outsider who should get in the way. The contrast with Semana Santa could not be greater. The *paso* is taken erratically in one direction and another, lost within a dusty, sweating heap of humanity, until everybody eventually calms down and the Virgin is processed round the brotherhoods. It should be added that, while ornate, the *paso* itself has nothing to compare with the Virgins of Seville.

With that, the *romería* is over for another year. The pilgrims who walked and rode still have the journey back, with more days of camp fires and partying, if less enthusiasm, since the anticipation is always more exciting than the fulfilment. You will meet *sevillanos* who go every year, *sevillanos* who have never been and don't intend to start, and *sevillanos* who go by car for the weekend and are lucky enough to be able to stay in a house in or near the village. No one can ignore it. Nicholás Salas recalls a letter written to *ABC* by a man complaining about the traffic jams the *rocieros* caused : 'We had angry letters from masses of people condemning him.' The press is full of the *Rocío*, with photographs, and interviews with stars, with sententious headlines like 'Lola Flores [a popular singer] is enjoying the *feria*, but she confesses that she prefers the *Rocío*.'

Salvador Rodríguez of Seville University believes that part of the success of the *Rocío* is because it has become the symbol of Andalusian unity. The old kingdoms of Córdoba, Jaén, Seville and Granada were only united over the past century or so to create the relatively new region of Andalusia; who better to express the new regionalism than the Virgen del Rocío? The *rocieros* have their traditional cries in praise of the Virgin : *'!Viva la Virgen del Rocío! ¡Viva la Blanca Paloma!'* ('Long live the white dove!') *'!Viva la Patrón de Almonte!'* ('Long live the patron saint of Almonte!') *'!Viva la Reina de las Marismas!'* ('Long live the queen of the marshes!') To this Salvador Rodríguez believes a new cry will soon be added: *'!Viva la Reina de Andalucía!'*

Seville celebrates the day of Fernando, its saint-king, on 30 May, one of the high days of the year when his body is put on display in the cathedral. Soon after, and sometimes coinciding with it, comes the joyous outburst of Corpus Christi. In 1990 the religious authorities moved the religious celebrations for Corpus to the nearest Sunday, but the civil authorities have decided to keep the traditional Thursday as a high-spirited holiday. Corpus Christi, which became in the sixteenth and seventeenth centuries an extravagant celebration of Christianity, is now more a celebration of the church's historic brilliance than its spiritual present. For all that, the procession makes, in the space of a morning, a vivid introduction to the life of Seville's brotherhoods.

The day starts the night before, when *sevillanos* turn out to admire their city. People living in the houses along the route drape their balconies with rugs and lengths of crimson velvet, while shopkeepers decorate their windows. The city council, which itself decorates the Plaza de San Francisco in traditional style, runs a competition for the best display, as it does for the temporary altars which are set up along the route.

The procession runs from the cathedral to calle Sierpes and back up calle Cuna to calle Placentines and the cathedral. As it passes, sedge, rosemary and other aromatic plants are strewn on the ground, adding to the scent of incense that fills the air. First come representatives from most of the brotherhoods and the religious orders in the city, as well as several *pasos*. In contrast with those of Semana Santa, most of the *pasos* of Corpus Christi are today drawn on wheels. The first represents the two martyred saints, the sisters Justa and Rufina, on either side of a model of the Giralda. The polymathic bishop of Visigothic Seville, San Isidoro, follows, as does a *paso* of his brother San Leandro. Following San Leandro are real representatives of the military and behind them a *paso* of San Fernando, carved by the master Pedro Roldán. Next comes civil Seville – the chief of police, the university, the city's consuls, aristocratic members of the Maestranza, the judiciary, the General Council of Brotherhoods – followed by a *paso* of the Virgin by Martínez Montañés, and another by the same sculptor of the child Jesus. The procession concludes triumphantly with a small silver monstrance, and the proud monstrance by Juan de Arfe, the centrepiece of the procession, an enormous Renaissance silver creation weighing 300 kilos.

Preceding the monstrance come the Church's dignitaries,

accompanied by the cathedral choir, and the *seises*, one of
Seville's most remarkable traditions, dating back more than
500 years. The *seises* (literally 'the sixes') are a group of ten
rather than six boys, unique in having papal dispensation to
dance in front of the high altar. They originally dressed as
pilgrims and then as shepherds, but in the sixteenth century
took on the fashion of the court of Austria. Thus they appear
in doubtlet, hose and white stockings, each topped with a large
hat with a pendulous feather. In the seventeenth century they
acquired silver castanets and they sing as well as dance in slow
formation to eighteenth-century church music during the mass
which precedes the monstrance's sortie round the city. At five
o'clock every afternoon for the following week, the *seises* dance
in front of the high altar. As payment the mayor gives one of
the boys an ancient gold coin, which is later exchanged in a
ceremony at City Hall for a small fee in today's money for
each boy.

The young Able Seaman George Melly joined a brief trip
to Seville in spring 1947 when HMS *Dido* dropped anchor at
Gibraltar. The *seises* earned his profound disapproval, when
he toured the cathedral and found:

. . . huge pop-eyed figures used in carnivals [Semana
Santa] which secretly, as an ex-C. of E. worshipper, I
found rather a shocking idea. The same was true of the
information, handed out by the priest in the most casual
way, that on certain feast days the choirboys . . . danced,
accompanying themselves on castanets, on the steps of the
altars. Nothing like that ever happened in Christ Church,
Linnet Lane, Liverpool 17, or the chapel at Stowe
School, Bucks. It sounded extremely frivolous . . . [But]
despite the dancing and pop-eyed carnival grotesques,
there was power here and religio-political horse-trading.
Franco was a good Catholic and, in exchange, the Church
were good Fascists.

The festivities of Corpus continue with equal merrymaking the following weekend in the parish of La Magdalena, and most notably in the Triana district. In the *Corpus Chico*, or 'little Corpus' of Triana, a monstrance and *pasos* have been processed round the *barrio* for the past 450 years. The procession is organised by the brotherhood of the Esperanza de Triana whose *costaleros* carry the *pasos*. The streets of the *barrio* are strewn with flowers and aromatic plants, and the buildings are all colourfully decorated.

Triana is out on the streets again in the third week in July for the *Velá de Santiago y Santa Ana*, the Fair of St James and St Anne, which is supposed to be based on a miracle performed by St Anne. There is another *feria* at this time on the same theme down the road in Dos Hermanas. Indeed, throughout the summer, there will be *ferias* and festivals practically every weekend in the province's villages and towns. In midsummer, on 15 August, when the city is like the inside of a gas-mark-9 oven at mid-afternoon and most sensible people have left for their holidays, there is still a good crowd to celebrate the feast of the Virgen de los Reyes, the patron saint of Seville, after whom one of the *plazas* outside the cathedral is named. Perhaps Seville's most intimate ceremony, it begins in the very early morning, when pilgrims come walking in from all the towns and villages of the Aljarafe on the outskirts of the city. By 6 a.m. there will be a crowd ready to hear mass in the cathedral's Royal Chapel and the Virgin will then be taken in procession round the cathedral.

Throughout the autumn there will be a series of festivals around the province ready to attract those in search of a party. Christmas is coming, but that, compared with what has gone before, is dull fare. More important in the religious and sentimental calendar of the city is the feast of the Immaculate Conception on 8 December. In any other city, this might pass more or less unremarked, but for Seville, as we shall discover in the next chapter, it is a day of historic signficance.

9. Living the legend

There are two women intertwined in the story of Seville, the one sacred, the other profane. The first is the Virgin Mary, who came down to Seville because she liked what she saw when she looked at her reflection in the old city's lagoons. The second is Carmen, a foreign devil, the creation of a hispanophile Frenchman. To the outside world for the last century, Carmen has been the more famous, the incarnation of Spanish womanhood. But to Seville for many centuries more, the Virgin has been pre-eminent.

Seville's worship of the Virgin Mary has always been intense, and undoubtedly has traces of the pagan worship of Venus and earlier female deities. It came to a head at the end of the sixteenth and the beginning of the seventeenth century, in the midst of the fever of anti-Protestantism. A strong groundswell of opinion developed in favour of the Immaculate Conception, arguing that the Virgin should be declared as having been born without original sin. The Dominicans, and a Padre Molina from a monastery on calle Regina in particular, opposed this, on the grounds that there was no biblical basis for it. However, the Jesuits and several other orders aroused great popular passion in favour of it and demonstrators in the street chanted:

> *Aunque se oponga Molina*
> *y los frailes de Regina*
> *con su Padres Provincial,*
> *María fue concebida*
> *sin pecado original.*

('Although Molina and the brothers of the Regina monastery and their Provincial Head are against it, Mary was conceived without original sin.')

The city council finally sent a deputation to the pope, who put off seeing them for two years and concluded in 1617 by refusing to make the Immaculate Conception a dogma of faith. The intensity of the campaigning explains the ubiquitousness of the Virgin in the art of the Sevillian school of the time. Murillo was one of the lobby's ardent supporters; his endless portraits of the Virgin, with or without cherubs, can be viewed not as art nor as faith, but as propaganda. The eminent sculptor Juan Martínez Montañés, who created some of the outstanding images of the Virgin, was also involved.

It took two centuries for the pope to change his mind. The city rejoiced, though I cannot help feeling that belief in the Immaculate Conception undermines the force of the incarnation of Christ as man. If Christ's mother was not just another ordinary woman, sin and all, then he cannot properly be said to be one of us. Nevertheless, the street songs of the seventeenth century were dusted off and adjusted:

> *Todo el mundo en general*
> *a voces, Reina escogida*
> *diga que sois concebida*
> *sin pecado original.*

('Let the whole world shout out, chosen Queen, that you are conceived without original sin.')

In 1917 the city proclaimed the dogma of the Immaculate Conception and, to mark the momentous event, erected a monument in the Plaza del Triunfo, widely ignored by the visitors who throng the Alcázar. Four of the seventeenth-century campaigners are commemorated on this monument: Juan de Pineda, the Jesuit who first made the petition; Juan Martínez Montañés; the writer Miguel del Cid; and Murillo. Also on the monument are carved the names of many well-known *sevillanos*, from cardinals to poets, who supported the campaign.

To any observer the devotion among the religious, and the merely superstitious, to the Virgin Mary in Seville is remarkable. It is inevitably easy to jump to conclusions about the connections between the *sevillanos'* attitudes to women, their relationships with their mothers and their devotion to the Virgin. More simply, I was repeatedly told that the shortest route to Christ is through his mother Mary. The quick answer to this is surely that the shortest route to Christ is through Christ himself, but even the supporters of the Gran Poder, the greatest image of Christ in the city, themselves take the Virgin's side. The *Hermano Mayor* of the Gran Poder summed it up for me: 'We all know that Christ is the goal of Christianity. For the *sevillano* the mother is the centre of everything. So the most direct route to Christ is through his mother Mary. The worship of Mary is so widespread, simply because everybody honours the mother. Christ is a much more austere figure to approach.' So while the temporal power of the Church wanes, the Virgin Mary remains a bright talisman for the *sevillano* traveller and his key ring.

The luscious Carmen is a much more dangerous creature. In 1845 the foreigner Prosper Mérimée captured the very essence of Andalusia, though the story is overwrought with every touristic cliché of the era – *bandoleros*, bullfighters, gypsies and the alluring girls of the tobacco factory. Carmen is the sensuous spirit of the *sevillana*, a gypsy vibrant with life yet ultimately destined for tragedy. Hers is the black hair, the white teeth, the flashing smile and seductive glance of the romantic travellers' dreams. She really only came to life in the hands of Bizet's librettists Henri Meilhac and Ludovic Halévy.

231

Bizet was another Frenchman, and what is more he had never visited Spain. His opera converted the story into a work of universal symbolism. Its first performance in 1875 shocked the audience, with its portrayal of women smoking and officers sitting with gypsies and prostitutes in Lilas Pastia's bar, and its 'un-French, un-Spanish' music. But it was soon accepted into the repertoire and became the portrait of Spain against which all other pictures of the country were assessed. Outside Spain, that is.

The curiosity is that inside Spain, Carmen was rejected. Rather than take part in the Age of Enlightenment, Spain had turned its back on Europe and the innovations taking place. Its prime concern was *casticismo*, the ensuring of purity and breeding, whether in fighting bulls or people. Carmen portrayed a gypsy society of forward women and Bizet's heroine was a dangerously independent spirit. For more than a century, 'Nobody studied Carmen,' says the academic Alberto González Troyano, who specialises in the myths of Andalusia and has recently published a book about *La Desventura de Carmen*, 'The Misfortune of Carmen'. Carmen's misfortune all these years, he argues, has been to be ignored by her countrymen. But very recently, her fortunes have begun to change. Where once she was a traitor, she is now a heroine; where she was denounced or ignored as a symbol of the wrong perceptions of untrustworthy foreigners, she can now be acclaimed as a symbol of a world that is in danger of disappearing.

'People were afraid to confront her,' Alberto González Troyano says, 'because they feared that they would lose their identity.' But now Carmen represents Seville's and Andalusia's – and even Spain's – defence against the creeping homogenisation of the developed world, as a powerful image of Spain, a heroine of unique stature. Nowadays, he concludes, given the demands placed upon Carmen to be a symbol for Andalusia, she is in a far stronger negotiating position. Now Spain has to pay attention to her, because it needs her. What's more, feminism and the general changes in women's lives ensure that she will not stand alone. In the conclusion to his book he writes that the fate of Carmen might be quite the reverse today: 'In the light of the new situation, it would be in Carmen's hands to wreak the vengeance of one who has been excluded . . . [If the story were acted out today] perhaps Carmen would read the cards differently this time, perhaps she would not see the shapes spelling out her death, perhaps her misfortunes would stop there, because this time her adventure would be shared.'

Flamenco, like Carmen, is another symbol of contemporary significance to Seville. Originally the music of an oppressed people, it became the sanitised entertainment of a dictatorship which was sold to the foreign tourists in commercialised *tablaos*. Today it has been reclaimed, in vigorous opposition to the homogenisation of western music. But flamenco itself is a living art, and it changes. It is no longer just the music of a band of gypsies in western Andalusia, but the popular music of the nation. Flamenco is identified as the music of Seville, it *is* Seville, as typical of the city as geraniums and the Giralda. But in the creation of flamenco Seville itself has never been very important – Jerez and the Triana district are the capitals of flamenco. Seville's importance lies in diffusion: recognition in Seville gives an artist the stamp of approval.

The basis of flamenco is the *copla*, a short song a few lines long, of which the *saeta*, sung during Semana Santa, is the popular religious variety. It is a very individual form of music-making which started with the gypsies and has its own classic forms and structures. Part of its fascination therefore comes from the individual styles of the singers in extending the basic song by their cries. An oral tradition like flamenco has encouraged a good deal of flannel amongst those who try to write about it. Even Camilo José Cela, the recent Nobel prizewinner and one of the few writers who remained in Spain under Franco, encouraged the mystique in his *Primer Viaje Andaluz*, a poetic pre-war portrait of the region. Singing flamenco, he says, 'like breathing, is something you don't learn. It's inherited.'

Much has changed since he first wrote about it. At the end of the nineteenth century, not long before he was writing, *cante jondo* ('deep song'), was in its golden age, sung in the long-lost *cafés cantantes* of Seville. This was the form so favoured by Federico García Lorca, which expresses the suffering of an impoverished and oppressed people. It had many variations, which are less common today, including the *caña*, the *seguiriya*, the *soleá*, the *debla* and the *martinete*. Flamenco, by contrast, is a lighter, more cheerful form, and was therefore sometimes regarded as trivial. Cela quotes the great singer Mañuel Torres, 'El Niño de Jerez', 'the boy from Jerez', condemning it with the greatest scorn that he could muster: '*Eso pa mí está en inglé*', 'In my view it's in English'.

Still, it was flamenco that prevailed, although there is another dominant strand of flamenco, the *sevillanas*, which have been taken up throughout Spain, aided partly by the *andaluces* who left their region to find work in other parts of Spain and took their music with them. At *ferias*, at parties and in bars people will be singing impromptu *sevillanas*, with couples dancing a sinuous, seductive dance and the crowd clapping to the distinctive rhythm.

In August 1983, soon after the socialist party came to power, an influential Reunión de Cante Jondo was held near Seville in Puebla de Cazalla, partly with the political intention of regaining the art of flamenco from the influences of nationalism. Yet nationalism had not swallowed it entirely. Wherever a group of friends got together, they could still sing and dance and clap their hands in the intoxicating rhythms, even if the cinema and television were censored and the cinema was banned altogether in Semana Santa.

One of those who attended the 1983 Reunión was Juan Alberto Fernández Bañuls, a secondary school teacher of Felipe González's generation who had acquired a taste for flamenco from his grandmother. He studied the *copla* from a philological point of view, and subsequently wrote a book about flamenco. He works with the Fundación Machado, which was founded in 1985 to study and promote Andalusian culture. One of its projects has involved collecting every *copla* that could be traced – so far, it has 66,000. His job as Co-ordinator of Flamenco Programmes for the Andalusian government illustrates the new political will to sponsor local culture. His role is to support anything to do with flamenco – *peñas* or clubs, festivals and publications, and to spread the culture of flamenco in schools. This last is still in its infancy, and materials and teaching strategies have to be sought, but it is just one example of the many ways the regions are attempting to foster their own history in schools under devolved government.

There are many difficulties with collecting flamenco, he agrees. 'People haven't thought about it. It is a living thing, but it was spread by people who were illiterate. There are many risks in attempting to write it down and to fit it in with a musical structure. But, at the same time, we have to look after it.' He is naturally afraid that it will remain simply another item for consumption by Seville's mass of tourists. 'Flamenco has to find a space for itself now. It was born into a stratified, romantic society. Now that has all changed and it doesn't have the creative impetus. It has became like any other kind of art. Flamenco was born out of pain and solitude. Art like this only comes out of marginalisation from society. Yet the professionals in flamenco are now – rightly – paid proper fees. They live well out of it, and that can take the edge off the agony.'

Performers may charge anything up to £2,500 for a session. Groups of friends club together in *peñas* to hire an artist to perform for them, typically in bars decorated with photographs of the singers and dancers. One such *peña* illustrates the way flamenco has spread throughout society, for it meets in the unlikely surroundings of the theatre of the University School of Education. Its members mainly work for the university, and each year they have a special session to give a gold medal to a flamenco artist.

Amongst the many flamenco activities sponsored in Seville is the biennial festival. This can, however, be too much of a good thing. It takes time to be enticed and seduced by flamenco. You need to give it an evening to let it exercise its

charms. The festival, on the other hand, is a barrage of performances, good, bad and outstanding, which is best avoided
except by *aficionados*. In many of the lively bars in the city
you will find young people singing and dancing *sevillanas*.
Often the barman or the dancers will be able to advise you
where to go to find flamenco, but it is worth remembering
that there is no such thing as one best flamenco. Flamenco is
typically Andalusian in that it is an individualistic art; it
expresses personal, not group, values. The performance relies
on one *cantaor* singing alone, or a solitary guitarist, or one or
perhaps two dancers. By contrast, the Catalán national dance,
the *sardana*, is performed in groups. The *andaluces*, when
they dance, dance alone. Even in the *sevillana*, where the
dancers dance in couples, each dancer dances for herself or
himself. In this, flamenco expresses the disdain for group
values which affects everything from politics to queuing (or,
rather, not queuing) and arguments about football in the bar.
Everyone has their own views and will defend them to the
death.

Which brings us very neatly to the *fiesta nacional*, as bullfighting is known, the ritual dance with death so identified
with Spain, even though the French also go in for it. The
outside world sees bullfighting as being as Sevillian as flamenco, but again, bullfighting was not invented in Seville,
nor do the very best bullfights necessarily happen in the city.
The city certainly may have the most beautiful *plaza de toros*
in the land, but it has no school for bullfighters. Ronda, in
the very heart of ranching country, has historically been pre-
eminent, and the bullfighting in Madrid, during its patronal
festival of San Isidoro, is usually of a high standard. But
Seville is the one with the reputation, which accounts for the
rows of miniature plastic bulls in El Corte Inglés.

The Roman historian F. J. Wiseman says the Arabs introduced modern bullfighting into Spain, although the Romans
found a cult of bull worship when they arrived in Spain and

enjoyed bull-running and -baiting of the kind still practised in Pamplona. Today's bullfighters still wear a small pigtail, real or false, in imitation of the Roman gladiators, who wore pigtails as a sign of their profession. With time it became an aristocratic sport; the fights were held in makeshift rings in the Arenal and the Plaza de San Francisco. But bullfighting was not without its critics, and eventually Felipe V of France, then King of Spain, banned nobles from the sport in the early eighteenth century, while the pope threatened participants with excommunication. With this, the style of fighting changed. Originally, the Arabs had fought the bulls on horseback in open country. Once bullfighting became the sport of the under-privileged, the working class, the toreros inevitably had to resort to fighting on foot.

Seville's golden age of bullfighting ended on 16 May 1920, when José Gómez Ortega, 'Joselito "el Gallo"' ('the cock'), was killed in the ring at Talavera de la Reina near Madrid. (The canon Muñoz y Pabón, the cleric who had so encouraged the growth of the *Romería del Rocío*, gave the funeral oration. So impressed were Joselito's supporters that they presented Muñoz y Pabón with a gold quill pen, and he in turn gave it to the Virgen de la Esperanza Macarena. She wears it clipped to the sash given her by Seville's nationalist 'liberator', General Queipo de Llano, who is buried in the Macarena's basilica.)

Joselito and Juan Belmonte had for almost ten years captivated the crowds. With Joselito's death, as Juan Belmonte recognised, the spice of competition had gone. Juan Belmonte became a successful *ganadero*, but tragically committed suicide in 1960. There have been a number of great bullfighters on the national stage since then – including Manolete, who was killed in the ring in 1947; Paquirri, whose father-in-law Antonio Ordóñez was also one of the greats; and even El Cordobés, who has turned into a rather seedy celebrity, but was nevertheless invited to the king's name day party at the Alcázar in 1991 – but Seville has never regained the sparkle of those early years of the twentieth century. Today the stars are Curro Romero, from the suburb of Camas, and Juan

Antonio Ruiz, known, with a nod to his gladiatorial antecedents, as 'Espartaco' or 'Spartacus'.

John Fulton deserves a mention here. He came as a young American to post-war Seville to be a bullfighter and succeeded in entering that closed world. James Michener gave him international fame in his book *Iberia* in 1968, and his art gallery in the Barrio de Santa Cruz remains popular to this day with American tourists seeking the romance of Ernest Hemingway's era.

However, anyone who attends a bullfight will be hard pressed to summon any of the enthusiasm felt by Hemingway. The bulls have a habit of falling down before they are pushed and the struggle seems as unequal as if the torero was fighting a guinea pig. The crowds are rightly, if harshly, derisive of any weakness in bull or fighter. Espartaco has said of fighting before the crowd in the Maestranza, 'What you fear in Seville is failure, not the pain of a goring.' I find it hard to stomach, though if you have the rare fortune to witness a great fight, then it is possible to appreciate the skill and science of the torero. But even for those who buy a season ticket and go every afternoon during the *feria*, such occasions are rare.

There are a number of reasons for the decline in standards. One is that in the period after the war, the appalling and treacherous practice of shaving the bull's horns was developed. When done with care, it can hardly be noticed. What happens is that the bull's horns are painfully shaved down to the nerve, blunting the point and foreshortening the bull's reach, thus reducing the risk to the fighter. There is no doubt, either, that the bulls have become weaker over the years, under the encouragement of the toreros' managers who don't want to lose their valuable clients, until the bulls can hardly make it to the final macabre dance with the matador. In the past, the *ganaderos* had extensive ranches and could pick their very best bulls for fights. Today many ranches are smaller and rearing fighting bulls is an expensive indulgence for a *ganadero*, who can earn much more selling his cattle at market. The crowd has also come to prefer a large, lumbering creature. It may look suitably terrifying, but it does not have the spirit of the earlier breeds, or the speed. As a result, after every bullfight the single topic of conversation among the crowd will be that bulls are not what they used to be. In terms of skill and art, bullfighting today does not deserve its status as one of the fundamental images of Seville.

What it does have is spectacle, and in abundance. The deep yellow of the sand, the yellow and white painting of the arches, the red of the ring contrast vividly, and the sun, as it moves across the ring, provides an impressive theatre of shadow. The parade of the matador and his supporters is a taste of Golden Age Spain too rapidly over. As the corrida opens, the matador (the leading torero, who kills the bull) enters to the sounds of the *paso doble* played to rather tinny effect by the band up in its box. (During the corrida the band will give a musical ovation of its own, if the matador deserves it.) The matador is led by the *alguacils*, mounted officials with nodding plumes in the clothing of the late sixteenth century. Behind him come his *cuadrilla*: the *banderilleros*, who poke beribboned sticks into the bull's shoulders, and the *picadors*, who do much the same on horseback. The horses are blindfolded and padded nowadays, and what with the plumed *alguacils* they give the event a very Don Quixote-ish air.

The matador is accompanied by two other toreros who will assist him as he prepares for the kill. Each torero is in his aptly named *traje de luces*, suit of lights, very tightly fitting, the jacket and side panels of the trousers encrusted with sequins and gold thread. The matador and his men bow to the judge in his box, who will award the matador one or both ears, or the tail of the bull if the fight has deserved it. Matadors' league tables are therefore compiled in terms of 'O' (*orejas*, the number of ears awarded) and 'R' (*rabos*, the number of tails).

At the outset the toreros working alone use their lipstick-pink capes lined with yellow to lure the bull. The *picadors* then take over to weary the bull further by stabbing it with their lances in the back of the neck. During this process the horse often falls heavily over on its side and has to be pushed back up again by the groundsmen. The *banderilleros* then enter to plant three sets of darts into the bull's shoulders so that they rise vertically in pairs. Finally comes the matador, backed up by the toreros. For the kill he changes to a red cape, stiffened across the top by a short stick, and a sword. His intention is to kill the bull by a sword thrust to the heart, but more often than not he has to repeat the move, and the bull is ultimately finished off by one of the attendants. Then, to the sound of much cracking of whips, three horses roped together drag the dead bull from the ring, led by attendants running before them, and the sand is swept clear of blood ready for the next fight. Each fight, with its ritual four phases, takes about twenty minutes, and there are six fights in a corrida. If the last fight is predictably unspectacular the crowd will abandon the matador to his fate, getting up to leave well before the bull has been despatched.

Outside, by contrast, the streets before a fight are full of interest. The bars are jammed with people, including many women in their smartest clothes. In the calle Iris round the corner a crowd gathers at the 'stage door' to watch the toreros and their *cuadrillas* enter. At the main entrance there are people selling headgear – panamas, berets, caps, flat hats – and umbrellas to shield those in the cheaper *sol* seats in the sun. There are the inevitable stalls selling nuts and sweets. They are also, surprisingly, selling Cadbury's creme eggs. Seville has many traditions, but the Easter egg is not one of them, and especially not creme eggs on a hot spring afternoon.

The television crews have set up their caravans and cameras are suspended on cranes over the ring. The *fiesta nacional* gets its own slot on television, though not as extensively as it used to do. Inside there are people selling cushions, to soften the immensely hard seats. Everyone gets up instantly each fight is finished to ease the discomfort. There is also much getting up and down to buy ice-creams and cold drinks, which are sold throughout the fight by men walking through the crowds.

The one moment of real atmosphere I felt was inside the Maestranza itself, before we had gone to our seats. In the arched tunnels that surround the ring, I felt that I was back in the Roman amphitheatre, and that I was the one about to be thrown to the lions.

Manolo Alvárez was a famous torero in the days of Manolete in the 1940s, and now lives in comfortable retirement in the Nervión district. With good reason, he regrets the old days. 'For one thing, seat prices weren't so high. [The best seats for Easter Sunday and the *feria* are around fifty-five pounds; a good seat in the shade will cost thirty, though seats can be had for twelve to fifteen pounds.] But it's elegant to go. People go to be seen. Women go – and they never used to. Nobody understands the science of it all nowadays.' This view would seem to add to the impression that bullfighting is increasingly an artificial plaything today.

Manolo started fighting when he was sixteen. He had always had a passion for it, and was forever practising. Eventually he got a chance to prove himself. For his first fight, 'Everybody came from Triana', and he was paid twenty *duros*, about 50p. He gradually became known but, as he discovered, 'There's no profession harder than being a torero. You can only be good or bad.' He also found it an expensive business. 'The torero may seem to earn a lot, but he has to pay everyone else. I used to earn £115 for a corrida, which then went up to £200, but out of that I had to pay my agent seven to fifteen per cent, and the *picadors*, the *banderilleros*, everyone else in the ring with me, and my hotel fees and expenses and theirs.' Out of these expenses also had to come the *trajes de luces*, which never last long. Towards the end of his time as a torero, bullfighting was taken over by a small group of businessmen who contracted the fighters to their stables. Where in the past Manolo might have complained of the difficulties of getting himself work, at least he was able to get it independently. The new group of businessmen have effectively acquired a monopoly of the bullrings, excluding fighters who are not on their lists.

Despite the inferior quality of the bulls and the lack of knowledge among the crowds, Manolo Alvárez has not lost his passion for fighting. Only recently he organised a corrida in Santiponce, outside Seville, not far from the Roman amphitheatre at Itálica, where the Romans would have seen bull-baiting. He wanted to show his son, who had never seen him fight, what the torero Manolo Alvárez had been like. 'I trained for three months, every day. We had a few friends along, and some of today's young fighters. Curro [Romero] came. It was a great party!'

Outside Spain there is a strong and growing body of opinion that condemns bullfighting completely. But it would be wrong to think that by contrast all *sevillanos* and all Spaniards are lusting for blood. I know many *sevillanos* who have no desire to go to a bullfight. Nevertheless they are as familiar with the vocabulary and the personalities as the English are with football, or the Americans with baseball, simply because bull-fighting is so fully reported in the media. Yet it has been condemned within Spain for centuries, particularly by the Church. Even before Felipe V banned the nobles from fight-ing, Isabella had wanted it banned. Today, there is far more opposition to it than there was. But the fact that the prime minister himself is a *sevillano*, brought up in a city within strong bullfighting traditions, ensures that any change in atti-tudes will be slow. As Federico García Lorca asked, 'What would happen to the Spanish spring, to Spanish blood, and even the Spanish language, if the trumpets of the bull-ring stopped sounding?'

In the glossy magazine *6 Toros 6*, launched in 1991, amongst the advertisements for watches, for Ricard and La Ina, today's bullfighters are sold like brands of whisky. With a soulful photograph and plenty of white space, each full-page adver-tisement gives a simple message: 'José María Manzanares. When bullfighting is a WORK of ART"; 'There are bull-fighters who give us hope. Jesulín de Ubrique'; 'Who's afraid of José Luis Bote?'; 'He fights with his soul. His body is his instrument. José Ortega Cano.' Bullfighters, as these adver-tisements show, are not just sportsmen, they are heroes. And while they remain heroes, and the public go on expecting that at least *next* time they will see a great duel between man and beast, then they will remain a symbol of the city which likes its theatre out in the open air.

Envoi

Seville is the focus of the world's fantasies about Spain. Latin lovers, treacherous beauties, gypsies, flamenco, a glorious past, bullfighting, excessive religiosity, white-painted streets scented with jasmine and orange blossom: every cliché crowds in. No other city carries the same weight of legend. Barcelona, Granada, Madrid, Marbella, Benidorm, Segovia, Torremolinos, Córdoba and Salamanca each contribute something to our idea of Spain, but Seville crowns them all. In Seville you can discover the history of Spain, real and fictional, but never forget that it is a living city.

For several centuries Seville has been regarded as being in decline – a city facing death as surely as its citizens, who feel death's shadow in the brightest of sunshine. Yet today Seville faces a new future under a transformed Spain. The democracy is young and Seville's economic and industrial base still weak in face of modern Europe. The city has to find an equilibrium between the foreign-currency earnings of mass tourism, and the need to preserve and protect its past glories.

Camilo José Cela, who wrote with great charm and perception about the city, nevertheless concluded that 'trying to count Seville's infinite grains would be like trying to count each one of the drops of the Guadalquivir'. 'One could,' he wrote, 'spend a whole lifetime talking about Seville without arriving at a single conclusion which one could accept as sure and certain. Seville is like the blue of the skies and the green of the olive trees, it changes.'

He was quite right, and this should be a cause for celebration. Seville is an ancient city, occupied for almost 3,000 years. Despite earthquakes, wars, floods and invasions, many of its great landmarks remain as records of its past glories and spurs to future greatness. Today it is adjusting to the invasion by Europe just as it yielded to and absorbed the Arabs, the Visigoths, the Romans . . . Contemporary architects vie to make their impression on the city. For it is the historic monuments that lure visitors to the city.

But the key to Seville is its people. Remember the blind seller of lottery tickets, the nun making *dulces*, the bartender with his obscure liqueurs, the politician in her flamenco dress, the fond family following the procession of Semana Santa, the bullfighter who came out of retirement, the Virgin Mary and Felipe González. They are all part of the fast-flowing river that is Seville. Step in.

Historical summary

Successive waves of Phoenician, Greek and Carthaginian occupation	8th c. BC	First settlement in Seville
	6th c. BC	Greek colonisers follow on from Phoenicians
	218–206 BC	Second Punic War. Rome defeats Carthage
Spain becomes province of Rome. Seville capital of Southern Baetica	206 BC	Itálica founded; becomes Rome's first colony in Spain
	45 BC	Seville raised to status of Roman colony
	287 AD	Saints Justa and Rufina martyred
	409	Germanic people invade Spain, soon followed by Visigoths

Visigothic Spain	5–7 c.	Hermenegildo of Seville murdered, later canonised as San Hermenegildo. San Leandro, San Isidoro, bishops of Seville
Muslim Spain	711	Muslims invade Spain
	718	Christians defeat Muslims at Covadonga, putting northern boundary to Muslim invasion. Muslim Spain known as Al-Andalus
	844	Normans raid Seville
	929	Córdoba becomes capital of Caliphate of the Western world
	1090	Almoravids invade
Reconquista or Christian conquest of Spain begins	1085	Christians capture Toledo
	c. 1145	Almohads invade
	1172	Building of Giralda begins
	1212	Christians defeat Almohads at Las Navas de Tolosa
	1248	Seville falls to the Christian Fernando III, later canonised as San Fernando
	1252	Fernando III dies; succeeded by his son Alfonso X, *el sabio*, 'the Wise'

	1364	Pedro *el Cruel* has the Alcázar rebuilt by *mudéjar* craftsmen
	1402	Building of cathedral begins
	1469	Fernando II of Aragón marries Isabella I of Castilla. After war over inheritance dispute, Spain united under one pair of monarchs: the *Reyes Católicos*
	1480	First office of the Inquisition set up in Seville
Reconquista ends. The Age of Discovery begins. Spain's rulers seek purity of blood and faith	1492	Catholic Monarchs take Granada, last outpost of the Muslim empire in Spain
		Columbus sails for New World
		Jews expelled from Spain
Artistic and economic Golden Age, when Seville has monpoly of trade with New World	1516	Carlos I, the Holy Roman Emperor Charles V and first of the Habsburgs, succeeds to throne
	1556	Felipe II succeeds to throne

Defeat ushers in four centuries of decline: war in Europe, loss of empire, disputes over the succession	1558	Spanish Armada defeated
	1571	Battle of Lepanto; Turks defeated
	1584	Building of the Archive of the Indies begins, originally as commodity exchange
	1609	Expulsion of the *moriscos*
	1702–13	War of the Spanish Succession. Bourbons take the throne
	1717	Seville loses monopoly of New World trade to Cádiz, and its decline begins
	1728	Building of Tobacco Factory begins
	1808	Napoleon installs brother Joseph as king of Spain. On 2 May *(dos de mayo)* people in Madrid rise up against French. War of Independence (or Peninsular War) begins. Seville briefly houses the new government
	1812	Liberal constitution declared in Cádiz

1814	Fernando VII returns from exile and repeals constitution
1830	Isabella II succeeds to throne
1833–9	First Carlist War
1847–9	Second Carlist War
1868	Isabella abdicates
1872–6	Third Carlist War
1873	First Republic
1874	Isabella's son Alfonso XII restored by military coup
1875	Bizet's Carmen premièred in Paris
1898	Spanish–American War
1902	Alfonso XIII succeeds to throne
1917	Seville proclaims dogma of Immaculate Conception
1923–30	Dictatorship of General Miguel Primo de Rivera
1929	Seville hosts Ibero-American Exhibition (Expo 29)
1931	Alfonso XIII abdicates. Second Republic declared

Spanish Civil War, followed by almost forty years of isolation

1936–9	Seville taken by General Queipo de Llano the day after the initial coup

	1939–75	Dictatorship of Franco
Democracy established	1975	Franco dies, Juan Carlos proclaimed king
	1982	Socialists win general election under their leader, *sevillano* Felipe González. Statute of Autonomy for Andalusia approved. Seville becomes capital of Andalusian government
	1986	Spain enters EC
Seville receives economic boost to take her into 21st century	1992	Seville hosts Expo 92 and celebrates quincentenary of Columbus' discovery of New World

Glossary

alameda	promenade
ataranzas	shipyards
Ayuntamiento	city council
azulejo	glazed, decorative tile
barrio	district, quarter
biblioteca	library
calle	street
callejón	alley
capilla	chapel; *capilla mayor*, chancel
cartuja	Carthusian monastery
Churrigueresque	extravagant Baroque architecture
ciudad	city, town
cofradía	brotherhood
converso	Jew converted to Christianity
cortes	parliament
costaleros	bearers who carry the floats at Semana Santa
cuesta	slope

Seville

custodia	monstrance
entrada	entrance
estación	station
fachada	façade
feria	spring fair
ferrocarril	railway
fuente	fountain
hermano	brother; *Hermano Mayor*, head of a *cofradía*
iglesia	church
jardín(es)	garden(s)
Judería	Jewish quarter, ghetto
Junta de Andalucía	Government of the Autonomous Community of Andalusia
lonja	commodity exchange
marismas	marshes
mercado	market
Morería	Moorish quarter of town after Christian conquest
morisco	Muslim nominally baptised as a Christian
mozárabe	Christian under Muslim rule, extended to describe their architecture
mudéjar	Muslim under Christian rule, extended to describe their architecture
muelle	quay
palacio	palace
paseo	stroll or walk; or a promenade
paso	float of sculpture(s) representing Passion of Christ, or the Virgin
patio	courtyard

plateresque	exuberant form of Renaissance architecture
plaza	square; *plaza mayor*, main square
puente	bridge
reja	iron grille
retablo	altar piece
río	river
salida	exit
sierra	mountain range
torre	tower
vega	alluvial plain

Further reading

Guidebooks and travellers' accounts

In English

Edmondo de Amicis, *Spain and the Spaniards*, transl. by Wilhelmina W. Cady, New York and London, 1881.

Hans Christian Andersen, *A Visit to Spain and North Africa, 1862*, transl. by Grace Thornton, London, 1975.

Eames, Andrew (ed.) Insight Guide: Southern Spain, Singapore 1990.

Richard Ford, *A Handbook for Travellers in Spain*, 3 vols, Arundel, Sussex, 1966.

Michael Jacobs, *A Guide to Andalusia*, London, 1990.

Vega McVeagh, Paul Harsh, Carlos Pascual, *Seville: Everything Under the Sun*, London, 1987.

George Melly, *Rum, Bum and Concertina*, London, 1977.

David Mitchell, *Travellers in Spain: An Illustrated Anthology*, London, 1990.

V. S. Pritchett, *The Spanish Temper*, London, 1984.

Ian Robertson, *Blue Guide to Spain*, London, 1989.

F. E. Sidney, *Anglican Innocents in Spain*, London, 1903.

J. Blanco White, *Letters from Spain*, London, 1822.

In Spanish

Antonio Burgos, *Guia secreta de Sevilla*, Barcelona, 1991.

Camilo José Cela, *Primer viaje andaluz*, Barcelona, 1959.

Francisco Morales Padrón, *Sevilla insolita*, Universidad de Sevilla, 1987.

Seville

In French

Gautier, Théophile, *Voyage en Espagne*, Paris, 1894.

History

In English

Henry Kamen, *A Concise History of Spain*, London, 1973.

Pierre Vilar, *Spain: A Brief History*, 2nd edn, Oxford, 1977.

J. Júdice Ganirto, *Social Complexity in South-West Iberia 800–300 BC: The Case of Tartessos*, Oxford: BAR International Series 439, 1988.

Richard J. Harrison, *Spain at the Dawn of History*, London, 1988.

H. V. Livermore, *The Origins of Spain and Portugal*, London, 1971.

Florence C. Lister and Robert H. Lister, *Andalusian Ceramics in Spain and New Spain, A Cultural Register from the Third Century BC to 1700*, Tucson, Arizona, 1987.

F. Wiseman, *Roman Spain*, London, 1956.

Simon Keay, *Roman Spain*, London, 1988.

John Elliott, *Imperial Spain 1469–1716*, Harmondsworth, 1970.

Clive Griffin, *The Crombergers of Seville: The History of a Printing and Merchant Dynasty*, Oxford, 1988.

Mary Elizabeth Perry, *Crime and Society in Early Modern Seville*, Hanover, New Hampshire, 1980.

Mary Elizabeth Perry, *Gender and Disorder in Early Modern Seville*, Princeton, 1990.

Ruth Pike, *Enterprise and Adventure. The Genoese in Seville and the Opening of the New World*, Ithaca and London, 1966.

Ruth Pike, *Aristocrats and Traders: Sevillian Society in the Sixteenth Century* Ithaca and London, 1972.

Henry Kamen, *The Spanish Inquisition*, New York, 1965.

John Lynch, *Spain Under the Habsburgs*, 2nd edn, vol. 1: *Empire and Absolutism 1516–1598* vol. 2: *Spain and America 1598–1700*, Oxford, 1981.

Richard L. Predmore, *Cervantes*, London, 1973.

Brown, Jonathan, *The Golden Age of Painting in Spain*, London, 1991.

Henry Kamen, *Spain in the Later Seventeenth Century, 1665–1700*, London, 1983.

Raymond Carr, *Spain 1808–1939*, Oxford, 1966.

Raymond Carr, *Modern Spain 1975–1980*, Oxford, 1980.

Ronald Fraser, *Blood of Spain*, Harmondsworth, 1979.

David Mitchell, *The Spanish Civil War*, London, 1982.

Hugh Thomas, *The Spanish Civil War*, Harmondsworth, 1965.

David Gilmour, *The Transformation of Spain*, London, 1985.

John Hooper, *The Spaniards A Portrait of the New Spain*, Harmondsworth, 1987.

In Spanish

Santiago Montoto, *Biografia de Sevilla*, Seville, 1990.

José Maria de Mena, *Historia de Sevilla*, 5th edn, Barcelona, 1989.

José Maria de Mena, *Personajes sevillanos célebres en la historia*, Seville, 1989.

Juan Campos Carrasco, *Excavaciones arqueológicas en la cuidad de Sevilla*, Seville, 1986.

J. Maluquier, *La civilización de Tartessos*, Seville, 1985.

Antonio Blanco Freijeiro, *La cuidad antigua*, 3rd edn, Seville, 1984.

Miguel Angel Ladero Quesada, *La cuidad medieval (1248–1492)*, 3rd edn, 1989.

Claudio Sánchez Albornoz, *De la Andalucia islámica a la de hoy*, Madrid, 1983.

Joaquin González Moreno, *Descubrimiento en Triana: las cuevas del jabon*, Seville, 1989.

Nicolás Salas, *Sevilla: cronicas del siglo XX*, tomo 1, 1895–1920, 2nd edn, Seville, 1991.

Francisco Morales Padrón, *Los corrales de vecinos de Sevilla*, 2nd edn, Universidad de Sevilla, 1991.

Nicolás Salas, *El Moscú sevillano*, 2nd edn, Seville, 1990. (Faction.)

Antonio León Lillo, *Palma del Rio 1936–52*, Cordoba, 1990.

Félix Moreno de la Cova, *Mi vida y mi tiempo: La guerra que yo vivi*, privately published in Seville, 1988.

Eduardo Chinarro, *Sindicatos prohibidos: Sevilla 1966–1975*, Seville, 1987.

Food

In English

Penelope Casas, *The Foods and Wines of Spain*, Harmondsworth, 1985.

In Spanish

Maria Luisa Fraga Iribarne, *Guia de dulces de los conventos sevillanos de clausura*, Córdoba, 1988.

Lourdes March, *La cocina meditérranea*, Madrid, 1989.

Lourdes March and Alicia Rios, *El libro del aceite y la aceituna*, Madrid, 1989.

Bullfighting

In Spanish

Alberto González Troyano, *El torero, héroe literario*, Colección Tauromaquia 12, Madrid, 1988.

Seville

Flamenco

In Spanish

José Luis Ortiz Nuevo, *Pensamiento Politico en el Cante Flamenco*, Seville, 1985.

Francisco Vallecillo, *Antonio Mairena*, Biblioteca de Estudios Flamencos *1*, Jerez, 1988.

Aurelio Verde, *Sevillanas para cantar y bailar, Antologia de letras 1969–89*, Seville, 1988.

Festivals

In Spanish

Hermandad . . . de la Esperanza Macarena, *Esperanza Macarena en el XXV aniversario de su coronación canónica*, Seville, 1989.

Manuel Serrano y Ortega, *Noticia historico-artistica de la sagrada imagen del Señor del Gran Poder*, Seville, 1898, repr. Seville, 1991.

Noticia historico-artistica de la sagrada imagen del señor del Gran Poder, Seville 1898, repr. 1990.

Salvador Rodriguez Bercerra, 'La Romeria del Rocio', *El folk-lore andaluz 3*, Seville, 1989.

Miscellaneous

In English

Hyland, Paul, *Purbeck: The Ingrained Island*, London, 1978.

In Spanish

Alberto González Troyano, *La desventura de Carmen*, Madrid, 1991.

Manuel Garcia Viñó, *Sevilla en la poesia*, 3 vols, Seville: Rodriguez Castillejo, 1988.

Index

Jaén 21, 225
jamón serrano 151, 162–3, 165
Jerez de la Frontera 98, 160, 233
Jews 18, 23–4, 25, 26–7
and Inquisition 32–3
anti-Semitic legislation 15
anti-Jewish riots 27
expelled from Spain 33–4
jornada intensiva 132
Joseph I 52, 54
Juan, Don xxi, 45, 84–5
Juan Carlos, King 57, 74, 82, 124
Juana *la Loca*, daughter of the
Catholic Monarchs 30
Junta de Andalucia *see* Andalusian
Government
Jurado, Rocio 125

Kamen, Henry 8, 42–3, 51
Keay, Simon 8

Ladino 33
land ownership 67
abolition of *mayorazgo* 58
desamortización reforms 58
reparto 58
Roman influences 7–8
see also latifundia, minifundia
Lara, Antonio 110–11
Larache 69
latifundia 12, 58
Lefèvre, Archbishop 123
León, Francisco de 71
León, Fray Luis de 24
lentejas 169
Letters from Spain 55
Lorca, Federico Garcia 66, 145, 234,
242
lotteries 141–2, 158
Loüys, Pierre 48–9
lunch 164–71
Lyon, Eugene 41

Macdonalds 194
Machado, Antonio 61–2
Machado, Manuel 61–2
Madres Irlandesas 120–2
school in Castilleja de la Cuesta
xvi, 120–1, 174
magdalenas 177, 181
Magellan 31, 41

Mairena, Antonio 125, 208
Mairena, Manolo 125
Mairena de Aljarafe 91
Mañara, Miguel de 45
manchego cheese 162, 165, 171
Manolete 237, 241
Manzanares, José Maria 242
manzanilla (sherry) xxi, 160, 163,
215
March, Lourdes 162
marmelade xv, 185–7
marranos 33
Marseilles 6
Martinez-Bordiú, Maria del Carmen 74
Martinez Montañés, Juan 46, 192,
226, 230, 231
Matalascañas 223
Montoto, Santiago 19
mayorazgo see land ownership
Medina del Corral, José Luis 126
Medina Sidonia, Duques de 26–7,
32, 78, 108
Medinaceli, Duques de 40, 62, 115,
125
Mediodia 66
Meilhac, Henri 231
Melilla 69
Melly, George 227
membrillo 171, 178
Mena, Gonzalo de, Archbishop 191
Mena, José Maria de 52, 73
Mérimée, Prosper 60, 231
Mesa, Juan de 46, 47, 192
Michener, James 238
military, the 119–20, 125
minifundia 58
Miura, Eduardo 125, 211
Molina, Padre 229–30
Molina, Tirso de 45
montilla wines 161
Morocco 30, 69, 70, 86, 184
Moreno de la Cova, Félix 78–81, 92,
93, 109–10, 117–18
Moreria 25
moriscos 46
Motilla, Marqués de 117, 125
Mozarabs 20
mudéjar 23, 25, 40
Muñoz y Pabón, Canon 237
Murillo, Bartolomé 13, 44–5, 53,
230, 231

Seville